The Letter of Violence

The Letter of Violence

Essays on Narrative, Ethics, and Politics

Idelbar Avelar

THE LETTER OF VIOLENCE: ESSAYS ON NARRATIVE, ETHICS, AND POLITICS

First published 2004 by
PALGRAVE MACMILLAN™
175 Fifth Avenue, New York, N.Y. 10010 and
Houndmills, Basingstoke, Hampshire, England RG21 6XS.
Companies and representatives throughout the world.

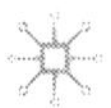

PALGRAVE MACMILLAN is the global academic imprint of the Palgrave Macmillan division of St. Martin's Press, LLC and of Palgrave Macmillan Ltd. Macmillan® is a registered trademark in the United States, United Kingdom and other countries. Palgrave is a registered trademark in the European Union and other countries.

ISBN 978-1-4039-6741-5 hardback
ISBN 978-1-4039-6742-3 paperback

Library of Congress Cataloging-in-Publication Data

Avelar, Idelbar, 1968-
The letter of violence: essays on narrative, ethics, and politics / Idelbar Avelar.
p. cm.
Includes bibliographical references and index
ISBN 978-1-4039-6741-5 — ISBN 978-1-4039-6742-3 (pbk.)
1. Violence. 2. Violence—Philosophy. 3. Torture. 4. Violence in literature.
5. Latin
American literature—History and criticism. 6. Ethics. I. Title.
HM886 .A84
303.6—dc22 2004049764

A catalogue record for this book is available from the British Library.

Design by Autobookcomp.

First edition: November 2004

Transferred to Digital Printing in 2011

Contents

To Alexandre and Laura

Acknowledgments

This book owes much to José Quiroga and Licia Fiol Matta's belief in it back when it was only a promise. Gabriella Pearce has seen the manuscript through from its early stages with impeccable professionalism. I thank the three of them, the anonymous reader who offered decisive insights, and Jen Simington for competent copyediting.

Three scholars have been with me every step of the way. George Yúdice has offered advice and inspiring conversation beyond all limits of generosity. I have also counted on Thomas Reese for that at the Stone Center for Latin American Studies, a generous source of research support for my work. There would probably be no book at all had I not been counting on the friendship, conversation, and joy of Christopher Dunn.

Whatever merits the chapter on the Colombian novel may have would not exist without the friendship and bibliographic guidance of Ana María Ochoa. I thank my Chilean friends Nelly Richard for the invitation to present the opening of the Derrida chapter, and Willy Thayer, Pablo Oyarzún, and Federico Galende for the invitation to present the reflection on Benjamin, both in lovely Santiago. For complicity and dialogue on all topics discussed here, I warmly thank my friend John Kraniauskas. Before she could ever put a face to my name, Jean Franco believed in my work, read me generously, and offered support and her unforgettable smile. I honor Jean Franco here with love and gratitude, hoping that my generation of critics will be worthy of her legacy.

Gratitude is due to my friend and student Aaron Lorenz, who translated a chapter originally written in Spanish. The provost's office at Tulane University provided means for bringing this project to completion by funding equipment and research assistants Colleen Sparks and Kerry Walsh. I thank both associate provosts, James MacLaren as well as friend, interlocutor, and comrade-in-Cultural-Studies Ana López.

In addition to a dear friend in Chris Dunn, the Department of Spanish and Portuguese at Tulane University has offered me the opportunity to work with Robert Irwin and Eleuterio Santiago-Díaz, and to continue to work with Tatjana Pavlovic, Maureen Shea, Laura Bass, Jean Dangler, Kathleen Davis, Marilyn Miller, and most recently John Charles and Gabriela Zapata, all of them so inspiring as friends and colleagues. I am also grateful to Christopher Soufas, Henry Sullivan, and the Dean of Liberal Arts and Sciences Teresa Soufas for taking the time to read my work, and to Teresa also for support with equipment. The heart and soul of the department is our administrative secretary, Claudia St. Marie, on whose help I have counted beyond the call of duty. At Tulane I have profited from dialogue with my colleagues Anthony Pereira and Martha Huggins in Brazilian studies, Leslie Snider in public health, Aoife Naughton in German studies, Felipe Smith, Gaurav Desai, Supriya Nair, Roseanne Adderley, and Richard Watts in African Diaspora studies. I have also counted on the competence of Guillermo Ñañez, Paul Bary, and most recently Hortensia Calvo in caring for a precious jewel, Tulane's Latin American Library.

At the risk of forgetting someone, I thank each colleague who offered interlocution and hospitality at institutions where I was invited to share ongoing work. For a delightful welcome to sections of chapter 4, I thank at Emory University José Quiroga, Tatjana Gajic, Carl Good, Karen Stolley, Ricardo Gutiérrez Mouat, Hazel Gold, and Ana Sofia Ganho. I thank Donna Jones and Franco Moretti for featuring *The Untimely Present* at Stanford University's Center for the Study of the Novel. For hospitality at Georgetown University I thank especially Horacio Legrás and also Vivaldo Santos. I warmly thank Jorge Brioso, Humberto Huergo, and Silvia López at Carleton College. For an engaging reception to a paper on xenophobia, I thank especially Carol Klee and a number of colleagues at the University of Minnesota: Fernando Arenas, Alberto Egea Fernández-Montesinos, Hernán Vidal, Nicholas Spadacchini, and René Jara. I am immensely grateful to an extraordinary group of students from Chile's Pedagogical Institute. For interlocution at the Duke—North Carolina consortium in Latin American studies I am especially grateful to John French as well as to John Chasteen, Walter Mignolo, Paulo Fontes, Gabriella Nouzeilles, and my mentor Fredric Jameson.

I am also grateful for the hospitality of Elzbieta Sklodowska at Washington University, Fernando Valerio at Colorado State University, Frederick de Armas at the University of Chicago, Christopher Conway, Julio Ortega, and a delightful group of graduate students at Brown University, Angel Loureiro, Arcadio Díaz-Quiñonez, Ricardo Piglia, and Paul Firbas at Princeton, and my friends Eva-Lynn Jagoe and Dara Goldman at the University of Illinois, Francine Masiello and Julio Ramos at the University of California, and Ana Lúcia Gazzolla at Federal University of Minas Gerais. In Brazil gratitude for scholarly hospitality or inspiring dialogue, live or electronic, is also due to Leda Maria Martins, Wander Melo Miranda, Graciela Ravetti, Júlio Pinto, César Guimarães, Paulo Henrique Caetano, Flávio Couto e Silva, and Inêidina Sobreira (Minas Gerais),

Denílson Lopes (Brasília), Raul Antelo, Jorge Wolff (Santa Catarina), Eneida Cunha Leal, Evelina Hoisel, Liv Sovik (Bahia), and in Rio de Janeiro, Silviano Santiago, Beatriz Resende, Italo Moriconi, Hermano Vianna, Fred Goes, Graça Coutinho, Evando Nascimento, Victor Hugo Adler Pereira, Júlio Diniz, Martha Jlhôa and most especially the wisdom of friend and countercultural legend Jorge Mautner. In Argentina thanks are due to Andrea Giunta, Noé Jitrik, and most especially my friends Florencia Garramuño, Alvaro Fernández Bravo, and Tununa Mercado. In addition to my comrade Kraniauskas sincere thanks are due to a hospitable and engaging community of Latin Americanists from the United Kingdom, including old friend Jon Beasley-Murray as well as Philip Derbyshire, Jens Andermann, Ana Alvarez, Lorraine Leu, Ben Bollig, and David Treece. For unfailingly good vibes in New York I thank Andreas Huyssen, Mary Louise Pratt, Robert Stam, and Fredrick Mohen. My work has counted on Carlos Alonso's supportive feedback and on Charles Perrone's keen editorial eye, and I thank them as well. I also thank invitations to contribute to collective endeavors from Elzbieta Sklodowska, Ana María Ochoa, Mary Beth Tierney-Tello, Marcy Schwartz, Mabel Moraña, Laura Demaría, Francine Masiello, Daniel Balderston, Harris Berger, Paul Greene, and Jeremy Wallach. It would be impossible to mention all my students, now proud doctors or soon-to-be-doctors, but I must thank my friends Felipe Victoriano, Alejandra Osorio, and Renata Nascimento.

Books, first books especially, *desire* certain readers, and *The Untimely Present* intensely wanted to be liked by three Argentine women critics who had been intellectual models to me from a distance, before it made any sense to let them know it. I thank them because receiving a Modern Language Association award from Sylvia Molloy, being warmly welcomed into *Punto de Vista* by Beatriz Sarlo, and becoming an interlocutor of Graciela Montaldo was more than I hoped when my writing set out to desire their readership. In political admiration I hope Sylvia, Beatriz, and Graciela like this book.

Outside academia, Drs. Paulo Antônio Vasconcelos, Catherine Lampard, and Elizabeth Timponi, each in a particular field, have been instrumental in helping me conclude this project. A section of chapter 1 was published, in earlier form, as "Five Theses on Torture." Trans. Philip Derbyshire. *Journal of Latin American Cultural Studies* 10.3 (2001): 253–71. A section of chapter 2 was published, in earlier form, as "The Ethics of Criticism and the International Division of Intellectual Labor." *Sub-Stance* 91 (2000): 80–103.

Closing a cycle of writings on atrocity and desiring a future book on Brazilian music, I dedicate *The Letter of Violence* to my son Alexandre and my daughter Laura, in the hopes that they will inherit a less violent world.

With their grace, love of life, and amazing intelligence, they are certainly doing their share. Believing—why not?—in the role of literature, philosophy, and Cultural Studies in getting grownups to do theirs, this book was made possible by two adorable cities. Thank you, New Orleans. Thank you, Belo Horizonte.

Introduction

> *[A]nd then war comes, and reveals that we have not yet crept out on all fours from the barbaric period of our history. We have learned how to wear suspenders, to write clever leading articles, and to make milk chocolate, but when we need to reach a serious decision about how a few different tribes are to live together on a well-endowed European peninsula, we are incapable of finding any other method than mutual extermination on a mass scale.*
>
> —*Leon Trotsky,* The Balkan Wars 1912–13, *qtd. Der Derian* 48

There was a time when it was common to think of violence as a set of hostilities taking place between comparable and symmetric forces. There was a time when Western philosophy—and disciplines such as anthropology, sociology, and psychology--thought that one could thoroughly explain violence through natural, biological, social, or political causes. There was a time when scholarly texts tended *either* to dream of a specific form of violence that could abolish violence once and for all *or* to combat it tout court as a temptation to which one should never cede. There was a time when it was far more acceptable to refer violence back to a unified set of causes. There was a time when the two extreme positions on violence were represented by thinkers who abhorred it in the name of ethic and universal tolerance (Hannah Arendt) and thinkers who forcefully justified it as the legitimate and inevitable right of the oppressed (Frantz Fanon). There was a time when things were far clearer on this matter.

Going back to Thomas Hobbes's concept of a state of war as the originary, enabling figure for all history, the problem of violence has occupied a key position in modern Western thought. It has now, however, acquired unprecedented centrality, as America's arrival to self-awareness as a potential victim of public, visible, *televised* violence has imposed renewed scrutiny upon the paradigms under which the topic had been examined. Debates about legal or illegal, legitimate or illegitimate, just or unjust, "real" or "symbolic" forms of violence have been revived, with positions, as rule, being now more entrenched than ever. Discussions that as recently as five years ago would have been unthinkable—for example,

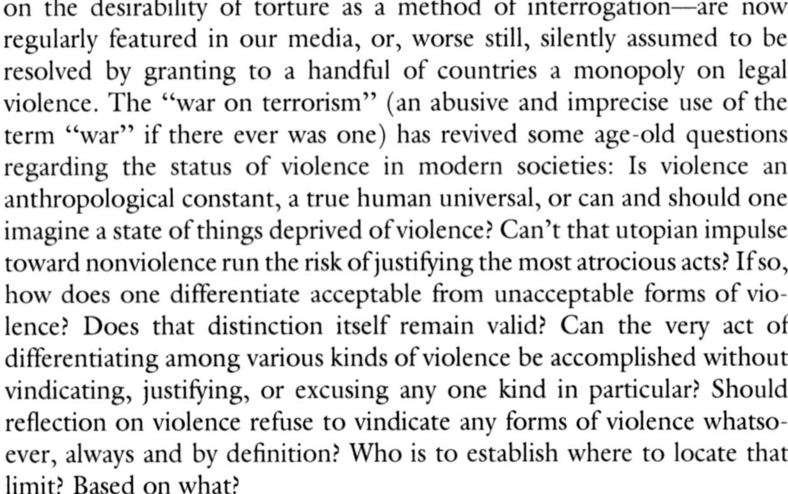

on the desirability of torture as a method of interrogation—are now regularly featured in our media, or, worse still, silently assumed to be resolved by granting to a handful of countries a monopoly on legal violence. The "war on terrorism" (an abusive and imprecise use of the term "war" if there ever was one) has revived some age-old questions regarding the status of violence in modern societies: Is violence an anthropological constant, a true human universal, or can and should one imagine a state of things deprived of violence? Can't that utopian impulse toward nonviolence run the risk of justifying the most atrocious acts? If so, how does one differentiate acceptable from unacceptable forms of violence? Does that distinction itself remain valid? Can the very act of differentiating among various kinds of violence be accomplished without vindicating, justifying, or excusing any one kind in particular? Should reflection on violence refuse to vindicate any forms of violence whatsoever, always and by definition? Who is to establish where to locate that limit? Based on what?

Influential among modern reflections on violence is German military strategist Carl von Clausewitz's unfinished treaty *On War* (1832). Next to the legendary *Art of War* published by Sun Tzu circa fourth century B.C., Clausewitz's is acknowledged by Left and Right as *the* greatest book ever on war. While there was and is abundant bibliography on war tactics, on the judicial, political, cultural, technological dimensions of war, or on the history of specific wars, Clausewitz's book stands out as one that brings together a host of voices, philosophical problems, reflection, and complexity not achieved before or since. In addition to political thought and military science, Clausewitz features the lexicon of modern physics, as war for him is not a form of violence "that explodes in a simple discharge" (87) but rather "a clash of forces freely operating and obedient to no law but their own"(78). Adding to the mix is the discourse of post-Kantian philosophy, present in the extensive featuring of the problem of "purpose and means" in war (90–9). Clausewitz, in fact, visits even the emerging discourse of philology, called upon to explain historical changes in the term "art of war" (133). All in all, Clausewitz remains indispensable not only because of the extraordinary intelligence of his treaty, but also because his book represents a true discursive panorama of early nineteenth-century Europe. His encyclopedic knowledge is deployed obsessively over the course of 125 chapters (grouped under eight different "Books"), all of them, for us, haunted by Clausewitz's claim that his treaty had remained unfinished. Go figure.

Much like Martin Heidegger's *Being and Time* and Robert Musil's *Man without Qualities,* roughly 100 years later, Clausewitz's *On War* belongs to that class of books whose unfinished status is built into the text itself, as a repeatedly announced possibility or as a central organizational principle.[1] In the case of *On War* it is hard to believe that the book is indeed unfinished, since to the contemporary reader it does not look like Clausewitz forgot much. As the key name in the codification of an entire set of laws and logistics of warfare, Clausewitz is still widely read in military academies, even as military science has made possible forms of destruction that no longer conform to his description. Understanding war as the maximum use of physical force with a view to a total subjection of the enemy, Clausewitz represented the pinnacle of an instrumentalist tradition that argued that war could indeed be the object of scientific knowledge.

Signatory of the famous dictum that "war is the continuation of politics by other means"(87),[2] Clausewitz remained as the fundamental reference for reflection on one specific kind of violence, namely the mutual violence perpetrated by warring factions. One of the challenges facing social thought is to understand clashes of forces that no longer conform to the classic political agents that he had in mind. Much of our current malaise harks back, in fact, to our witnessing forms of violence that do not follow the Clausewitzian-Napoleonic paradigm of two comparable, symmetric warring sides. One could argue that the Clausewitzian model, based on modern European wars between nation states, now stands for a form of violence that has been definitively abolished. The African interethnic wars, the Empire's "war on terrorism," Islamic *jihad*, the global "narco-war" (to mention four contemporary paradigms) all can be said to follow patterns *other than* the modern European, territorial, Clausewitzian-Napoleonic type war. In any case, Clausewitz remains key to the understanding of the pragmatics of war, even as tactics and strategy have changed beyond recognition since his time.

Naturally, if one is looking to pose *ethical* questions regarding violence, one is better served by another bibliography. Clausewitz very emphatically proposes war as the terrain where all ethics dissolve and all ethical consideration is not only unnecessary but also dangerous. His is, rather, a philosophy thoroughly saturated by the will to power proper to total war. For Clausewitz, war is precisely the moment of complete ceasing of ethical concerns in politics. War is the culmination of politics in a brutal game of force. There may be a pragmatics of warfare but there may never be—except due to a tremendous irresponsibility—an ethics of war. As Paul Virilio later explained, "going to extremes is one of Clausewitz's concepts. It designates the relation he draws between war and politics . . . the tendency of war to go beyond all limits" (*Pure War* 48). Although one might see Clausewitz as a Hobbesian theorist of the untrammeled clash of forces, the Prussian strategist is careful to differentiate between the suspension of ethics *during* the war and the absolutely necessary ethical moment *before* the war, in the period when war is still being justified and planned. In Clausewitz's point of view, for example, no one should go to war based on a lie or on a false accusation. Although war suspends ethics, it should not follow that one can or should make do without ethics *when going to* war.

The interesting story is that the twentieth century's thinking on violence has been, in a way, a succession of parodic variations on Clausewitz's understanding of war as the continuation of politics by other means. In Michel Foucault's 1975–6 lecture course on sovereignty and war, *Society Must Be Defended,* he argued for a reversal of Clausewitz's most famous dictum: We should now understand *politics itself* as a *continuation of war by other means.* While Clausewitz mapped war as a conflict that *overflows,* that cannot be contained by "regular" politics and therefore *leads politics into an elsewhere,* Foucault wrote in a time where one had come to think of politics, of political activity itself, fundamentally according to the model of war. In a way, Foucault's great reversal is precisely that instead of understanding power along the lines of a whole republican tradition of sovereignty that runs from Machiavelli to Montesquieu, he rethinks politics itself in Clausewitzian fashion, as an act of war.

Less than ten years after Foucault's critique of sovereignty, the leading theorist of war, Paul Virilio, observed the cold war and the nuclear race and remarked: "the Total Peace of deterrence is Total War pursued by other means" (*Pure War* 25). Years earlier philosopher Emmanuel Levinas had taken definitive distance from "modern contract theories and their postulation of an originary war of all against all" (Vries 339), and proposed a meditation where surprisingly and boldly *peace not violence was the originary state.* This propelled Jacques Derrida to note that if anything, for Levinas, *war was a continuation of peace by other means.* When confronted with the need to find a metaphor for sexual violence and gender inequality as a continuation of German fascism, Austrian feminist Elfriede Jelinek forcefully argued that "institutionalized love and marriage were our times' true continuation of war by other means" (qtd. Hanssen, *Critique* 211). Depending on the twist given by each twentieth-century thinker to Clausewitz's witty phrase, one can very much locate that thinker within the century's most important polemics.

Foucault, for example, *reverses* Clausewitz's dictum: Politics is the continuation of war by other means. For Foucault, war saturates the field of experience in such a way that it becomes a paradigm for all political activity. Deemphasizing historical in favor of geographical categories, Foucault no longer understands violence according to that eminently temporal, Hegelian thing we call "revolution" (which always exists as a moment in a progression of change in history), but rather as that far more geographical, spatial event we call "war." The result is Foucault's remarkable critique of the paradigm of sovereignty, hitherto dominant in a gamut of Western political theories. Foucault argued that multiple and mobile power relations could not be captured by the contractual, juridical theories of sovereignty. Only by understanding political relations through the paradigm of war could one capture the various layers of action proper to political dispute. In other words, for Foucault politics is the terrain that "sanctions and reproduces the disiquilibrium of forces manifested in war" (*Society* 16). The primary, fundamental event is war; politics is simply the legitimation and consolidation of the hierarchy imposed in war. Foucault's reversal of Clausewitz is, then, clearly inspired by Nietzsche's *Genealogy of Morals.*[3]

Less than a couple of decades after the publication of Clausewitz's treaty, anarchism and Marxism began to redefine the understanding of violence, taking as their fundamental paradigm not wars between nations and armies, but the violence between classes. Still based on the model of the "Napoleonic battle," Proudhon's radical anarchosyndicalism conceived the workers' uprising as the total annihilation of the enemy, a goal toward which every form of violence would in principle be justified. Calling attention to the daily, institutionalized violence to which the working class was subjected, Marx's framing of history was grounded in a double gesture. On the one hand it showed the violence upon which the present capitalist order of things was founded (the horrors of past, primitive expropriation and accumulation, duly reproduced in the present). On the other hand it offered the definitive rationale for revolutionary violence in the future. It started from the premise that revolutionary violence was the only particular manifestation of the universal "violence" that could abolish the concept once and for all by abolishing the reality that it designates. In Marxism it is axiomatic that revolutionary violence brings with itself, by definition, the promise of an end to violence as such. This is the *ethical* basis for the vindication of violence in Marxism, however brutally so-called Marxist regimes around the world have manipulated or made use of that claim. If for Marx the theory of history was the primary justification for the validity of a one-time, revolutionary recourse to violence, Fredrick Engels, in *Anti-Dühring*, preferred to add his own, considerably more mechanical vindication of violence as the very motor of permanent historical evolution. Engels's vindication of violence proudly evolved through analogies with the Darwinian natural sciences, which in Marx's texts are far more rare and careful.

In opposition to accounts of violence as an expression of natural, irrational aggression, for Marx the abolition of class exploitation should spell the end of all violence, or at least of "violence" as all human history so far has known it. It is probably true that today, well over a century after the Paris Commune and near the ninetieth anniversary of the first successful socialist revolution, the prospect of a utopian end to violence seems as distant as ever. But it is also true that Marx's text remains a crucial source of tools to understand why history has turned out that way. Marx's oeuvre is in fact filled with pages *both* advocating the thesis that no transformation will happen without violence *and* warning that a simple and voluntaristic recourse to violence means little and probably will accomplish nothing. Be that as it may, thinking on violence has never been the same since Marx, as he establishes a permanent suspicion, asking: Whose violence? Acting in whose interests? Is it complicit with the horrors of primitive accumulation—the expropriation and enslaving of vast numbers of human beings for the privilege of a few (daily reproduced, in its turn, by ideological and real forms of violence)? Or is it annunciatory of the revolutionary, redeeming violence that brings with it the promise of the end of violence as such?

The stability of the Marxian theory of the revolution remains, naturally, dependent on the assumption that it is always *possible* to discern and distinguish between the endless reproduction of the violence of primitive accumulation and the redeeming, promising violence of the revolution. Today, many of us are convinced that those two forms of violence cannot be neatly separated, not even in speculative theory. This is why the success of the Marxian vindication of violence has been, throughout the twentieth century, proportional to the separability between the oppressors and the oppressed. The more dichotomously split a society is, the more a general vindication of violence in Marxist terms is likely to be heard and supported. For this reason, the rich Euro-American societies of the North Atlantic, by managing to create large and solid middle classes, have also, by and large, succeeded in preventing revolutionary outbreaks within their own borders. Not only cheap labor, but also various forms of atrocity have been, over the course of modernity, progressively "outsourced" to the Third World.

Facing different needs at various moments in history, Lenin, Trotsky, Mao, and other Marxists presented explicit justifications of violence or calls for a well-targeted use thereof. But no Marxist thinker has been more associated with the vindication of violent action than Franz Fanon. The momentous encounter between Marxist theory and decolonization in Africa made for the twentieth century's most uncompromising reflection on revolutionary violence.

The colonial world is "a world cut in two" where the dividing line between camps is watched over by "barracks and police stations" (Fanon 38). In colonialism the crude daily violence upon which capitalism is rooted makes itself fully visible, without the thick cushion granted to the North Atlantic societies by their rich and large middle classes. For Fanon, colonial violence is the name of that particular manifestation that makes us see the true universality of the concept. In colonial situations the system and its victims agree that violence is absolutely inevitable and necessary. The system knows it must deploy it daily and implacably just to sustain itself. The oppressed know that no liberation will be given to them for free, that they will need to fight for it with all their weapons. ***In the colonial world we understand that violence is ubiquitous.*** In its extremely atrocious nature, colonialism makes us see that violence not only happens in the colonial world.

Atrocities happen in the colonies with an intensity unknown in the First World, not because there is a moral or cultural difference between the two spaces, but because colonial, scandalous violence helps keep invisible the daily, institutionalized economic and political violence in the metropolis. Anchored in Marx, Frantz Fanon was the thinker who made us understand that *global dialectic of violence* implemented by colonialism. Postcolonial and critical race theories would later unmask the many ways in which the recounting of Western modernity has been blind to its colonial conditions of possibility.[4] In any case, Fanon's *The Wretched of the Earth* inaugurated the understanding that there was a unique locus of enunciation, a unique voice, proper to the colonial subject's unmasking and unveiling of the truly global nature of violence. Drawing upon his experience as a psychiatrist in Algeria, Fanon dismantled stereotypical claims about native violence by accounting for them "not as physiological characteristics as in the theories of biological determinists, nor as cultural differences as in the theories of the anthropologists, nor even as moral shortcomings as in the allegations of the missionaries, but rather as political and psychological consequences of a colonial system that alienated the native" (Desai, *Subject*, 49).

The fundamental issue for Fanon is that as long as there is capitalism, violence is not only ubiquitous but also, by definition, predicated on colonial or neocolonial forms of exploitation. Although he never explicitly theorized it as such, the resolution of Fanon's account of violence—the endpoint of the colonial master-slave dialectic—demanded a Trotskyite-type permanent revolution. In Fanon's work the violent destruction of colonial and neocolonial structures is not, from the standpoint of the oppressed, something over which much of a choice remains. For the native the process of violently destroying colonialism is not a contingent, unimportant one but rather the very process through which s/he accedes to subjectivity. This is nothing but the dialectical flip side of colonialism itself, for "the settler has shown him [the native] the way he should be if he is to become free" (Fanon 84). Fanon's version of the master-slave dialectic is forcefully promising an ending to all slavery. Claiming that violence is an inevitable historical reality of colonial capitalism, Fanon also furiously champions it as a source of "illumination" for the consciousness of the people (94), an integral part of what the oppressed should engage in if they are to overcome oppression at all. Violence is global, ubiquitous as well as by definition futural, promised. For Fanon, violence is the foundation of all good and all evil, but it is, in itself, *beyond good and evil.*

If the backdrop for Frantz Fanon's reflection was decolonization, for Hannah Arendt it was the Holocaust. From the end of World War II to her death in 1975, Arendt set herself the task of challenging those who "glorified" violence. One of the results of that effort was the pamphlet *On Violence* (1970), Western philosophy's terrified attempt to make sense of the violence of 1968. Writing for the "first generation to grow up under the shadow of the atomic bomb" (14), Arendt fiercely reacted to the impact of Fanon's book. She also reacted to a political context in which Europe's most prestigious thinker, Jean Paul Sartre, was insisting that "to shoot down an European is to kill two birds with one stone" for "there remain[ed] a dead man and a free man" (Sartre 22). In her critique of Sartre and Fanon, Arendt faults them for not being faithful to Marx when appealing to violence in his name.

Schooled in Nietzsche and, naturally, in her teacher Heidegger, Arendt saw the emergence of violence as the consequence of a failure in *power*: "I am inclined to think that much of the present glorification of violence is caused by the severe frustration of the faculty of action in the modern world" (83). For Arendt, violence is a compensatory surrogate for lack of real power. Proportional to a decrease in power, the justification of violence represented, for Arendt, a capitulation predicated on a betrayal of Marx's original insight. It was a bit odd, for sure, to see a European student of Heidegger censoring an African Marxist for betraying Marx when appealing to revolutionary violence, or for not reading Marx well enough in the course of a struggle against colonialism. In any case, while Arendt polemicized with Sartre's and Fanon's appropriations of Marx, she made, herself, a few poor readings of the world around her, as when she claimed that only weaker, non-nuclear-bomb-holding nations could "still afford" war (6). Clearly misunderstanding what the cold war was about, Arendt continued to think of conflict according to the Napoleonic model that culminated in World War II. It remained invisible to her what many post-1945 wars already announced, namely the shifting of the paradigm of war from symmetrical hostilities between comparable armies to a newer model, that of a sequence of methodical "strikes" by powerful nations upon a smaller enemy. In her eagerness to combat Fanonian Third

Worldism, Arendt may have gone, in fact, a bit far in her axiom that "the Third World is not a reality but an ideology" (21). Since the time of her writing, the rift between First and Third Worlds has only grown, showing that perhaps there was indeed something to the claims made by the first generation of African thinkers of decolonization. In any case, Arendt's pamphlet reads more like a testimony to a mode of reflection now definitely buried than as a source of possible insights for today's thinking. In our age, her universalistic belief in the ultimate comparability of different forms of violence—as in her insistent condemnations of racism, "white or black"—tends to strike us as a naive justification of institutionalized forms of violence, not as an effective antidote against them.

Some of Clausewitz's most forceful formulations have been rephrased with unprecedented brilliance in the late twentieth and early twenty-first centuries by French architect and urbanist Paul Virilio. Encompassing philosophy, urban studies, art criticism, and political and film theory, Virilio is the signatory of the definitive philosophical account of contemporary, global, electronic forms of violence. For him all urbanism can be divided in two major schools, the one that sustains that cities emerged out of commerce, and the one that claims that cities emerged out of war (*Pure War* 3). Not only does Virilio side with the latter current, but he also makes war the fundamental paradigm for the understanding of our *dromological* society, one that is organized primarily around speed. Since the early 1980s Virilio's research has anticipated features of warfare subsequently made popular by the war machinery itself. For over 20 years he has commented in uniquely lucid fashion on themes such as: the new centrality of electronics and telecommunications to warfare, the consolidation of *speed, instantaneity,* and *virtuality* as attributes of all war machinery, the decline of the paradigm of war of state against state, the rise of today's endless and asymmetrical wars, the complete collapse of the distinction between warfare and law enforcement (allowing for powerful nations repeatedly to wage war in the name of law enforcement), the systematic decline of international legal and political forums, and the full globalization of war against an invisible or virtual enemy. All of these traces of the contemporary technology of warfare have been analyzed and often *predicted* in the work of Paul Virilio. This is a thinker who, quite rigorously, and following strict protocols of scholarship, has led us to the nightmarish realization that "in the future war will be waged by answering machines" (Virilio, *Desert*)

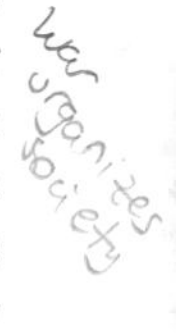

Over 20 years ago, Virilio noted that one of the new paradigms of warfare was "interstate delinquency." It had become increasingly difficult, argued Virilio, to separate state actions of war from organized delinquency. The attack carried out by Israeli paratroopers on the Beirut

Airport in 1969 inaugurated a model in which the "State has strengthened itself against individual terrorism . . . by developing its own brand of terrorism" (*Pure War* 28). Interstate forms of delinquency—some of which get to be called "incursions," others get to be called "intelligent strikes" with some "collateral damages"—have now become *criminal enough* to be condemned by almost the entire community of nations yet *legal enough* to continue to subsist unhampered by any international tribunal. No doubt that the profound crisis of international legality and diplomacy is strictly related to what states such as the United States and Israel have been able to get away with in recent years. The line that separates law enforcement from military action has become increasingly blurred, with strong states repeatedly *waging acts of war in the name of law enforcement.* This is the moment in which war abandons once and for all the Clausewitzian paradigm of symmetrical forces. Rather, it takes the shape predicted by Virilio, that of an "infinite spreading of State crimes, of acts of war without war" (28). The dissemination of "war without war," that is, the methodical waging of international aggression without the acknowledgement of such acts as war, has been one of Virilio's most pointed and well-formulated predictions. In the early 1980s, he insisted that war had become continuous, endless, and now dispensed with declarations of any kind. The doctrine of preemptive strikes later confirmed Virilio's most Orwellian predictions by fully ushering war into the era of military-media-entertainment industries of global and catastrophic reach.

Virilio is the thinker who fully accounts for the decline of the modern symmetrical and territorial wars. For Virilio, that model begins to collapse with the nuclear weapon, which inaugurates a period in which there remains no distinction between wartime and peacetime. The philosophy of deterrence "fills" peacetime with war, to such an extent that peace itself becomes war by other means. Along with the erasure of the line between peace and war, the "ultimate weapon" inflicts a blow in a particularly modern concept, that of the *just war,* an idea that only subsisted alive and well until the anti-fascist effort in World War II. Whereas up until World War II the concept of "just war" had maintained its prestige and delivered considerable legitimacy to the allies, Virilio notes that the nuclear bomb increasingly introduces the notion of a war *beyond politics,* a war that could be, in fact, *sheer technology*: "before nuclear power, the 'just war' had meaning. It had meaning in politics. Technological war, on the other hand, is complete release" (*Pure War* 50). In that regard Virilio echoed Soviet physicist Andrei Sakharov, who argued that a nuclear war, unlike the wars that Clausewitz had in mind, could never be a continuation of politics. It simply was universal suicide (qtd. Arendt 10). If for Fanon the war of decolonization is the beyond of morality, for Virilio contemporary war is the realm of sheer technological speed beyond politics itself. In a friendly aside to the work of Michel Foucault, Virilio insisted that "before knowing-power, there is always moving-power" (*Pure War* 55). That is to say, the decisive datum is not the articulation of power with various forms of knowledge (as crucial as that can be) but rather the articulation of power with movement and speed.[5]

According to Virilio, the history of war encompasses three major periods: tactics (coinciding with nomadism), strategy (coinciding with the appearance of politics in Greek democracy), and war economy, emerging around 1870 (*Pure War* 15). A meticulous student of war technology and communications, Virilio has been drawing conclusions from the observation of all major wars of the past decades, be they Vietnam, Iran-Iraq, NATO vs. Yugoslavia, Gulf Wars I and II, or the occupation of Palestine. Of NATO's bombings against Yugoslavia Virilio noted, in an implacable analysis entitled *Strategy of Deception,* that it marked the emergence of the paradigm of intervention by "silent consensus"—a tool in the process of making the enemy completely invisible. Kosovo also represented, for Virilio, the consolidation of one particular feature of contemporary warfare, namely *the absence of contact between soldiers of warring factions.* Unlike the modern wars, where it was conceivable for soldiers to switch sides when convinced that the enemy's was a just cause (much like, say, many Czarist soldiers joined the Bolsheviks during the revolutionary insurrection in Russia), the *technological war* renders the enemy invisible as a human being and only visible as a target. That is to say, *the battlefield has disappeared* and the enemy is no longer someone with whom you *exchange* anything (Virilio, *Ground,* 43). In the contemporary technology of warfare Virilio finds confirmation of the essentially *dromological* character of our times, the primacy of speed as the central category for the understanding of our society. A contemporary pragmatics of war, then, would be nothing but a phenomenology of electronic speed, if such a formula, given phenomenology's morose and methodical form of thinking, were not oxymoronic in itself. In the scholarship that follows Virilio we see that the history of warfare in the twentieth century has been, in way, the history of the attempt technologically to produce the one-hit fight.

Having finished his book on the concept of "virtuous war" a little before 9/11, James Der Derian capped a fascinating research through Bosnia, Iraq, Kosovo, and various U.S. army headquarters with the theory of a new "military-industrial-media-entertainment network" of warfare. Der Derian's phrase *virtuous war* alludes both to the virtuality (immateriality) of new forms of destruction *as well as* to the fact that these new technologies of death operate primarily through a recourse to the moral concept of *virtue*. Capturing both the virtuality and the presumed virtuosity of new technologies of destruction, Der Derian takes a step beyond French philosopher of disappearance and *enfant terrible* Jean Baudrillard. Whereas in Baudrillard one has a sense that there is a *celebration of new simulacra* over the old and tired empirical reality (the latter perhaps now abolished once and for all), Der Derian prefers to ask whether the new, simulated forms would not have the power to produce the very reality that they presumably came to abolish and replace: "is it possible that new—let us say digitally improved—simulations can precede and engender the reality of war that they were intended to model and prepare for? To reinvoke and upend Clausewitz: can the strategic effects of digitized means predetermine policy intentions?" (Der Derian 16). Instead of a celebration of the simulacra we get a more serious investigation into how new forms of simulation are themselves *producing* a quite distinct experience of the real.

A voluminous body of literature continues to address current juridical, political, and technological transformations of warfare, as well as the terrifying development of ever-tighter systems of global surveillance. This bibliography ranges from John Arquilla and David Ronfeldt's secretary of defense–sponsored research on new forms of cyberwar and electronic terrorism (see especially their edited volume *Networks and Netwars*) to a host of extensive philosophical and anthropological meditations on the relations between violence and religion by Hent de Vries. From a Pan and Latin American perspective, George Yúdice has shown how culture has become "expedient" in a number of ways, including post-9/11 uses of it both to foment jingoism as well as to mourn the dead or critique government and media handling of the "war on terrorism" (Yúdice, *Expediency*, 338–62). Not discussing contemporary wars directly, but certainly feeling their impact, *The Letter of Violence* will engage these and other moments of Continental critical theory, Anglo American philosophy, and Latin American literature to propose strategies to think through the aporias and dead-ends of current reflections on violence.

Chapter 1, "From Plato to Pinochet: Torture, Confession, and the History of Truth," takes up the question of the widespread practice of torture in the world. Rather than focusing on historical facts, sociological statistics, or moral principles, I choose to study the technology of torture in its relationship with a host of issues including voice, narrative, sexual difference, and philosophical truth (*alethêia*) as such. I take my cue from a revolutionary book entitled *Torture and Truth*, where Page DuBois explores the mutual complicity between the juridical sanctioning of torture upon slaves in Ancient Greek democracy and the emergence of the properly philosophical, Greek concept of truth. DuBois inherits the Foucauldian premise of a mutual relationship between the regimes through which the true is defined and the regimes through which power is reproduced. She also operates with the Benjaminian premise that what we call "culture" is inseparable from the daily reproduction of the worst forms of barbarism. DuBois's historical research into Plato, Demosthenes, Aeschilus, Licurgus, and others encompasses different genres and all periods of Classical Greece. Her research leads her compellingly to map out the slave's body in the Greek juridical system as a body liable to being tortured—and most decisively, *a body that will be necessarily truthful when tortured.* In a quite strict and specific way, the first tribunals of democracy linked the torturing of slaves with the emergence of truth. This has important consequences for the understanding of the gendering and the historicity of democracy and philosophy. I will attempt to flesh some of them out in the chapter.

Mobilized as a tool to fix the perennially unstable distinction between slave and free man, the practice of torture played a role, argues DuBois, in the very concoction of what philosophy and jurisprudence have come to define as truth. The gendered metaphor of extraction, of dragging out with violence, informs the very juridical and philosophical emergence of *alethêia.* I spell out some implications of that insight with an analysis of Roman Polanski and Ariel Dorfman's *Death and the Maiden,* a masculinist filmic representation of the impact of torture upon *woman.* I then move on to a debate with psychoanalytic accounts of the relation between trauma and narrative. Both of these arguments resort to a critical dialogue with Elaine Scarry's phenomenology of pain such as put forth in her *The Body in Pain,* a book where she depicts torture as the destruction of a pre-existing domesticity of civilization, effected by the pain of a voice ruling over a body. Against the liberal Arendtian tradition of reflection on violence—a school whose literary-critical pinnacle is Scarry's phenomenology of pain—this chapter takes its cue from an insight that links Walter Benjamin's thinking on violence with Foucault's preference for understanding politics as a mobile war (and not as a contract of sovereignty). Studying the specific manifestation of this war in the practice of torture, DuBois extracted from her Foucauldian inspiration a fundamentally Benjaminian insight: High culture and its philosophical, academic, legal, and ideological institutions have been, from the beginning, complicit with the calculated and organized infliction of human suffering. Although DuBois's work would be unthinkable also without deconstruction, it would not be unfair, I believe, to argue that in this particular debate Derrida would be closer to Arendt and Scarry than to DuBois and Foucault. *The Letter of Violence* goes on to suggest some directions for the study of violence in culture that would be in keeping with that insight, capped by lengthy engagement with Derrida's *Force of Law* in chapter 3.

Foucault's recently published seminars, especially the 1975–6 lecture course *Society Must Be Defended,* have been useful here. Arguing that modern European politics had been structured primarily around the notion of sovereignty (a territorial and static concept), Foucault mapped out an alternative model, anchored on the understanding of politics as *war,* that is as a permanent conflict of mobile forces. Following Nietzsche's lead—the key insight that all morality can be referred back to a clash of forces, to the imposition of a political will upon another—Foucault reverses Clausewitz's dictum. For Foucault, *politics is the continuation of war by other means.* Whereas Nietzsche had referred all morality back to politics, Foucault continues his legacy by referring politics itself back to its roots in war. For Foucault violence is not something that happens *to* politics from the outside. It is, rather, the very essence of politics. Politics is, in fact, the name given to the set of struggles around the territorial and populational managing of violence.

Chapter 2, "Thinking Ethics across Neocolonial Borders: Borges, Ethical Theory, and the International Division of Intellectual Labor," continues that argument from another angle by reading a blind kernel in the ethics of liberal universalism. The specific case in point is Anglo American ethical theory's response to the rhetorical, self-reflexive, and deconstructive turns of continental philosophy and literary theory. Unable to absorb and respond to the challenges presented by those schools of thought, Anglo American ethical theorists have appealed to a "defense" of ethics or a "return" to ethics phrased in terms that are intellectually and politically quite suspicious. Martha Nussbaum and Wayne Booth are two illustrious and erudite representatives of that position, both more sophisticated than the doctrinaires of moral philosophy with whom they often see themselves allied. My chapter chooses, then, to focus the critique not on the hysterical defenders of "reason," "the classics," or "American values," but on distinguished (albeit profoundly misguided) thinkers such as Nussbaum and Booth. My critique of their work takes its inspiration from a scene, a predicament to which liberal ethics remains blinded: what I call the "international division of intellectual labor," an asymmetric, previous division of labor between different languages and national traditions that makes possible liberal Anglo America's own quite regional brand of universalism. This is a phenomenon by definition harder to be observed by those working in the dominant North Atlantic intellectual traditions, especially in the U.S. American, where the phrase *monolingual scholar* does not describe an oxymoron or a contradiction in terms, but rather an actually and profusely existent referent. My polemic with defenders of the universality of categories such as "the human" or "reason" targets specifically their anxious responses to the terrain gained by "theory," a body of texts governed by premises not regularly studied in U.S. philosophy departments (as the latter are bastions still dominated by analytic orthodoxy).

In this polemic I engage primarily Wayne Booth's treatise on ethical literary criticism, as well as Martha Nussbaum's writings on cosmopolitanism. My critical dialogue with them is prefaced by an analysis of the problem of intercultural translation such as dramatized in Jorge Luis Borges's "The Ethnographer." This superb play on anthropology was part of the 1969 collection of prose and poetry entitled *In Praise of Shadow*. It relates graduate student Fred Murdock's impossibility of writing his ethnographic thesis due to his all-too-perfect experience going native amongst a South American tribe. He returns to the United States but renounces the task of writing the thesis, dedicating himself instead to marrying, divorcing, and working as a Yale University librarian. Offering a powerful allegory of silent violence across cultural and political borders, "El etnógrafo" was Borges's great contribution to postcolonial literature. Written from the point of view of an unbridgeable rift between experience and narrative, Borges's tale offers a healthy cautionary note vis-à-vis universalistic, liberal understandings of cross-cultural translation. The blindness with which First World spokespeople for concepts such "the human" or "democracy" attempt to understand the difficulty faced by Borges's character (forced to translate an experience that was *truthful only insofar as it was untranslatable*) is perhaps not unrelated to the cross-cultural blindness that informs much of the violence carried out today around the world. Borges's tale dwells on the aporia that universalistic ethics cannot transcend: the fact that universals such as "reason," "language" or "culture" *simultaneously* get constituted and emptied out, for they depend on a previous, internationally organized division of labor to which spokespeople for such universals have been, more often than not, completely blind. This is the lesson taught by Fanonian Third Worldism, but also by poststructuralist and deconstructive currents of thought. Having engaged deconstruction to discuss torture and to critique liberal ethical theory in chapters 1 and 2, I then move on to a confrontation with Jacques Derrida's work itself in chapter 3. I engage in most detail what I consider Derrida's fecund and symptomatic inability fully to engage Walter Benjamin.

Chapter 3, "Specters of Walter Benjamin: Mourning, Labor, and Violence in Jacques Derrida," tackles Derrida's reading of Benjamin's "Critique of Violence" (1921) in his *Force of Law* (1990), a crucial text for American critical legal studies. My analysis is not antagonistic but supplementary to more sympathetic readings of the same text by, for example, Drucilla Cornell. While engaging *Force of Law* I also discuss Derrida's

Specters of Marx as well as his "Interpretations at War: Kant, the Jew, the German," an essay first presented as a talk in Jerusalem in 1988. I slowly flesh out a complex, multilayered context in which Derrida's *Force of Law* reads a 1921 Benjamin essay written during the Weimar Republic's disillusionment with the "shameful peace" of Versailles. Derrida's reading proleptically refers the essay to the "Final Solution" of Nazism 20 years later. In the process, Derrida says and does not say a few important things about the context in which some important distinctions are made in another one of his essays, "Interpretations at War," delivered during the first Intifada against the Israeli occupation.

In 1920s Germany, the peace of Versailles, coupled with the bloody defeat of the Spartacus socialist Revolution, had come to express a serious crisis of liberalism, characteristic of that moment of European history but particularly acute in Germany. Under fire from left- and right-wing critics, liberalism was no longer able to mount a successful defense of its universalistic utopia of moderation and dialogue. Both Carl Schmitt and Walter Benjamin, rather different figures, are signatories of critiques of liberal understandings of violence that have gained increased attention in recent years. The often-remarked kinship between the two has become, in fact, emblematic of the convergence between conservative-traditionalist *and* revolutionary-left-wing vindications of a *certain recourse* to violence in that era. What that *certain* meant precisely, that is, what exactly were those moments of history or kinds of violence that genuinely qualified, was always a hard question to establish and a difficult border to draw. Schmitt and Benjamin's radically different styles—the former encyclopedic and treaty-like, the latter fragmentary and allusive—attempted to respond to that challenge. *The Letter of Violence* will argue that we must be careful before collapsing Benjamin's thought into Schmitt's decisionism, as thinkers as sophisticated as Derrida have often done in recent years.

Schmitt's *The Crisis of Parliamentary Democracy* (1923) testified to a coincidence between the "great struggle" promised by anarchists such as Proudhon and conservative Catholics such as Donoso-Cortés, both in opposition to liberal pacifism, while his *Concept of the Political* (1927) defined the condition of possibility of the sovereign state in the antithesis between friend and enemy—in the course of which he explicitly established liberalism as the enemy on the other side of the philosophical barricades. Most often remembered in the current revival of interest in the conservative jurist's work are the antinomy between friend and enemy and his concept of sovereignty as the prerogative to decide on the state of exception, developed in his *Political Theology* (1922). Interest in Carl Schmitt is understandable, to be sure, in our own historical moment, when the rift between "the West" and its other is more insurmountable than ever, when the "state of exception" represented by extreme violence is the rule, and the decision on what constitutes legitimate violence depends solely on a relation of forces characterized by unprecedented hegemony of one single empire. The thread weaving through Schmitt's work is the constant rewriting of political antagonisms with *moral* categories. That turn is particularly palatable to our times' dominant reality and ideology, marked by the universalization of violence and its permanent deployment against an enemy understood in moral rather than political terms.

Jacques Derrida, among others, chose to interpret Benjamin's early "Critique of Violence" (1921) in the light of its presumed kinship with Schmitt's decisionism, and as part of a "wave" of disdain for parliamentary democracy in Weimar Germany. Having indeed elicited a complimentary response from the conservative jurist, Benjamin's essay did participate in a cultural zeitgeist in which revolutionary and reactionary vindications of violence seemed to share a common horizon, in a moment of profound crisis in the liberal ranks. As Derrida well points out, "Critique of Violence" was written in the Kantian tradition of *critique,* understood not only as an investigation of the conditions of possibility of a phenomenon (in this case violence) but also as the judgment and evaluation *(krinen)* to which that phenomenon can lend itself. The piece showed clear signs of Benjamin's enthusiasm for George Sorel's work *Reflections on Violence,* where Sorel discerned between different types of violence and championed proletarian revolutionary violence. At that moment the difference between the moderate, social democratic take on social transformation and the revolutionary, Communist one hinged, to a great extent, on their respective positions on the need and justifiability of violent action. This was so in spite of the fact that the Communists themselves, when faced with the possibility and need to consider violent action, also failed miserably.

In any case, both Sorel and the young Benjamin show suspicion of universalistic liberal treatments of "violence" as such and announce *another kind* of violence to come, endowed with redeeming potential. In Sorel, for sure, the theory is heavily anchored in the anarchist and in the Marxist traditions as well as in the experience of French trade unionism. As for Benjamin, his direct contacts with Marxism at that point did not go much further, in fact, than Sorel's own book. He still had not experienced the maddening love for Bolshevik activist Asja Lacis that would inaugurate his complex, life-defining engagement with Marxist thought.[6] By January 1921, when he finished "Critique of Violence," Benjamin was already schooled in a number of discourses articulated through the topic of violent rupture, as he had come out of earlier engagements with Kant and the

German Romantics. By the time Benjamin attempted his critique of violence, he had set himself the task of exploring one particular manifestation of that universal—the particular form of violence he would name "divine." His hope was to unsettle and dismantle the oppositions plaguing philosophical and anthropological discussions of violence. Among those are the logical deadlock between means and ends, and the political antagonism between conservative ("law-preserving") and reformist ("law-making") violence. I take Derrida to task for the elision of some of the conceptual differentiations made by Benjamin in that process.

The chapter is divided in two parts. The first outlines Derrida's turn to Marx (in the aftermath of Francis Fukuyama's "end of history") via Hamlet and Benjamin through the notions of the messianic and the New International in anonymity. The second part revisits Benjamin's attempt to think though violence by raising a few doubts about Derrida's interpretation of that essay. I am not, to be sure, the first one do so, as Giorgio Agamben, among others, has made critical remarks about Derrida's reading of Benjamin. However, I attempt to draw from that critique a few insights for the study of Derrida's oeuvre itself.

Much as Hannah Arendt had done in *On Violence* (1970) Derrida made sense of Benjamin's piece by referring it back to a state of things that, in its contempt for parliamentary democracy, presumably opened doors to National Socialism and the Holocaust. The decades that followed the publication of Benjamin's piece in 1921 operate, for Derrida, both as a retrospective lens through which to read Benjamin's essay as well as an object of what the essay "anticipates." Derrida's reading is therefore both retrospective and proleptic. This is not in itself worthy of note, as these operations with temporality may well be a protocol of any interpretation. I will point out, however, what I see as fundamental problems with Derrida's raising of a certain cultural horizon of reading (especially the presumed kinship or intersection between vindications of violence on Right and Left) to the status of explanatory key to Benjamin's essay. *Force of Law* is, I would contend, the space where a rift opens up and *a missed encounter* takes place between Derrida and Benjamin. My reading is not meant as antagonistic to Drucilla Cornell's, who has cast *Force of Law* as a key text in developing the deconstructive axiom on the irreducibility of justice to law. However, I do refer *Force of Law* back to Derrida's systematic failure to read Weimar Germany (and specifically Benjamin) beyond the inscription left by Heidegger in his—Derrida's—own thought. This collapse often leads Derrida to see the Heidegger mark or frame there where it *is nowhere to be seen.*[7]

My hypothesis is that Benjamin is a spectral figure in Derrida's work, informing, almost silently (but no less powerfully), his reading of Marx, if not of other thinkers to whom Derrida devoted attention before and since his turn to Marx. The second half of the chapter, devoted to Derrida's reading of Benjamin's essay, is prefaced by my own reading of "Critique of Violence." I argue that more crucial than Sorel's influence or the kinship with Schmitt is Benjamin's painstaking attempt to operate simultaneously *within* and *outside* the means-ends dialectic on which all discussions of violence tended and still tend to hinge. This is a question that occupied both Sorel's and Schmitt's attention, for sure, but for which neither had as forceful a response as Benjamin. The area of intersection among contemporaries such as Benjamin, Schmitt, and even Heidegger (whose specter organizes Derrida's reading of the Weimar "wave" of antiliberalism) is well known and has been belabored. Among these "intersections" are their common rejection of liberalism, an appeal to decision and rupture, and a general disdain for parliamentary democracy. However, my argument is that today it is far more productive to read Heidegger, Benjamin, and Schmitt in their irreducibility to one another.

Derrida could have but has not been the reader of that irreducibility. Notwithstanding Benjamin's inspirational (but relatively silent) role in *Specters of Marx* as well as his presence in his superb piece on translation (*Des tours de Babel*), Derrida's work repeatedly frustrates the full encounter, the definitive "having it out with" Walter Benjamin that the work itself announces and demands. The emblematic moment for that nonencounter is, for me, Derrida's referring of Benjamin back to a Weimar Republic cultural horizon of reading in which Heidegger still occupies the fundamental, organizational position. The absence of a "full encounter" with Benjamin—or his dilution within a Heideggerian problematic—might be of direct import, the chapter goes on to argue, for understanding the very real violence that informs the context in which Derrida returns to those questions. This context is that of the piece subtitled "Kant, 'the Jew,' and the 'German'" delivered in Jerusalem in 1988, during the Intifada against the Israeli occupation, as part of a conference where Palestinians were not allowed to participate.

Chapter 4, "Transculturation and Civil War: The Origins of the Novel in Colombia," is, strictly speaking, the only chapter of literary criticism in the book, although the major premises of *The Letter of Violence* all come from literary theory. "Transculturation and Civil War" analyzes nineteenth-century Colombian representations of "processes of transculturation," that is, moments of conflictive cultural give-and-takes where the hegemony and the direction taken by the exchange is never given in advance. Building on the Latin American essayism devoted to the nineteenth century, I analyze foundational texts in the prose fiction of the four major regions of Colombia: the Caribbean Coast, the Andean Center-East,

Antioquia, and the Cauca Valley. Colombia has come to represent Latin America's ultimate instance of violence as a constant, pervasive element in the nation's self-definition, and the study of its early fiction can be a corrective to contemporary critiques of violence that unilaterally link it to state and nationhood. Because it is a nation with a rich tradition of reflection on violence precisely as a consequence of the *absence* of a truly unified nation-state, Colombia's becomes a particularly fruitful literature to examine in that regard. Its narrative canons emerged *prior to* the establishment of a reasonably unified state apparatus, something that cannot be said to have existed as a full reality in Colombia before the 1930s. The study of Colombia foregrounds the need to rethink the relation between state and violence, as older Weberian or Schmittian definitions of the state as the agent of a monopoly on the legal use of violence no longer hold true today—be it because large organized sectors within given states dispute that legality violently, be it because *international* state violence has become legitimate only insofar as it is carried out by *certain* states. In an age where modern, universalistic definitions of the state as the monopolic agent of violence have seen their decadence, nineteenth-century Colombian literature offers us interesting instances of violence before the unified nation—with often the worst violence resulting precisely from the desire and the struggle for a state.

This chapter offers close readings of the novels that inaugurate Colombia's four major regional canons. Juan José Nieto's *Ingermina* (1844) is an exile novel (written and published in Jamaica) about the Spaniards' colonial invasion of the Calamar kingdom, on the Caribbean Coast of Colombia. The novel recounts the love between an indigenous woman and a Spanish official, but it differs significantly from most tales of the sort, such as the Mexican Malinche or the Brazilian Iracema. Nieto's novel devotes itself extensively to depicting the rift *internal* to the indigenous population, between resisting and dying or negotiating in servitude. *Ingermina* paints Colombia's first novelistic heroine (an illustrious tradition later continued by the likes of Manuela and María) but first and foremost it is a key, inaugural novel about the Caribbean Coast's colonial heritage. Nieto's text articulates and mirrors the limits of what Colombia's radical brands of liberalism could accomplish in the mid-nineteenth century. My reading focuses primarily on the ways in which the novel dissolves the political conflict between colonizers and colonized (as well as the cultural and political rift between revolted and submissive colonial subjects) *into the moral conflict between ruthless and magnanimous colonizers.*

Published in Bogotá more than a decade later, Eugenio Díaz Castro's *Manuela* (1856) was the nineteenth century's great novel of manners about the age-old Colombian rift between liberals and conservatives. The novel was particularly important as a mark of how provincial Díaz Castro's own arrival to Bogotá provided the city's lettered elite with a character, a figure, and an emblem of provincial life. That figure offered, with *Manuela,* the novel that the capital city's literary circles had needed for a whole decade and had not been able to produce. Díaz Castro's novel is filled with an excessive, chaotic proliferation of discourses, as the Enlightenment, religious conservatism, civil wars, Colombian regionalism, superstitions, national or international musical traditions, feminism, and antifeminism are all featured prominently. *Manuela* was primarily a love tale about a class alliance responsible for one of the few and ephemeral moments of political stability in Colombia, the mid-century pact that had united conservatives and moderate liberals and isolated the more radical brand of liberalism. I read *Manuela* as a cousin of the Argentine novel *Amalia* (1853), by José Mármol; both of them are prestatehood novels filled with an immediate political clash that just a few years later would begin to be depicted in a far more indirect, "autonomous" fashion.

Jorge Isaacs's *María* (1867) is the novel that marks, in Colombia, that full autonomization of fiction vis-à-vis the political sphere, the reason why, in fact, the novel has been so effective politically. *María* is a Cauca Valley idyll that almost immediately became the national novel of Colombia. It depicts an announced but failed semi-incestuous love between cousins raised together in the same Big House of a land-owning family. This is a canonical Romantic text about which stylistic, historiographic, and sociological approaches have said quite a bit. In keeping with the thread organizing these essays, however, my reading explores an understudied element in the novel: the violent and traumatic moment of conversion as the origin of it all. In *María,* conversion operates as the very metaphor of violence, the image of all the unspoken horror running underneath the peaceful and melancholy love idyll. In short, my reading locates *María* in the tradition of "the novel of violence," a key thread in the history of Colombian narrative to which Isaacs's novel has not been usually associated. As the father hands María over to his cousin after her mother's death, María sets off on a unique path, bound for conversion but also for becoming the very mark of an increasingly erased Jewish origin. Narrative allusions, images of her *hereditary* epilepsy, and deliberate operations on a host of proper names all suggest that in fact the novel engages Jewishness in ways not yet fully fleshed out in Colombian criticism, where the question has been, by and large, avoided. On the other hand, I also take issue with Doris Sommer's recent suggestion that Jewishness in *María* is a coded representation of a rift between black and white. As my discussion both of Isaacs's novel and of the racial context of nineteenth-century Cauca will show, Jewishness and blackness could only occupy rather different positions in the novel. Jewishness appears in the novel as an allegory of the otherness that continues to operate within the tropical Christian love idyll. Blackness is a fully silenced otherness in Isaacs's text, one that only is allowed to exist as *the name of a limit*.

Finally, Tomás Carrasquilla's *Frutos de mi tierra* (1898) is a belated literary translation of the foundational myths of entrepreneurship proper to the Antioquia region. I am tempted to argue that precisely *because* the region was so prosperous economically the inauguration of its novelistic tradition happened so belatedly. Representing the rise of a pair of siblings, Filomena and Agustín, who accumulate wealth by expropriating and robbing those around them (including their own family), Carrasquilla establishes, very much in dialogue with Antioquia's dominant culture, the representation of *exchange value, money, wealth,* as the structuring principle in fiction. In accomplishing that incorporation Carrasquilla closes the era of picturesque narratives of manners and inaugurates the tradition of realist social fiction. The particular tension in the novel takes place between *exchange value* and *love value*. There is a perennial ambiguity whereby we never know, for either of the two couples constituted in the text, whether characters are truly in love or simply attempting to make use of their partner. In that dialectic, I read Carrasquilla very much in the light of broader continental realist tradition that includes Chilean Blest Gana and the early novels of Brazilian Machado de Assis. In all of these cases, the tension and mutual translation between exchange value and love value do not take place without eliciting a considerable amount of violence.

In Nieto, Díaz Castro, Isaacs, and Carrasquilla we have, respectively, colonial occupation, internal national displacement, cultural-religious conversion, and monetary transactions as dominant emblems of transculturation. The former two take the explicit form of violence upon the body of a victim, whereas the latter two rewrite religious conversion and economic trade as privileged forms of the often-violent entrance of subaltern or premodern groups into modernity or statehood. In Colombian criticism, little has been said about Carrasquilla and Díaz Castro, Nieto has been completely ignored, and only Isaacs has been extensively studied. Reading these novels simultaneously and contrastively is, therefore, of particular importance for understanding what triggers and sustains the often-assumed link between the proliferation of violence and the absence or feebleness of the state in Colombia. In this sense the study of literature is of import for all of those who are concerned with the generalized and entrenched violence in the country. Likewise, for general criticism of nineteenth-century Latin American literature—often seen in relation with its state-building functions—it can only be instructive to turn its eyes to the one continental example where literature did not carry through the role of helping constitute a unified national state in the nineteenth century.

The four essays that comprise this book share more than the concern with violence. They share the assumption that rhetorical (symbolic, literary) are to be linked with social (political, juridical) instances of violence in ways that go beyond a functionalist or cause-and-effect scheme. In this sense, the lesson that the crafting of the language of philosophy and jurisprudence was part and parcel of the political establishment of torture upon the slave (chapter 1) is a good corrective and supplement to Derrida's somewhat hasty linkage of rhetoric and politics in his attempt to read the Holocaust retrospectively in Benjamin's essay (chapter 3). Likewise, attention to the crystallization of universals such as humankind, the state, freedom (an awareness that is invariably absent in First World universalist ethical theories, as analyzed in chapter 2) can also help us intervene in the field of Latin American criticism, where the quasi-universal shadow of the state hovers over most of the guiding questions, especially when it comes to nineteenth-century literature (chapter 4). In these different instances, I continually insist that that the ubiquitous presence of violence should never serve as an excuse for naturalizing it or taking for granted the ways in which it operates through language and rhetoric. After all, much of the senseless and unilateralist violence that has proliferated in the world in recent years is anchored in particular linguistic operations involving notions such as democracy, freedom, justice, and security.

I conceive of *The Letter of Violence* as a contribution to ethical theory, to deconstruction, to gender studies, and to Latin American literary criticism. Although the original versions of the essays collected here were written for separate and independent occasions, they have been set to dialogue with one another in ways that were not conceivable when the book project first arose. A common concern with the ***rhetoric and politics of violence*** has made them all communicate in novel and unexpected ways. The journey begins with a study of the infliction of torture as an illustrious chapter in the history of philosophy.

Chapter 1

From Plato to Pinochet

Torture, Confession, and the History of Truth

Torture and Voice

Between the initial version of this chapter, composed in 2000 and published as an article in Chile in 2001, and the significantly rewritten version that appears in this book, much has changed in the discussion of the theme of torture, as the "war on terrorism" has revived debates that one thought were definitively buried in Western democracies. Since the bombing of Afghanistan we have witnessed the resurgence of the scandalous conversation (all the more scandalous when "reasonably" posed by written and televised media) about the legitimacy, legality, or desirability of torture as a method of interrogation. As will be demonstrated in what follows, torture has never been foreign to what we call democracy. It was, in fact, part and parcel of the establishment of democracy in Ancient Greece and was universally used by modern Western democracies in their colonial and neocolonial enterprises. The scandalous revelation of the recent years has not been, therefore, that Western democracy and the practice of torture are not antonyms—we knew that from the work of a host of philosophers and historians from Michel Foucault to Page DuBois. The recent scandal is that the disguised practice and legitimation of torture has been replaced, to a great extent, with its outright justification and barefaced practice, even as it still goes largely unreported in corporate media, the vast majority's only source of information. Torture is now one of our truly universal categories, from Guantánamo to Moscow.

A mass of testimonies, journalistic inquiries, and Amnesty International reports have told us a great deal about the worldwide practice of torture. Not only Third World dictatorships but also First World countries have systematically resorted to it, legally or not. Although preferably used in colonial and neocolonial territories, methodically cruel forms of punishment have also appeared in the developed world throughout modern history. We have learned more and more about the frequent recourse to it as a form of punishment undergone by poorer populations, especially minorities and immigrants, in the very democratic countries that often present themselves as bearers of human rights. This is worthwhile to point out because in the hegemonic nations it is often easy to fall into the comfort of believing torture to be a monopoly of "terrorist" regimes, and so see it, in a second moment of the dialectic of bad faith, as an otherworldly aberration present in Cuba 1985 but not in Guatemala 1985, in Cambodia 1980 but not in East Timor 1980, in Iraq 2000 but not in Iraq 1983, in "terrorist" Arab states but not in Israel. As I write, article 5 of the Universal Declaration of Human Rights—"No one shall be subjected to torture or to cruel, inhuman or degrading treatment or punishment"—continues to be universally mocked. Thousands or perhaps millions of human beings continue to be victims of torture around the world. The difference between states that practice torture (and should be called "dictatorships" or "tyrannies") and states where such practice has no place (and are thus deserving of the epithet "democracy") is a distinction that has been steadily collapsing as of late, even as a plausible ideological fantasy in which one might have once been at liberty to believe. If we understand state-sponsored torture as the deliberate infliction of physical or *psychological* suffering by an agent that acts *in the name of the law,* it would be difficult to deny that the practice is now as global as it has ever been.

The first scholarly history of torture was written by an Englishman who explained it as the manifestation of a "primitive urge" to inflict pain. G. R. Scott's *The History of Torture,* published in 1940, includes in his recount "savage and primitive races," Asiatic societies, and ancient through early modern Europe. Sir Scott wrote in a time when it was still possible to believe that human civilizations progressively become more enlightened and therefore were in the process of abandoning such things. As anthropologist Talal Asad notes in his critique, Scott's description of the encounter between "savage races" and modern Euro-Americans simply assumes "that 'torture' is something the former do to the latter," ("The Concept" 287) this perhaps being the reason why the atrocities committed against Native Americans, for example, have no place in his history. Scholars such as Iranian political scientist Darius Rejali later came around to set the record straight. In his *Torture and Modernity* he showed that in fact torture was far from being a mere barbaric survival in modern civilization, one that would be abolished once we all became moderns, liberals, and enlightened. Torture, Rejali argued, was an integral part of the modern disciplinary state as such. It was, therefore, a particularly modern technology.

According to Michel Foucault's *Discipline and Punish*, the history of punishment has evolved from a premodern moment of *public* display of violence (to viewers that witnessed it as a spectacle of suffering) to a modern moment, where the condemned have been displaced, confined, hidden in prison cells. In premodern times the prisoner was a "herald of his own condemnation." That is to say, "a successful public execution justified justice, in that it published the truth of the crime in the very body of the man about to be executed" (*Discipline* 44). Premodern punishment was first and foremost a performance. Classical torture was "the regulated mechanism of an ordeal: a physical challenge that must define the truth; if the patient is guilty, the pains that it imposes are not unjust; but it is also a mark of exculpation if he is innocent" (41). The performance at the scaffold combined punishment and investigation. In reproducing the crime upon the visible, publicly displayed body of the condemned subject, classical torture had not, Foucault claims, followed an economy of example. Torture was meant to "make everyone aware, through the body of the criminal, of the unrestrained presence of the sovereign" (49).

It was only with the modern technologies of punishment that the infliction of pain acquired the presumption of being a pedagogical and moral force. Modernity maintained the equation between truth and punishment but withdrew the infliction of suffering from the public sphere. While in premodern times "execution [had been] the moment of truth" (43), modern technologies of torture made of the punitive inscription a *piece of information* that could now be appropriated and monopolized by the state, most often as a justification for the act of torture itself. In pre-eighteenth-century punishment, the reinscription of the crime on the body of the condemned had attempted to reactivate power more than reestablish justice. "If torture was so strongly embedded in legal practice, it was because it revealed truth and showed the operation of power" (55). The sovereign, often physically present at public executions, presided over the recasting and annulling of the crime through its doubling in representation. For Foucault, what the nineteenth century progressively did was "to strive to put as much distance as possible between the 'serene' search for truth and the violence that cannot be entirely effaced from punishment" (56). Unlike the public theater that unleashed the power of the sovereign upon the body of the criminal as a *revenge* for the crime, modern apparatuses of punishment developed a pedagogical dimension. Taking "into account not the past offence, but the future disorder" (93), modern punishment intended to produce the "most intense effects on those who have not committed the crime" (95). Modern punishment found its raison d'être in breaking all *future* resistance: Much like classical torture had done, modern penal practice inscribed punishment on the body of the condemned. The difference was that it continued to be a state prerogative but was invariably carried out within four walls. Even though it was hidden from view, it was meant to address a *third, absent* subject upon whom its effects were supposed to make themselves felt as a warning and a moral lesson.

The perusal of Amnesty International reports shows one crude repetition in the modern apparatus of torture: *its exhibition to the tortured subject*. In different moments of the technology of punishment, torture has rested upon self-representations that are not *subsequent to the acts of the executioner but their constitutive moment*. The technique of torture systematically includes, as a central element of the apparatus of terror, its own doubling in the realm of signs, its own farcical replica, its own display, from the forced contemplation of the machinery of torture in the Greece of the Junta (1967–71) to the insistent sound of locks opening and announcing the arrival of the torturer in the Basque Country, from hysterical verbalizations by its practitioners to visual exhibition of tortured subjects to their loved ones in the Southern Cone of Latin America. This surplus of cruelty is a fundamental component of terror itself. That is to say, without being excessive, obscene, absurd, terror is simply not terror. Torture exists in that excess, the reason why all attempts to "measure" different degrees of torture will by definition be obscene.

The pain of anticipation is frequently reported by survivors as one of the worst forms of pain. The modern technology of torture soon discovered that a calculated manipulation of that announced representation often succeeded in producing collaborators. In contemporary disciplinary societies torture is usually not judged in tribunals or reported in domestic media *while it is happening*. In that confined space power can hardly be contested. This considerably magnifies the torturer's power inside the chamber, and in spite of a number of heroic acts of resistance by tortured subjects, the struggle against torture is first and foremost a matter of winning a battle in the public sphere. At least so it has been since the transition mapped out by Michel Foucault, from the state-sponsored public scaffold to the state-sponsored private torture chamber.

Delivered as a series of five lectures in Rio de Janeiro in 1973, at the height of the Brazilian military regime, Foucault's "Truth and Juridical Forms" is a key to the trajectory of its author and an important essay for the intellectual milieu to which it was first presented as a talk. Consolidating Foucault's turn from the descriptive and archeological work of the late 1960s to the later, more politicized genealogical work—as well as consolidating Brazilian humanistic academy's transition from structuralism to poststructuralist thought—"Truth and Juridical Forms" was above all a tale about two ways of telling the truth.[1] Foucault did not quite claim that they were the *only two ways* in which Western societies—literary and juridical traditions in particular—have understood and posed truth. But he came very close from claiming precisely that, and gave us in fact a rough chronology of how the transition from one truth mode to the other took place. In the thinking that leads from Foucault's "Truth and Juridical Forms" to *Discipline and Punish* (1975) and *History of Sexuality* (1976), the mapping of the history of truth is first and foremost a story about how European thought travels from one understanding of truth to the other.

What are these two modes of posing the truth? For Foucault, first truth was conceived as a *proof* to be overcome, a *game*, a *contest*. There was no sense, then, in determining truth by checking a representation against a pre-existing reality, as truth was primarily a *game of force*. The privileged paradigm of truth as a game of force, for Foucault, was the Homeric epic, where the "responsibility for deciding—not who spoke the truth, but who was right—was entrusted to the fight, the challenge, the risk that each one would run" ("Truth" 33). On the other hand, Sophoklean tragedy gave signs of a paradigm that later became dominant: *the understanding of truth as unveiling, dragging, and bringing to light something hidden*. In mapping that second moment of the history of truth—truth as the extraction of an inside kernel hitherto concealed—Foucault's work opened up wide avenues of research: How was the *dragging out, bringing to light* metaphor itself complicitous with the history of punishment in modern, disciplinary societies? Did the image of truth as dragging out not endow modern torture with its privileged image and fantasy of justification? Could one not perhaps postulate that torture is a key chapter in the history of truth? Is the entire metaphorics of penetrating, dragging out, and extracting not gendered in ways perhaps yet not fully understood? What does all this tell us about the connections between philosophy and jurisprudence?

Paralleling many of Foucault's concerns, Elaine Scarry's *The Body in Pain: The Making and Unmaking of the World* (1985) was the definitive contribution of literary and critical theory to the phenomenology of pain. Starting from Virginia Woolf's observation that we rarely read about pain in literature, that fiction seems utterly lacking in mechanisms that would allow writers to represent extreme pain, Scarry takes her reader back to the biblical pattern of representation of violence, namely the repeated action of God's *voice* upon human *bodies*. To be God is, in a sense, to lack a body. To be God in the Hebrew Bible is to speak as a being that only has a voice, as when God appears in a burning bush in Deuteronomy 4:12. To be human is, on the other hand, to have a body on which the divine voice is imprinted. As the voice commands the body, the word is impressed upon the flesh. In Scarry's reading the Bible depicts "the experienceable 'reality' of the body that can be read . . . as an attribute of its metaphysical referent" (184). The metaphysical truth imprinted by the divine word makes of the body little more than a vehicle. Pain stamps belief onto human flesh. Scarry's intelligent reading of the Bible allows us to draw a psychoanalytic insight in tune with much of Lacan's reading of Freud: The function of pain in the Bible is to provide the *link that ties the subject to belief.* The subject is bound to his/her belief the moment that s/he offers him/herself as a body upon which the immaterial divine voice will painfully imprint the truth of the word. The imprinting of God's voice on the flesh is, in that sense, the very image of the entrance into the Law. The belief that binds the subject to the Law is not, then, a natural datum but a result of a process of systematic infliction of pain.

Scarry takes us into a reading of the Bible in which there is no clear separation between divine creation and pain, or, as Scarry calls them, between *generation* and *wounding*: "Apart from the human body, God himself has no material reality except for the countless weapons that he exists on the invisible and disembodied side of" (200). The transcendent reality of God's voice makes itself present as the pain felt by the body: "God ordinarily permits himself to be materialized in one of two places, either in the bodies of men or women, or in the weapon" (235). The weapon that wounds the body is one of the privileged emblems through which God appears in the biblical text. His infinite power depends upon his being maintained in a vocal realm of bodilessness. The commandment not to represent God, not to confer upon him a body or a name, is then coherent with his existence as a sheer voice.

For Scarry, the voice-body paradigm is also the one that reappears in the modern technology of torture. "The structure of torture is . . . the transformation of the body into voice" (46–51). The magnification of the body for the tortured subject, caused by the experience of extreme pain, converts him/her into a subject deprived of a world, deprived of a voice and of a self. "The transformation of body into voice" is the operation carried out by the torturer: His body is not present. He monopolizes the world, the voice, and the self. According to Scarry's axiom, the torturer has no body, only a voice, and the tortured subject has no voice, only a body. The executioner becomes first and foremost a voice, while the tortured subject has been converted into a body: "the very voice of the torturer, the demand or the question itself, is obviously, whatever its content, an act of wounding" (46). Wounding attempts, according to the odious calculation of torture, to produce in the subject a separation, an alienation from his/her body that would make of the subject a traitor or collaborator. This is why in Scarry's restorative conception, recovering voice becomes a key in the battle to deprive torture of its political legitimacy and to make its horror visible.

The remarkable point here is that in the very origins of Judeo-Christian civilization Scarry finds the subjection characteristic of the act of torture, the infliction of pain by a voice upon a body. Even though she herself does not draw this conclusion—and perhaps would not consciously subscribe to it—Scarry's research lends further credence to the Nietzschean, Benjaminian, and Foucauldian postulates regarding the complete imbrication between the high, venerable institutions of Western civilization and the low, despicable barbarism of its torture chambers. In spite of Scarry's occasionally naive belief that torture "unmakes" the world (as if this world had ever been constituted independently of pain), her research into the Bible shows that the modes in which Judeo-Christian civilization has imagined the human subject's access to belief do not substantially differ from how it has featured punishment in its most methodical and cruel forms.

It is well known that torture does not happen because the victim possesses some information that the torturer might find useful. In the modern technology of pain the question is always a component of pain itself. The questioning is never there for some pragmatic reason, that is, to elicit the revelation of a piece of information. The interrogation is not something that, once resolved to the torturer's satisfaction, would signify the end of the other's subjection to torture. In the modern technology of torture the moment of interrogation is constitutive of the infliction of pain. That is to say, questioning is justified not because it produces truth, but it because it produces pain. Herein lies its entire truth, in fact. Its purpose is to lead the tortured subject to self-incrimination—often the betrayal of a loved one—and trap him/her in a perennial circle of guilt. Such forced production of statements in the tortured subject is the *act of torture itself*. As any perusal of the copious corpus of testimonies of tortured subjects indicates, nothing is more frequently unmasked as a lie than the idea that torture happens because it may be useful for the state to secure a piece of information.

Scarry knows this but insists on recounting the act of torture through a phenomenology that describes the *unmaking* of the world. She supports her thesis by noting how the world of the tortured person loses its functional character: "a refrigerator is no longer a refrigerator, a chair is no longer a chair." Even if such a pragmatic content to objects is indeed lost, it would still be a risky step, it seems to me, to postulate that this is equivalent to a "suspension of civilization," a civilization by now already hypostasized as something necessarily "opposed" to such a practice (121). Every time one poses the atrocity as the suspension of civilization one is taking a politically and theoretically risky step. One is, in fact, obliging oneself to determine what is it that takes place in that territory where "civilization" rests, uncontaminated by the atrocity.

Scarry's *The Body in Pain* is a most important book on the devastating effects of torture on language and on the world around us. I do take distance, however, from her understanding of terms such as "world," "language," "representation," and "body" as contents already constituted in advance and only subsequently threatened and destroyed by torture. Since she assumes that there is a civilization already ordered and *then* destroyed by torture, she cannot question whether there might not be some connection or complicity between civilization and atrocity. For Scarry, civilization exists precisely because it is *the opposite* of torture. As an alternative to Scarry's thesis, I follow thinkers such as Page DuBois in arguing that torture has always entered into the very construction of what is understood and experienced anthropologically as "civilization," politically as "democracy," and philosophically and juridically as "truth." These are concepts whose history is quite indebted to the development of technologies of pain.

My difference with Scarry becomes apparent when it comes to reading Franz Kafka's allegory of modern torture, "In the Penal Colony." For Scary, tales such as Kafka's "record the fact that the unmaking of civilization inevitably requires a return to and mutilation of the domestic, the ground of all making" (45). For Scarry, the construction of the torture apparatus in the Kafka story implies a destruction of domesticity. But this seems to me precisely *not to be* what Kafka's story is saying. When read carefully, the tale suggests exactly the opposite, namely that the modern technology of torture does not consist in the simple technical perfecting of the apparatus but in its conversion into an apparatus that can be possessed, *that is to say its conversion into a domestic, private gadget that need not be subsumed or justified by state intelligence*. If there is one thing that Kafka's story makes clear—however enigmatic it may otherwise be—is that the torture apparatus *belongs* to the official, it is his personal project, one that is quite independent of any collective approval by the polis.

Torture in Kafka is thus not something that comes to destroy an uncorrupted domesticity, a hypostasized and pre-existing *making*. It is, rather, something that is constitutive of domesticity as such. Kafka does *not* portray a happy family existing prior to the arrival of atrocity. In Kafka's story torture does not come to interrupt the existence of civilization, but rather *makes and remakes* civilization in its own image and resemblance. In fact, as the official quite proudly presents it to us, the machinery of pain is the culmination of civilization as such. This is politically important because it prevents us from holding any illusions regarding the presumed separation between, on the one hand, an enlightened "civilization" that preserves the "domesticity" that allows for the "making" of the world, and on the other hand a technology of torture presumed to be opposed to and destructive of said civilization. As a copious bibliography does not cease to demonstrate, none of the major institutions of our democracy emerged without spilling a considerable amount of blood.[2]

Opposing the idea of "the unmaking of civilization by torture" is not merely a philosophical dispute carried out at a distance from the hard truth of atrocity. It is a political debate that leads not only to a different understanding of what constitutes Western modernity, but also to a different therapeutic engagement with the victims. If we hypostasize a subject and a civilization constituted in advance, presumably expressing themselves in a "voice" subsequently destroyed by torture, we can only be led to a nostalgic and defeatist therapeutic practice, one that is haunted by the project of an impossible restoration of pre-traumatic subjectivity. We will later discuss in more detail these therapeutic consequences through a dialogue with Slavoj Zizek's work and Roman Polanski's film adaptation of Ariel Dorfman's *Death and the Maiden*. For the moment we need to flesh out better our disagreement with Scarry about torture's relationship with "civilization." An invaluable source for that is the work of critic Page DuBois, who has shown how the very emergence of Western philosophy and jurisprudence is directly implicated in the systematic infliction of pain.

Torture and the Origins of Philosophy

Torture and Truth is a revolutionary book by Page DuBois about the judicial practice of torture in the production of the Western, philosophical notion of truth, as well as in the production of the binary opposition between slave and free citizen. The book starts from a premise that is clearly rooted in the Benjaminian insistence on the impossibility of separating culture from barbarism: "So-called high culture—philosophical, forensic, civil discourses and practices—is of a piece, from the beginning, from classical antiquity, with the deliberate infliction of human suffering" (4). DuBois goes on to map out the process through which, in the Athenian polis, the body of the slave is juridically converted into an object of torture and at the same time a privileged conveyor of truth. The key piece of historical information here is the rule that in the Athenian tribunal the free man could not be tortured but the slave could. In fact, not only was it customary practice to torture slaves, but it was assumed that the slave would *produce truth once tortured.*

According to DuBois, the word that designates "torture" in Greek, *basanos*, evolved from older uses meaning "touchstone that tests gold," to the broader meaning of "a test which defines whether something is genuine or real." Over time it came to signify "interrogation through torture" as well as the act of torture itself (21). Through an insightful reconstruction DuBois maps out the contexts in which *basanos* appears in the Homeric epic, in aristocratic poets such as Theognis and Pindar, in tragic poets such as Sophokles and Aeschylus, in Aristophanes' satire, in Herodotus' historiography, in the speeches of Demosthenes, Lycurgus, and Antiphon, and in the philosophical works of Plato and Aristotle. It is in Sophokles that DuBois observes a transition of the meaning of *basanos* from "test" to "torture" (21). In a number of later texts, philosophical, forensic, and literary, DuBois compellingly shows that torture was not only widely practiced in Greek democracy but was a fundamental component of how truth came to be conceived and of how the difference between slave and free man came to be conceptualized. DuBois's research gives us, then, a key chapter of a Nietzschean project of reconstitution of what has been the history of truth in the West (a history that naturally cannot be written without calling into question the very process through which the boundaries of the "West" are constituted and named).

In Greek democracy, the juridical testimony of the slave was equated with truth if and only if such testimony was extracted under torture. As the slave was "a valuable piece of property, liable to damage from torture" (38), it was the master's prerogative to offer his slave to the practice of torture. This practice could not be applied to citizens, to free men. DuBois demonstrates that torture thus acted to fix and control the very instability of the binary between citizen and slave: "the discourse on the use of torture in ancient Athenian law . . . betrays both need and anxiety: need to have a clear boundary between servile and free, anxiety about the impossibility of maintaining the difference" (41). In Greek thought, the separation between free men and slaves could never be completely naturalized. Today's free men could be converted, through defeat in war, into tomorrow's slaves. Greek thought could not, therefore, ground the social fact of slavery biologically or ontologically. It could never justify it in terms of a predetermined essence, despite Aristotle's best efforts, which flounder in the attempt to ground in some essential manner the rift between the slave and the free man. Aristotle stumbles repeatedly when trying to explain why slaves are deprived of reason: If there is a natural difference between free man and slave, how come free men can become slaves when defeated in war? How to justify ontologically the political structure that allows the systematic infliction of pain upon certain human beings but not others?

Book III of Aristotle's *Politics* starts with this most unfortunate of all tasks, namely defining what the heck really is a citizen, and what is it that sets a citizen apart from a noncitizen. To my knowledge neither Derrida nor the major thinkers influenced by him have yet devoted deconstructive attention to Aristotle's ontologizing of citizenship in *Politics* (Derrida's engagement of Aristotle has focused primarily on questions related to friendship), but Book III opens up ***demanding*** a deconstructive reading:

> Resident aliens [*metoikoi*] . . . do but imperfectly participate in citizenship, and we call them citizens only in a qualified sense, as we might apply the term to children who are too young to be on the register, or to old men who have been relieved from state duties. Of these we do not say quite simply that they are citizens, but add in the one case that they are not of age, and in the other, that they are past the age, or something of that sort; the precise expression is immaterial, for our meaning is clear. (*Politics* 1275a)

Metoikoi is the masculine plural nominative form derived from the Greek verb *metoikos,* which means "changing one's abode, emigrating and settling elsewhere." The more Aristotle believes that the exact expression is "immaterial," and the more he believes that his "meaning is clear," the more blurred and confusing the border becomes. His attempt to separate the "citizen" and the "resident alien" is itself curiously mirrored in Benjamin Jowett's choice to translate *metoikoi* as "resident alien." The context of Jowett's lexical election is the translation of Aristotle prepared under the editorship of W. D. Ross for Oxford University Press (copyrighted 1941). "Resident aliens" for *metokoi* is itself a translation choice that bears interesting traces of modern, twentieth-century configurations of Anglo American immigration policy. Before we digress into speculations on Aristotle translations in the age of the Immigration and Naturalization Service, let us continue quoting Aristotle's attempts to naturalize the rift between the citizen and the noncitizen, for that will bring us back to the invention of torture in philosophy and in democracy. After comparing the *metoikoi,* or the "resident alien," with children and old folk, Aristotle continues:

> Similar difficulties to those which I have mentioned may be raised and answered about deprived citizens and about exiles. But the citizen whom we are seeking to define is a citizen in the strictest sense, against whom no such exception can be taken, and his special characteristic is that he shares in the administration of justice. . . Let us, for the sake of distinction, call it "indefinite office," and we will assume that those who share in such office are citizens. (1275a)

One does not need to have read Derrida's complete works to know that once Aristotle is done excluding women, slaves, children, old fellows, "resident aliens," exiles, and other noncitizens, we are left with a *category that seems to be collapsing*. It is certainly not a matter that little by little, after eliminating everyone, nobody has remained.[3] Someone always qualifies as "citizen," even if the ontological grounds for that qualifying is shaky. The clear ruling of Athenian-born, Greek-speaking, property-holding adult males in Ancient Greek democracy shows that the ontology may be crippled, but its incoherence does not preclude it from *politically* working to favor the most powerful. On the other hand, the justification of that dichotomy is certainly one of the most shaky of all classical thought. I would have to know more Greek language, history, and jurisprudence to push this any further, but we have approached a quite delicious hypothesis: What Aristotle calls a "citizen" is that *virtually empty place* that remains once one eliminates all noncitizens. The horror of noncitizenship is also a void, a voluptuous void that threatens to engulf all citizens, either because they can become old, or because they can lose their property, or because they can be exiled or, along with all their national contemporaries, defeated in war. How can one differentiate citizens from noncitizens if the destiny of each one of the former is to become again one of the latter once they grow old, or get exiled, or defeated in war? How truly stable could the category of citizenship ever really have been in the Greek polis?

Be that as it may, the fascinating hypothesis of DuBois's research is that the practice of torture played a role in fixing that binarism between citizen and slave. The slave is that person who can be tortured. Why are slaves tortured? Because out of torture *(basanos)* emerges truth *(alethêia)*. Beyond Aristotle's slippages ontoligizing citizenship, it was Demosthenes who most clearly articulated the justification for the practice of torture in ancient Greece, with the argument that "no statements made as a result of *basanos* have ever proved to be untrue" (qtd. Du Bois 50). The absurdity of the argument, which turns a contingent link into an essential one, probably did not escape Demosthenes' sharp intelligence. But intelligence is often content to take a break in these situations. In fact, as DuBois shows, the desirability and necessity of torture on the slave in court was not, for Greek thought, something that needed explicit defense. It belonged, rather, to the realm of what was presupposed in advance and taken for granted. In Lycurgus, the equation between the practice of torture and the revelation of truth (when, and only when, the witness was a slave) needed no rhetorical defense either. In order to prove Leocrates' guilt, Lycurgus tells us that he made an offer that the proof in the case should depend on Leocrates' own slaves being tortured. The accused man's rejection of this offer proves his guilt without any doubt since "naturally [*kata physin*] when they [the slaves] had been tortured they would have told the whole truth [*pasan tên alêtheian*] about the crimes" (qtd. DuBois 52). The fact that one should torture slaves and the fact that truth would be revealed through their torture were not, therefore, ever in question.

DuBois's hypothesis is that the establishment of the slave body as one that can be tortured (and furthermore as one that will be necessarily *truthful* when tortured) was instrumental in the *very constitution* of the concept of *alêtheia* (truth) in ancient Greece. If we recall Michel Foucault's "Truth and Juridical Forms," two different conceptions of truth clashed in Greek thought. On the one hand there is the older understanding of truth as the product of a struggle, a battle, an *ordeal* through which something emerges. On the other, there is the conception of truth as a hidden and buried essence waiting to be unveiled and brought to light, extracted from an unknown interior that knowledge attempts to penetrate. The latter is the gendered concept of truth that eventually prevails. According to DuBois, this process of *extracting the truth* is profoundly indebted to the torture unleashed upon the body of the slave. The juridical sanctioning of torture endows philosophy with the metaphor that organizes its central concept, truth.

Basanos dissolves resistance, brings to light, drags into visibility. The metaphor deployed to describe torture replicates the same movement of the philosopher who drags truth from its condition as buried and unknown. It is in Plato's *The Sophist* that we can best see the link between the *extortion* of truth (a procedure through which the philosopher brings to light, out of the sophist, a truth of which the latter remains unconscious) likened to the process characteristic of the juridical production of truth through the body of the slave: "the best way to obtain a confession of the truth would be to put the statement itself to a mild degree of torture [*basanistheis*]" (237b). The relationship between the ordeal undergone by the slave in court and the one imposed upon the Sophist are clear enough: "like the slave, the Sophist yields truth only under violent interrogation and stress" (115). DuBois suggests that we could map, in Greek thought, an antidemocratic conception of truth as that which is unveiled through the body of the other. This conception is implicated in the instrumentalization of the other in the philosophical route toward a truth reified, buried, in need of being dragged into light. Clearly, the process cannot but evoke torture, *basanos* in its legal context. The following question, then, imposes itself: to what extent does the very conception of truth installed in Western philosophy take us back to this procedure carried out on a bastard body? The Platonic metaphor transforms the Sophist's argument into a body that must undergo suffering, harassment by the attack of Logos. *Logic and dialectic are arts of torture,* they are implicated in it, and are so theorized by Plato in a quite explicit way, in fact, in the very moment of their constitution and systematization. Plato's hunting and cornering of the Sophist inaugurates a long tradition of metaphorization of truth as *imprisonment* in Western philosophy, a metaphor that would reappear, for example, in Descartes's epic struggle to impose a crushing defeat on *doubt.*[4]

It has not escaped the attention of feminist scholars that the violence through which the concept of truth emerges is itself highly gendered. Greek thought established extensive links between truth and "hiddenness, secrecy, female potentiality, the tempting enclosed interiority of the human body, links with both treasure and death, with the mysteries of the other" (DuBois 91). Both woman and slave are *receptacles, containers* of truth that do not themselves have access to it as subjects. Their function is to provide such access to the free man, the citizen. Truth is thus constituted through the abjection of these containers. The manufacturing of the concept of truth is thus contemporaneous with and constitutive of the invention of sexual difference as such. The metaphors of imprisonment and dragging to light are not only sexualized. They found the sexual as such by granting to the masculine pole the prerogative of extracting the truth from a feminized interiority. Both poles come to be dialectically constituted in an asymmetrical and violent process: The feminine is the hidden inside that will be penetrated and illuminated by the masculine. The very production of the opposition masculine/feminine takes place by resort to the metaphor of *being caught, locked up,* circumscribed as interiority. The virile task of the philosopher is to extract truth from that container and bring it to light in a process of *extortion.*

Noting the sexualized nature of the metaphor, however, is not enough if one does not submit both terms to a critical genealogy. There is a clear difference in the treatment of this metaphor in the works of thinkers usually lumped together under the misleading label "French feminism." In *Revolution in Poetic Language,* Julia Kristeva *accepts* beforehand the split between rationality (understood as the masculine realm of the symbolic) and the corporeal indifferentiation of the *khora* (understood as the feminine realm of the semiotic). Kristeva then goes on to romanticize the latter as the source of a "subversion" that in fact keeps the Platonic binary intact. Her "transgression" does not go very far because it is based on a mere inversion of the negative and positive marks assigned to each term by Platonism. Instead of the Western-philosophical privileging of rationality, Kristeva offers us the eulogy of the corporeal *khora,* a presumed escape from the cage of masculine rationality into the freer feminine spaces of poetic language. The association of each term with maleness and femaleness remains unquestioned. *Revolution in Poetic Language* was as Platonic as you could get in the radical, experimental, post-Maoist and post-structuralist French literary criticism of the early 1970s. Much less easily dated was the radical critique of Platonism and Freudism by psychoanalyst Luce Irigaray.

In Luce Irigaray's far more sophisticated thinking one finds a rather different position from Kristeva's. In *Speculum of the Other Woman* and *This Sex Which Is Not One,* Irigaray sets herself a more complex task than Kristeva's, namely to map out the process through which the binarism itself comes into being only by abjecting and excluding the feminine. The abjected feminine is then naturalized and incorporated as the hiddenness of interiority. The very emergence of the body-mind split, for Irigaray, is a gendered operation in which the feminine is devalued and silenced. Unlike Kristeva, who is all too content to accept the Platonic binarism as long as the value judgements are reversed, Irigaray argues that the very attributes with which we have grown accustomed to associate the feminine are a product of the violent exclusion that founds Western philosophy. In Irigaray there is no corporeal *khora* to which one might choose to return. The task of the critic is not, as in Kristeva, a simple return to a pure and uncontaminated feminity, but the rather more complex one of genealogically showing how male and female are concepts that emerge in the midst of violent operations of subjection. In line with thinkers who have, for example, argued that no concept of "race" exists independently of the history of racism, Irigaray shows that the very category of "woman" needs to be understood as a chapter in the history of sexism. We will demonstrate how these connections operate in a film particularly useful for our purposes, Ariel Dorfman and Roman Polanski's *Death and the Maiden.*

Torture and Sexual Difference

The Roman Polanski adaptation of Ariel Dorfman's play *Death and the Maiden* (1994) is an instance of what Michel Foucault characterizes as modernity's "juridico-discursive paradigm." For Foucault, what distinguishes this particularly modern epistemic structure is the *convergence or collapse between confession and truth.* Set in an unnamed postdictatorial South American country, Polanski's film assumes the identity between truth and confession by announcing, imagining, and finally depicting a scene where truth can only emerge by confession. For Foucault, this collapse is part of a paradigm that disciplines subjects into speaking in the first person, recounting experience, and thereby producing truth. The figure of the interrogation is key here: Drawing upon the understanding of truth as hidden interiority, the practice of the interrogation is one of the major instances through which subjects are constituted for Foucault. As we have seen, both the metaphor of truth as that-which-is-hidden-and-covered and the scene of confession are heavily gendered. We are back, then, in the relations historically established between torture, confession, sexual difference, and truth. Let us see how these relations are depicted in Dorfman/Polanski's film.

The dramatic tension of the film lies in the portrayal of a scene of restitution and demand for payment that comes about quite by chance. Said promising and demanding is formally expressed by a particular kind of camera work that combines the most naturalistic Hollywood conventions with abrupt and vertiginous cuts that *suggest* that viewpoint is constantly changing, although the two dominant options presented to the viewer remain the same throughout. Gerardo Escobar (played by Stuart Wilson) is an important lawyer and head of a new government commission on the violation of human rights under the recent dictatorship. He is married to Paulina Lorca (Sigourney Weaver), a former political prisoner who was tortured by the military. Although tortured, she never revealed the name of her activist husband. In a way, then, she undergoes torture *for* her husband, the same one who would later, as a lawyer, have a chance to prosecute and punish those responsible for it. While Escobar is driving back home under a heavy storm, his name is announced on the radio as the new human rights commissioner. He gets a flat tire and receives a saving ride home from Roberto Miranda (Ben Kingsley), represented as a good and personable samaritan. This is the nice occasion for the unpredictable workings of chance. As Miranda and Escobar reach the latter's home and begin talking in the living room, Paulina recognizes Miranda's voice as that of the doctor who had raped her during and after the torture sessions she had suffered under the military regime. This recognition presumably belongs to Paulina alone, as neither the film nor the spectator necessarily share it. Almost the entire action of the film unfolds inside Paulina and Gerardo's house and takes place between the two of them and the former torturer Roberto Miranda. More precisely it takes place between Paulina and the two men, until the final resolution, overlooking a cliff, in one of the film's few external scenes. Despite appearances, though, we are not dealing with a triangle here.

The opening shows us the inside of a theatre where a small ensemble plays the Schubert quartet that names the film. In the audience, revealed by closeups that alternate with mid-distance shots of the musicians, we see Sigourney Weaver and Stuart Wilson. Weaver's body and facial reactions are shown as clearly more central for the film than her husband's, a difference indicated by the closeup of her hand as she grabs his. He unsuccessfully tries to decipher the emotional tension in her features. This powerlessness is subsequently reproduced throughout the film to the point of implausibility. The curious coincidence is that a shot frames Weaver frontally at the opening scene, and another frontal closeup reappears for the end of the film, when the torturer finally confesses his crimes (this time the closeup is more mobile, capturing from above the face that it frames). From the beginning, the film makes extensive use of melodramatic aesthetics in order to produce a certain truth effect. The coincidence of similar camera movements framing both Weaver's confession at the beginning and Kingsley's confession at the end is part of what is ideologically and politically most problematic about the film: the validation of the woman's confession was, and could only be, granted by the torturer's confession at the end. The film does not present us with an enigma. It lies to us.

The opening scene is interrupted by a cut and a violent image of water striking rocks during a nighttime storm. Over the image that indicates the beginning of diagetic time we see the caption "A country in South America, after the fall of *the* dictatorship" (emphasis added). Within this more or less standard rhetorical procedure for indicating time and place in cinema (in itself not necessarily worthy of note) my attention was drawn to the incongruous uses of the definite and indefinite articles. If we are in *a* country in South America, somewhere imprecise, why is the reference to *a* moment in the history of this undefined country made by the definite article "the"? What could "*the* dictatorship" mean if we are in *a country* in South America? Even if this undefined country only had a single dictatorship in its history, wouldn't the very structure of the utterance still require the use of the indefinite article? Again the formal question opens up a political one: Only in *one* South American country could the reference to *the* dictatorship be made like this, without qualification. Brazilians, Argentines, Peruvians, Ecuadorians—they have all known many dictatorships. Only in *one* South American country could the reference to *the* dictatorship be maintained in the absolute singularity of the definite article. This is of no little importance, as the achievements and failures of the Polanski/Dorfman film hark back to the ways in which it symptomatizes and betrays the experience that the indefinite article ("a country") at once designates and hides, namely the Chilean experience. This act of allusion and elision (that is of elision of its constitutive allusions) is the backbone of the film's rhetoric.

Paulina's trauma is established right at the opening scene and emblematized by the Schubert quartet. It returns in the following scene, which shows Gerardo arriving home just after his acceptance of the job as head of the truth commission. Paulina has heard the news and does not like it. Represented in the film as an almost "mad" woman, Paulina is "unreasonably" opposed to her husband's acceptance of the job. Something tells her that her experience will be betrayed. When Gerardo is given a ride home by Roberto Miranda, Paulina sees the car headlights in the distance and begins desperately to rush around closing all the doors, putting out the lights and candles, and getting out a gun that she keeps in a drawer. In Paulina's actions, Polanksi/Dorfman rehearse the Hollywood cliché of the upper-class character who defends "his/her property" against the invasion of a "criminal" or supernatural threat. The property itself is a suburban mansion, built in the best U.S. American style and situated to the side of a country road more reminiscent of Illinois or Iowa than of Chile. The lighting of the film, alternating between suburban, semirural darkness outside and intense artificial light inside, further contributes to make the film far more *gringo* that Chilean. The female character's reaction to "defend her property" has nothing to do with what would be plausible behavior in a Latin American activist (unthinkable even in an upper-class woman who is now the wife of a minister of state). Paulina's "false alarm" is repeated a few minutes later, when Miranda returns with Gerardo's spare tire. In a series of shots and countershots we see an alternation between the two environments, the brightly lit living room where the two reasonable males talk about the future of the country and the dark bedroom where the madwoman is frantically getting her clothes together for what is made to look like a frenzied flight. Her escape is in fact the preparation for the insane theft of Miranda's car, which Paulina will then push all the way to the cliff, in a scene where the lack of plausibility reaches its highest.

Paulina's "unreasonable" reactions begin to form a pattern in the film. She systematically displays an "obsession" that seems invisible to herself but visible to the male characters and the implied spectator, whom the film likewise assumes to be male. We see the female character's "madness" as she gets the revolver out before the car arrives, as she throws her husband's meal away when he refuses to disclose his conversation with the president, and as she yells out "I don't exist" when her husband suggests a legal, rational, parliamentary solution to the postdictatorial dilemma of restitution and justice. Her insanity culminates in her pushing, like *a mad woman,* Miranda's car over the cliff—the very car that has brought her husband back to the house. If we were to sum up the position of the female character, we might see that Dorfman/Polanski locate her in the place of the *hysteric:* the one who symptomatizes the truth but who is ultimately incapable of speaking it, of articulating it. Such a reduction of the feminine to an experience that is fetishized and hystericized is contradictory, because the film very clearly wants to make a gesture toward feminism. For this it reserves the melodramatic confirmation of the ending, which shows that Paulina was right in her identification of Miranda's voice. *This confirmation only emerges, however, with the torturer's confession, and is only valid inasmuch as it comes from his own mouth*. Moreover, this is the only possible way out for the film, since whatever the resolution of the status of Paulina's testimony this can only be cleared up with the torturer's verification. We go from the question of whether or not her testimony is true to the question of whether it is true *despite* the fact that she is insane or *because* she is insane.

At stake here is what Foucault maps as proper to the juridico-discursive paradigm of truth, namely the equation between confession and truth. Such an equation is not only presupposed by the film but transposed in a sordid manner into the torturer's confession and placed at the end as the key to the resolution of the pseudo-suspense constructed at the cost of stereotyping the female character. Throughout the film, Paulina's irrational body and her hystericized experience are incapable of completely convincing the male virtual spectator (imagined by the film) of Miranda's guilt. In truth, the presumption of a lack of resolution to this question represents the only invitation that the film makes us to keep watching. The spectator imagined by the film is therefore a replica of Gerardo, the husband, the hopeless fool incapable of learning the truth that his hysterical wife screams out. The pseudo-feminism of the resolution is of a piece, then, with the caricatured portrait of the husband. He comes off as almost mentally retarded, incapable of seeing the absolutely obvious, incapable of believing the wife who went through torture on his behalf. Gerardo is the head of a commission on human rights set up by the postdictatorial government, and yet at the same time *he ignores what any Latin American would know about torture,* namely that the torture of women invariably included rape and sexual violence. In other words, the Polanski/Dorfman film can only attempt to make a feminist gesture by imagining a couple composed of a hysteric and an idiot. The only one of Dorfman's gallery of characters who is not pathological, the only one who is rationally credible, the only one who reasons and is plausible, is the torturer—a fact with important political consequences. The film that claims to be a validation of the experience of the tortured woman ends up being no more than a psychology of the torturer, crowned by the image of the "ordinary paterfamilias" who attends a concert with his wife and children, the odious shot that closes the film.

The greater part of the film is devoted to the "cage of justice" created by Paulina. After pushing Miranda's car over the cliff, she overpowers him and ties him to a chair. Screaming hysterically, she demands a confession.

Her husband oscillates between defending the torturer and asking for a "fair trial." Talking in private with her husband on the porch, Paulina confesses to him that she was raped by the doctor who is now tied up. Roman Polanski's circular travelling shot cannot conceal the fact that the scene's assumed viewpoint is male. Paulina has omitted the "detail" of the rape during her previous conversations with Gerardo. She now confesses and further reinforces the sordid paradigm by which the film equates torturer and tortured under the sign of confession. The conversation between Paulina and Gerardo is as follows:

—I want him. . .to talk to me, I want him to confess.

—To confess?

—Yes, I want. . .I want to have him on video, confessing everything he did, not just to me but *to all of us.*

—And after he's confessed, you let him go?

—Yes.

—I don't believe you.

The husband who utters this "I don't believe you" is the same person who has just received Paulina's confession that she has been raped. Her confession therefore is completely invalidated. This implausible idiotization of the male character (with a concomitant devaluation of the female) contrasts with the cinematic atmosphere of production of truth that surrounds the torturer's confession at the end, after an hour's worth of denials, with alibis uttered in a "convincing" way as to keep the spectator "in suspense." The atmosphere of production of truth is constructed through a series of technical clichés, used by the film to validate the torturer's confession and confer on it the status of resolution: its placement at the finale, presumably resolving a dramatic tension; the slow movement close-up of Ben Kingsley framed from above; his "humanized" face marked by emotion; the muzak music in the background; the rain on his face; the confession of "feelings" ("I enjoyed it, I was excited"). The melodramatic apparatus produces the truth of the torturer's confession and forces us, as spectators, to read his confession as true, and thereby implicitly to equate the confessed and the true. That "confirms" the tortured female character, but only at a point when she has already been irredeemably lost and betrayed by the film.[5]

That space of truth, such as validated by the torturer's confession, is the only one the film can assign to the feminine. As argued above, the equation between confession and truth is not something unique to

Dorfman and Polanski's film. In fact, that equation is what characterizes the modern episteme as such, if we follow Foucault in the matter. What is most singular about the film is how literally it stages the torturer's fantasy, that is, the power of reducing truth to confession through a coarse metaphor of penetration. The film thus reduces the issue of torture to the psychology of the torturer. In attempting to grant a "voice" to the tortured female character, the Dorfman/Polanski film stages the fantasy of the torturer. Confessional Hollywood cinema, in alliance with pseudo-leftist and self-indulgent "exile" writing, pretends that it gives us the truth about torture precisely at the moment in which its stages, melodramatically, the torturer's confession. The equation of confession and truth, mapped out by Foucault as distinctive of modernity, takes here a particularly obscene form. No wonder, then, that in spite of its tremendous success in the grandiose framework of Broadway, the Dorfman play that originated the film was a resounding failure among the public that it had attempted, secretly and in bad faith, to translate and express, the Chilean population.[6]

Torture, Trauma, and Narrative

Can this philosophical and cultural knowledge tell us anything of value for the therapeutic task of overcoming trauma? Can literature, film, and philosophy say anything "practically" relevant to trauma studies? After reading human rights reports, Amnesty International documents, and historical accounts of the origins and development of torture in the West, what is the cultural critic left with? Why study *representations* of torture if the *reality* of cruel punishment around the world invariably leaves us with a sour taste of powerlessness? Is it legitimate to speak of torture from the point of view of philosophy, literature, and film? Is it valid to speak of a "language" of torture? This final section will address some of these questions through a short excursion into the terrain of trauma studies.

A fundamental component of torture is the production of statements by the tortured subject, his/her transformation into a mouthpiece for the statements of the torturer. The technology of torture is the *calculated* production of an *effect*. As argued above, the betrayal extracted under torture is only rarely of use for torturers' designation of their next victims. Invariably, the objective is to produce an *effect* within the tortured subject him/herself: one of self-loathing, self-hatred, and shame. The forced production of utterances during the act of torture may lead to a trauma that eventually buries the subject into silence altogether. Torturers make you speak so you will forever hate speaking, so you will never want to speak again. Torture produces speech in order to produce silence. It produces language so as to manufacture the absence of language. Torturers know that as long as that subject does not tell that experience, its tyranny is perpetuated.

The dilemma of the tortured subject, then, is always one of representability. How can one speak of the unspeakable? How can one relate that which is by definition designed to be unnarratable? The complexity of this question cannot be overestimated. The worst insult to the experience of the victims is what Claude Lanzmann once called "the obscenity of understanding," (Caruth, *Trauma* 200–20) namely the all-too-facile pretension that one "understands" what the victim has gone through.[7] Nothing insults the experience of the victim more than the assumption that the trauma is easily representable and understandable. To that fallacy of transparency, traumatized subjects often insist on the untranslatability of their experience. Cathy Caruth, one of the most lucid voices in the field of trauma studies, has summed up this predicament as follows:

> to cure oneself—whether by drugs, or the telling one's history or both—seems to many survivors to imply the giving-up of an important reality, or the dilution of a special truth into the reassuring terms of therapy. Indeed, in Freud's early writings on trauma, the possibility of integrating the lost event into a series of associative memories, as part of the cure, was seen precisely as a way to permit the event to be forgotten. ("Preface" vii)

The aim of therapeutic reminiscence is the eventual production of forgetting, the anticipation of which produces a profound suspicion in the traumatized subject. "Forgetting" here is to be understood in purely linguistic terms: An experience is "integrated" and "forgotten" once one has found a *metaphor* that is able to translate it. No genuine work of mourning can proceed without attempting such metaphorization. The predicament of the traumatized subject is, then, that there can be no elaboration and overcoming of the trauma without the articulation of a narrative in which the traumatic experience is inserted. But this very insertion can only be perceived by the subject as a real betrayal of the intractability of the experience. This is the particular bind with which trauma studies is confronted: The survivor fore-experiences cure as betrayal. Undoing that foreexperience *without betraying the truth expressed therein* is the patient, endless labor of the pscyhoanalysis of trauma.

The survivor is then caught in a struggle to *resist metaphor* and preserve the *proper name* that names the traumatic experience. The name of an atrocity—Holocaust, Apartheid—is always a proper name, capitalized and by definition untranslatable. One does not "translate" those words into any language, for translating them would automatically amount to losing their meaning entirely. If there is indeed something proper to every *proper name* it is that it preserves something singular and unconvertable. The nature of the proper name as always recalcitrant to conversion into a *common* noun indicates that a clash takes place inside language. The resistance to metaphorization, characteristic of proper names and held onto by survivors in their attempt to preserve the singularity of their memory, cannot but clash with the very nature of linguistic signs as gregarious beings par excellence, that is, beings whose very nature is to stand for other being. In other words, what Roland Barthes once called "the gregarious nature of the sign" will inevitably threaten all proper name with conversion into *metaphors,* a first step toward their naturalization in language as *common* nouns. Survivors will fiercely resist that gregariousness, as nothing can be more insulting to, say, a Holocaust survivor than seeing that word in the dictionary, written in lower case, transformed into a metaphor for "atrocity" in general.

For survivors there is, then, a struggle taking place within language between, on the one hand, the tendency to exchange that would force us to read in, say, "Apartheid" nothing more than a *metaphor* for racism, and on the other, the experience of the survivors who insist on maintaining "Apartheid" as a capitalized name that designates an untranslatable experience. On the one hand there is the movement that propels the proper name to become a common noun and enter into the abode of substantives that can be put in the dictionary and defined semantically. On the other hand there is a countercurrent of resistance to metaphoricity within the name, a force of entropy toward the maintenance of its nature as proper name. The "resistance to language" often observed in testimonies of survivors is not a simple resistance to all language but rather a particularly linguistic strategy whereby the proper name wages a war against the gregarious power of the sign, against the facile dilution of experience in metaphor, against the tranquilizing effect of all dictionaries.

For all survivors this war against metaphorization is particularly urgent and gives rise to the sensation of powerlessness common in memoirs of survivors. The traumatized subject perceives that the experience stained language irreversibly and made narrative an impossible endeavor. Any true therapy has to labor against the effects of the perception that the cleanliness of language has been compromised. Any real effort to confront trauma must labor on that resistance to all language and to all narrative, even if one must also remain on guard against narratives that all too easily put things in place.

The latter suspicion was formulated most forcefully by Slavoj Zizek:

> the ultimate goal of psychoanalytic treatment is *not* that the analysand comes to organize his confused experience of life into (another) coherent narrative, with all of its traumas properly integrated, and that narrativization itself would have to be regarded as suspect, as a symptom, given that *narrative as such* emerges so as to resolve some fundamental antagonism by rearranging its terms into a temporal succession. (*Plague* 32–33)

Zizek may be correct, but then again for victims of atrocities such as torture, narrativization is an indispensable therapeutic moment. Even when narrative obscures the traumatic truth, even when it keeps the subject blind to it, or unable to name it, the very fact that the contours of a story have emerged signals to us that the battle is not yet lost, that a locus of a confrontation with the trauma is promised for the future.

Zizek's insistence on narrativization as something that can also be part of the worst ideological edifice is welcome. Readers of Walter Benjamin would agree with Zizek that narrativization is often what masks the most. For Zizek, the standard case is the obsessive, whose mask of denial consists precisely in the fact that he is "active all the while, tells stories, presents symptoms and so on, *so things will remain the same*, so that nothing will really change, so that the analysts will remain immobile and will not effectively intervene—what he is most afraid of is the moment of silence which will reveal the utter vacuousness of his incessant activity" (*Plague* 34). Zizek's argument about narrativization in the neurotic reveals its nature as an act of denial, its role in the production of an ideological fantasy. Zizek is in fact less interested in a therapeutic argument than in a theoretical attack on a great part of contemporary thought that he sees as desperately attempting to organize antagonisms and breaks into a story that ultimately masks the inability to come to terms with a traumatic, Real kernel. It is the facile suturing of contemporary narrativizing interpretations of psychoanalysis that Zizek targets. Trauma studies scholars agree but remain on guard.

Zizek may well be right that weaving tales has become a way of avoiding confrontation with the unnarratable void. When we are in the terrain of trauma studies, however, Zizek's insistence on a Lacanian critique of narrativity is only welcome insofar as it does not endanger survivors' promise of a narrative. For survivors, this promise takes the form of a *retrospective construction of a witness,* right there where all witnessing had been eliminated. Torture produces a world in which one can no longer be a witness, since the very act of imagining the other, the very postulation of a "you" has been cancelled in advance. The modern technology of torture is the atrocity in its completely privatized form. The destruction of the possibility of witnessing heightens the sensation of guilt that terrorizes the survivor. The task of constructing narratability must be understood, then, less as the elaboration of a coherent, comforting sequence about the past (the sort of narrativization whose ideological effects Zizek warns us against), and more as the postulation of narrative as a possibility, that is, a virtual *place of a witness*. One is here reminded of a famous child survivor of the Holocaust who clung to a photograph of his mother, knowing that there, in that photograph, he was constituted as a witness, he was promised the act of testimony that the atrocity had tried to eliminate.

Manufacturing a narrative that is not complicitous with the perpetuation of trauma again includes, as one of its moments, a linguistic war that takes place around the act of naming. When the Argentine generals succeeded in spreading *their* name, their signature, *Proceso*, shorthand for "Process of National Reorganization," as a supposedly neutral and descriptive name (so much so that even a great number of the victims came to refer to the period 1976–83 as the *Proceso* years), their victory on the level of language was considerable. The torturer's great victory is to define the language in which the atrocity will be named. As Tununa Mercado has remarked, setting aside the term "dictatorship" and picking up the name that the torture apparatus itself created already means to experience an important defeat (2). Any individual or collective therapeutic effort must confront that defeat. To confront trauma is to conquer a space of narratability in which even the unmasking of narrativization can have a place. Securing this place of narratability depends on a permanent operation on language. For the political and therapeutic task of confronting trauma, languages and dictionaries are battlefields. The future of democracy is not indifferent to the outcome of the confrontation that therein continues to take place.

Chapter 2

Thinking Ethics across Neocolonial Borders

Borges, Ethical Theory, and the International Division of Intellectual Labor

Bellicose Philosophy

Again world events caught the revision of one of this book's chapters in a quite particular moment. Drafted in 1999 and published in 2000, the first version of this essay on the international division of intellectual labor included an ominous foreshadowing of possible consequences coming from Anglo American narrow unilateralism in the understanding of some basic concepts of ethics and politics. Certainly I could not imagine that the critique of unilateralism would be, a few years later, a matter of such urgent and important global concern. The original piece published in *SubStance* argued on several fronts, but it was moved by a specific struggle, namely the need to defend literary theory in general and deconstruction in particular from attacks by resentful analytic philosophers who often spoke, curiously enough, in the name of ethics. That struggle is now far less urgent than it was in 1999. The debate between analytic philosophy and critical theory is now a bit outdated, and this is so in part because we have won it. That win has been, to be sure, limited, as it has not translated into a real transformation of the American philosophical establishment: with a few exceptions here and there, U.S. philosophy departments continue to be dominated primarily by analytic orthodoxy. But now the inadequacy of that philosophical establishment to understand the world around it has become so obvious that Derridas, de Mans, and Butlers are no longer needed to make it visible. On the other hand, the mythologies on which such philosophies have traditionally rested—frozen and reified concepts of "humanity," "freedom," "reason," "logic," "morality"—remain alive and well, way stronger now than four years ago. But the debate *outside* moral philosophy has moved forward.

This has convinced me that although moral philosophy is now not nearly as important an adversary as it was when this essay was first drafted, it was worth my while to update and clarify the argument extensively. What follows is, therefore, a critical and deconstrutive engagement with the debates that occupied Anglo American ethical philosophy in the 1990s, conceived in 1999/2000, and rewritten and rethought in 2004. Although the philosophical trend critiqued here has limited reach in our academia (it is by and large limited to departments of philosophy and classics, but modern literature programs have not been immune to it), its intellectual authority is not to be doubted or downplayed. The recent political climate has, in fact, strengthened the trademark ethnocentric combination of U.S. nationalism and universalism associated with some of its philosophical claims. The police state implemented by the Bush administration relies, quite explicitly, on linguistic strategies analogous to the ones used by Anglo American moral philosophy, in spite of the fact that much of the latter is of liberal inspiration. In addition to the military, economic, juridical, and extrajuridical activities we have witnessed in the past few years, the oil-weaponry-insurance coalition currently in power has effected one of the most radical operations on *language* known in modern history. Historians and linguists, in the future, will have to track down the subtle displacements imposed on the meaning and usage of terms such as "security," "democracy," and "terrorism." This research would show how important the manipulation of language has become to the current operation of war, deceit, and propaganda. Be that as it may, if a few years ago it was possible for some to think that the deconstruction of concepts such as "freedom," "reason," or "the West" was an apolitical game in which lit crit types engaged themselves, many have now seen what is at stake in the careful and attentive study of the history of how concepts have arisen, evolved, and been used over the years. We have now had a sour taste of where an ethnocentric abuse of certain words can take us.

When critical theory of Continental inspiration began to dominate English, comparative literature, and other humanities departments, the U.S. analytic philosophy establishment reacted with such fury and resentment that the reaction itself was a symptom that could not go unnoticed by anyone observing the discussion. The typical attack went as follows: "deconstruction and other 'radical' brands of literary criticism foster the dangerous belief that everything can be reduced to language; they foster an 'anything goes' that can lead youth to a catastrophic relativism; they have abandoned moral and ethical concerns in favor of formalistic language games." Of course those were the *sophisticated* attacks, since I am ignoring the ones who insisted that deconstruction was a perilous form of neo-Heideggerian Nazism. One would be surprised at how many of the responses to deconstruction offered by the U.S. American moral philosophy have been more or less unfortunate versions of this *Newsweek*-level nonsense. Such nonsense prospered in some ill-informed quarters, however, primarily because it voiced a *real* malaise in the division of labor between philosophy and literature departments, related to the growing resentment over the attraction exerted on philosophy students by more theoretical, "hipper" comparative literature programs.

One of the most common accusations—that deconstruction abandoned ethics—was particularly perplexing, as it seems fairly clear to anyone who reads Derrida that his is a sustained effort to think of ethics on fresher grounds, a clear attempt to engage ethical questions from an angle that would allow us to rethink them anew. In the hasty gathering of buzzwords for facile attack, the notion of undecidability—Derrida's image for the aporia, the abyss that haunts and makes possible every decision—often served rather well as the strawman. Under attack from a hasty morality that equated careful conceptual labor with political omission, the notion of undecidability remains as crucial today—when so many impossible choices confront us in the world—as it did when Derrida began to develop it in the 1970s. The same philosophers who speak in the name of "rigor" have not taken the scholarly trouble to inform themselves about the substantial impact of deconstruction in large sectors of, for example, American legal studies.[1]

The deconstructive notion of the undecidable is predicated upon a simple paradox: If one could establish any rules for decision, if decision were in that sense ever "rational" and "explainable," then it would not have been, ever, for a single moment even, a decision at all, but simply an application of a predetermined set of rules and norms. In order for decision to exist, then, the choice has to rest upon a ground that has been literally blasted open by the undecidable. In other words, the more rigorously grounded in law and rules a decision is, the less of a decision it is. It is the very nature of decision not to be grounded at all, while of necessity retrospectively engaging in the postulation of said grounding. Every genuine choice must, then, dwell upon and go through the *ordeal* of the undecidable. I will feature the representation of that ordeal in a short story by Jorge Luis Borges, on my way to demonstrating how deconstruction can breach open a number of ethical issues that have been historically repressed by the U.S. American philosophical establishment.

Borges, Undecidability, and the Critique of Ethnography

In "The Ethnographer," published in his 1969 collection of poetry and prose entitled *In Praise of Shadow*, Jorge Luis Borges offers us an elegant allegory. This is a tale about a student's failure/success to read the wholly other, the most radical and distant alterity. Our hero is Fred Murdock, a doctoral student in a U.S. university, a young man about whom there is nothing singular, not even a "feigned singularity" the narrator associates with young men (265/334).[2] Borges's gesture of exaggerating Murdock's ordinariness establishes a contrast with the character's unique, singular destiny. He was respectful and did not distrust books or their writers. Uncertain about his research, he is advised to study indigenous languages, observe their rites, and discover the secret revealed by the medicine men "to the initiates" (265/334). He sets out on this mission, presumably in order to come back and write a dissertation. Borges's genius is to make, in two pages, the very success of the mission implode the possibility of any dissertation.

This is, then, a story about anthropological legibility. It depicts an encounter with otherness and the retranslation of that encounter back into the language of sameness. The image of the conversibility of the knowledge acquired in his fieldwork is, naturally, the doctoral dissertation that Murdock is expected to write once he returns. His ethnographic journey was a successful immersion in indigenous otherness, as he lived for more than two years on the prairie and acquired all cultural habits of the indigenous population. The narrator tells us that he came to dream in a language "that was not that of his fathers" (266/334) and to think in a way that his previous logic completely rejected. After some time the tribe's priest tells him to start remembering his dreams. At last, the secret doctrine of the tribe is revealed to him. Precisely at the moment when the reader expects Murdock to have become a full time Indian, he departs from the reservation without saying a word to anyone.

In this initial moment the story seems to confirm the possibility that the other may turn out to be transparently legible, if one just made sure that all the protocols of an efficacious ethnography are followed. Murdock becomes one with the tribe in a utopian fusion with his object of study. His dreaming in another language offers the seemingly definitive proof that the great divide had been overcome. As the ending of the story makes clear, however, his immersion in his object (the horizon of perfection for all anthropology) also represented the retrospective implosion and dismantling of his research project. At the very moment when he seemed to offer the image of ethnography as a space of translation across neocolonial borders, Borges takes us back to ground zero. Murdock fails as a anthropologist not because there was anything wrong with his experience, but because he simply walks away from the discipline's rite of passage, the doctoral dissertation. The richness of the story stems from the fact that Borges suggests that he never wrote the dissertation precisely *because* his experience as an anthropologist had been too perfect. In other words, Borges portrays anthropology's moment of perfection precisely as its moment of definitive collapse. The distance between researcher and native informant, when collapsed, threatens the very process as such. Much like mimesis, anthropology *requires* a certain degree of imperfection that allows it to exist as such. If it achieves full success, it collapses instantaneously and irretrievably.

Upon his return to the city following the revelation of the indigenous secret, Murdock visits his professor and tells him that he knew the secret and had resolved not to reveal it. After being asked if he was bound by any oaths, or if the English language was inadequate to convey the secret, Murdock assures his professor that neither was his true reason, and that now that he possessed the secret he could tell it in a hundred different and even contradictory ways, adding that the secret was not as important as the paths that led him to it. To the professor's final question as to whether or not he now plans to live among the indigenous population, Murdock replies that what the men of the prairie taught him "was good" [*vale*] anywhere and for any circumstances. The teachings seem to be good for any purpose indeed, except for the original one, that of providing him with the means to produce a piece of ethnographic knowledge. The narrator laconically closes the story by saying that Fred married, divorced and was now "one of the librarians at Yale" (267/336).

The difficulty of interpreting "The Ethnographer" stems from Borges's refusal to offer any anchoring points that could turn the story into a transparent parable. Everything impels us toward reading it as a parable, except that one is not quite sure of what it means. In that matter-of-fact tone characteristic of Borges's narrators, the reader is confronted with a tale that prevents any moralization as to a "proper" way of approaching the other. Fred approached the indigenous in the most successful and respectful way, but the fascination provoked by the story derives from its leaving unanswered the question that could make the text reducible to an ethical imperative: Did Murdock return because he could now live, *in the United States*, according to principles learned among the indigenous (thus carrying and caring for the seeds of their teaching), or did he choose the detached-from-experience job of librarian at an elite university as the sign of a recoil, a refusal that ultimately canceled out the very lessons learned on the journey? Moreover, who is in a position to decide, since the content of his learning remains shielded from the reader?

It seems fairly obvious that the story is talking about ethics, but unlike most tales that thematize ethical codes, Borges's does not advocate any choice in particular. In fact, the story *implodes* the common association between ethics and morality. The story depicts an election presented to a subject and then the undermining of the only choice that would seem appropriate to us. In the space of two pages, an impeccable mode of approaching the other has been presented to us and voided of meaning. In attempting to make sense of Murdock's failure to write his dissertation (due to the *success* of his field work) we continually ask questions that the story refuses to answer: Could it be that giving up the project of studying the natives was the very ethical content learned on the journey? Could it be that in fact turning away from the other, letting the other be (as in the Heideggerian axiom for that most ethical of all tasks, "letting things be"), represented the only possibility of truly responding to the call of the other? The remark that the secret was not, for him, worth as much as the paths that led him to it suggests a primacy of experience over the knowledge that attempts to translate it. The story highlights a fundamental incommensurability between the lesson learned in the tribe and the initial project of writing a dissertation about it. It exposes the rift, or let us say with Leibniz, the *incompossibility* between experience and narrative. If we take this suggestion to be the structuring principle behind Murdock's final choice, we would then be forced to admit that *his giving up the dissertation is the locus of the ethical par excellence.* The ethical is then expressed here only negatively, through an act of renunciation.

The rift that separates Murdock-turned-indigenous and Murdock-the-ethnographer is the zone designated by the deconstructive notion of undecidability. Murdock would not be worth his salt as an ethnographer without "having become" a genuine indigenous subject for some time. But the excessive genuineness of his "indigenous experience" undermines the very possibility of ethnography as such. This is a classic undecidable structure: By "undecidability" deconstructionists do not mean that a decision is impossible or that it will not be made. On the contrary, once an undecidable ground opens up, *there and right there*, a decision is not only possible but always demanded and necessary. The word "undecidable" is simply the reminder that, first of all, there is no guarantee behind Murdock's choice, and second,the choice of remaining true to the indigenous lesson exists, but it implies breaking with the ethnography that originally allowed him to approach that lesson to begin with. The rigorously rational choice does exist, but only at the price of imploding the space of choice as such. Try explaining that to rational choice scholars in economics departments in the North Atlantic countries, and you will have a sense of the profound limits of interdisciplinary dialogue. In "The Ethnographer" Borges is critiquing anthropology, certainly, but he is also, in a way, portraying anthropology as the privileged space for that kind of interrogation to arise.

The Borges story rests upon the indissociability between Murdock's *successful* experience going native and the impossibility of writing the dissertation. His success is his failure. The story rests on undecidable grounds not because it is merely "ambiguous," as one would say in New Critical fashion. It is, rather, that it establishes a *determinate* relationship—it may be worthwhile to stress again that undecidability has nothing to do with "indeterminacy"—between the success of the journey (true knowledge of the other) and the failure of the purposes behind the journey (a dissertation presenting the knowledge acquired). For Murdock there is no simple choosing between the immanent knowledge of his experience in the plains and the external knowledge of the doctoral dissertation. The former is initially thought of as a precondition for the latter, but the successful completion of the journey preempts the very possibility of translating it into academic language. This is one of those cases of trips that you needed to take in order to realize that the trip was useless and empty all along—albeit strictly necessary in its emptiness.

I know of no story more efficacious to introduce students into the pleasures and perils of cross-cultural (mis)understanding. Putting in crisis all hasty desire for facile legibility, "The Ethnographer" depicts an asymmetrical relationship. For Murdock it is possible to produce knowledge about the indigenous tribe by entering it from an outside position, by penetrating it. The reverse is not true, not because the indigenous do not produce knowledge about Murdock, but rather because they can only do so endotopically. They only know the other as the one who is occupying their land. The divide is not between those who think and those who do not, as if the story did not make clear how much thinking actually goes on in the tribe. The split is not, either, between one culture that could, by virtue of its own intrinsic properties, absorb others, and another culture that could not do the same—as in the common revamping of old theses regarding the "West's" superiority.[3] The point is that an uneven balance of power makes it possible and inevitable that indigenous thinking be appropriated outside by a metalanguage that turns it into raw material, without that metalanguage having to go through the same process. The language that does the appropriating is not seen as one language among others. Unlike the indigenous thinking, that language is assumed to be universal. There is no symmetry, no two-way street, therefore, between those who study and those who are studied. While the anthropologist comes from the outside to find a niche that allows him to become *one of them*, indigenous thinking has endotopic knowledge of the one who comes from outside. That knowledge may be privileged epistemologically, but it is also much more painful.

This highly gendered asymmetry has, of course, occupied much of modern anthropology's self-examination, and the unreciprocal nature of the anthropological endeavor is a theme that dates back at least to the disciplinary crisis provoked by decolonization (Leiris; Asad, *Anthropology*). Brazilian writer Silviano Santiago has referred to anthropology as a manifestation of "Europe's guilty conscience" (*Vale* 25), and the discipline has certainly been haunted by the need to come to terms with the imbalance that lies at its foundation. The recent "literary turn" of cultural anthropology has reflected upon this imbalance, most fruitfully, with rhetorical categories. In James Clifford's probing into the various modes of constitution of "ethnographic authority," the notion of *allegory* comes in precisely to signify the fact that such authority always relies on the imaginary suturing of a broken, fragmented process of representation. Clifford highlights in fact that the constitution of such authority was indebted, in the early days of anthropology, to the avant-gardist scenario where "the 'primitive' societies of the planet were increasingly available as aesthetic, cosmological, and scientific resources" ("Allegory" 120). Clifford's work is the moment when anthropology's self-examination decides to highlight the rhetorical nature of the imbalance that makes the discipline possible.

Another key moment in the history of anthropology's self-examination is Johannes Fabian's demonstration of how the discipline constitutes its object by converting spatial into temporal distance. By denying the other that it studies all coexistence in time—the neocolonial epistemic mechanism that Fabian calls "denial of coevalness"—anthropology creates the fiction of an evolutionary line at the end of which lies the anthropologist's own culture. Anthropology's guilty conscience over the asymmetry that makes it possible—and rich scholarly elaboration thereof—represents an instance of the ethical problems posed by what I call the international division of intellectual labor. These should not be seen, of course, as a privilege or a damnation unique or particular to anthropology.[4] Given anthropology's singular relationship with the phenomenon of colonialism, the discipline might dramatize this imbalance more visibly, perhaps, than most others. Anthropologists certainly have been more aware and willing to address that imbalance in metadisciplinary discussion more often and more effectively than most other folks in the humanities. The point, however, is that the international division of intellectual labor produces certain *real* effects: a hierarchy of worldviews, the presumption of universality of certain concepts, the reification and naturalization of certain categories. In other words, a host of issues that demand to be *thought philosophically*, or not be thought at all.

The abyss that separates Murdock-the-indigenous from Murdock-the-ethnographer in the Borges story restages *the philosophical rift between experience and knowledge*. Based on the fact that for Borges all knowing takes the form of a story, I have been referring to that binarism in "The Ethnographer" as one between experience and narrative. For Borges, ethnography is possible due to the fact that the rift is unbridgeable. Awareness of such rift, when taken to its ultimate logical consequences, would necessarily have to entail the dynamiting of the ground that sustains the discipline. This rift, once looked at from the point of view of its *international* imbalance, places in crisis certain ethical formulations produced on the dominant side of the cultural and political divide. Let us say that the asymmetry highlighted by Borges, when taken to the arena of contemporary academic knowledge, is a variation on a split reproduced in the university between national traditions expected to produce thought (philosophy, "theory") and those traditions expected to provide objects for the thinking learned elsewhere. Let us say that this is a variation, then, on the split between *producers of thought* and *producers of objects for thought*.

In the colonized vernaculars and in the European languages where national philosophical traditions were not constituted—Spanish, Catalan, Portuguese[5]—one systematically faces the effects of a perverse division of labor according to which those traditions could produce unique objects for thought, but not original thinking themselves. Thought itself would always be, in those languages, an application of a set of techniques learned elsewhere. In so far as the absence of philosophy in these traditions is very real and has lasting effects, this division of labor is not simply a myth or a mistake otherwise avoidable. In other words, one cannot exorcise this problem simply by saying that we should "pay more attention" to "Latin American thought," or that we should cease to "privilege" thinkers who wrote in the hegemonic European languages, as though it made no difference whether or not you share a native language with Kant, Rousseau, or Locke. The problem cannot be brushed away, either, by the claim that in peripheral national and linguistic traditions, literature, and not philosophy, does most of the thinking. All of these arguments are quite worn out and are easily appropriated by a self-satisfied and compensatory aestheticism.

In the marginal European languages that do not have philosophical traditions of their own, to substitute for an absent philosophy has been, in fact, one of literature's most consistent claims to self-legitimation. In these languages, in which all philosophy exists in the form of *translation* or *commentary*, literature has claimed to be the unique and original door into thinking. The rhetoric that usually accompanies this compensatory ideology of the literary, far from questioning the international division of intellectual labor, makes the phenomenon all the harder to fight. The separation between producers of thought and producers of objects for thought is somehow turned into a presumed asset, a fecund void to be filled by a "great" literature all too satisfied to occupy a position previously assigned in a rather perverse international division of labor (the "boom" of Latin American literature, for example, mastered that dialectic to great effect by presenting its fiction as the philosophy the continent had never had). This reinforces, in its turn, exotic expectations by those on the other side of the spectrum, that is, the dominant traditions: "give us more García Márquez, more magical realism, give us what we don't have, after all there are plenty of people doing this theoretical stuff in English departments!"[6] No matter how sympathetic exotic expectations may be, the power asymmetry that makes them possible cannot be brushed aside by nativist or folklorist affirmations of originality or "difference."

One must not refuse to think in the void left by the absence of philosophy. Refusing to think through that void has been the gesture of many a Latin American intellectual who has chosen to claim that "we have original thinking here too" while going on with life as though they did not, in fact, as though the affirmation of originality were merely one that they needed to make. The challenge is, in other words, to learn to think of the *absence of philosophy as the most philosophical moment of these traditions*. Whereas in the hegemonic languages it is fairly easy to live in monolingual oblivion and happiness (as we will see soon with our examination of American moral philosophers), certain traditions are endowed with the possibility of thinking what it means to exist in a language deprived of philosophy. As Chilean philosopher and essayist Pablo Oyarzún has shown, one of the only books by a Latin American "philosopher" to have garnered a bit of attention recently is, ironically, predicated on *the forgetting* of that difference ("Heidegger" 84–100). Victor Farías's *Heidegger and Nazism*, the book that was used to reignite a rather ill-informed campaign against deconstruction and against "Heidegger-the-Nazi," is not really a book worthy of any attention except in what it forgets.

In a quick but brilliant passage of an essay devoted to the question of *tone* in Heidegger, Oyarzún shows how Farías's book exists as a tribute to Farías's incapacity to respond to a question and an invitation that had been posed to him by Heidegger himself. Farías explains in an interview that *twenty years before* the publication of *Heidegger and Nazism*, he was confronted with Heidegger's invitation to translate *Being and Time* into Spanish. In his own words, he refused because "I didn't want to dedicate twenty years to this task, and looked for an excuse. I said: 'Professor, by reading Plato I learn Greek, by reading Heidegger I learn German.'" (Farías qtd. Oyarzún, "Heidegger," 88). Here Oyarzún understands and poses the fundamental question by reading precisely what begs reading, that is, Farías's refusal to translate *Being and Time* for 20 years, followed by his publishing—*20 years later*—a pitiful and opportunistic book "denouncing" Heidegger-the-Nazi on the basis of zero original research[7]: "The weight here is that of the original, the *value* of the original, differently from the translation. And two questions resonate in their absence. How to learn Spanish, that is, by reading whom, that is, by reading which philosopher? There is no answer. But also: why not learn Spanish by translating (for example, Heidegger)? There is no answer" (Oyarzún, "Heidegger," 88). What we learn from Oyarzún's felicitous critique is that in his refusal to *translate* Heidegger, Farías already announced the disastrous result that we would see 20 years later: an obscurantist book that contributes to a ill-informed campaign directed against the very thinker that it attempts to study. In his incapacity to accept the task of translating Heidegger into Spanish, Farías pays the philosophical price. He fails to see that he is coming from a tradition in which the *ethics of knowledge* is absolutely inseparable from the *ethics of translation*. In not being able to see the importance of the question of translation, Farías was already setting himself up to make a poor reading of Heidegger, one that simply repeated the cliché of Heidegger-the-Nazi.

Borges's story also allows us to see how the international division of intellectual labor bears crucial implications for this relationship between *ethos* and *episteme*. For the tribe in Borges's story, as for objects of ethnographic narratives in general, mode of being is construed as inseparable from knowledge. After all, it is by *living* that Murdock learns it; he only becomes one of them when experience and knowledge become one. That is to say, in the tribe there is no separation between *ethos* and *episteme*. Murdock-the-anthropologist, on the other hand, lives in a modern world where social spheres have been clearly marked off, and morality, aesthetics, and the sciences are three distinct domains. The consequence is that unlike the tribe (construed as the producers of objects for thought), the anthropologist (the producer of thought), is in a situation that allows him to sever *ethos* from *episteme*, knowledge from morality, *Wissenschaft* from *Sittlichkeit*, and thus produce truth beyond ethics, that is, elaborate a truth content that would then only a posteriori come to be assigned a moral content. To the tribe, to those whose only knowledge of the other is endotopic, that possibility is structurally precluded. This is the abyssal rift where all declarations of liberal good will turn out to crumble down.

Murdock, however, learns a lesson. His theoretical apparatus does not remain intact but undergoes a total change when confronted with his new object. The ideal of a successful ethnographic immersion in the other, the dream of becoming one with the object, of achieving that completely internal knowledge fully respectful of the other, ends up dynamiting all roads back to the safe external knowledge of the doctoral dissertation. The study of the other is, then, a necessarily failed enterprise, not in the banal sense that full knowledge of the other is impossible but in the more fundamental sense that in its failure resides its condition of possibility; its success forcibly entails the undermining of knowledge as such. The story's pedagogical potential stems from the fact that it brings us dangerously close to that abyss where knowledge faces its wholly other, that sustaining ground that no longer belongs to knowledge as such.

Is it too ambitious a task for our times to formulate a pedagogical ethics that invites students to experience the vertigo that one's knowledge about the other may very well undermine the very position from which one has been granted the possibility of producing that knowledge? If a multicultural climate has generated a student population ever hungrier for otherness, why limit oneself to a liberal benevolence that quiets guilty consciences and changes nothing in the terms of the debate? Why not take the truly risky step of unconditionally welcoming that otherness in ways that can produce a radical epistemic crisis in the classroom? If that other cannot be truly welcomed today, all talk of ethics will have been nothing more than empty chatter, for the *unconditional* welcoming of the other is simply axiomatic for ethics as such. Precisely because suspicion of the other is at the highest, hospitality and good will must govern all choices in the terrain of international politics and ethics. As deconstruction makes clear, there is no merit in being hospitable when *danger is zero*. If the other to be welcomed is not truly an *other*, then we are not really talking about hospitality, are we? A situation of complete predictability would simply represent a moment when, properly speaking, hospitality would no longer be at stake. The concept of hospitality pressuposes the welcoming of *an other*, and the concept of otherness by definition includes a risk.

If Murdock is prey to the paradox of a full knowledge that undermines the channels through which that knowledge could be encoded and circulated, readers of the story, in their turn, replicate the paradox in the very act of reading it. For how can the indigenous secret, presumably unique and untranslatable, be converted into Murdock's dissertation without losing that which defines it? How can the reader of the story accede to the secret learned by Murdock if our only contact with him takes place through literature, this most Western of all discourses? The impossibility of canceling out the undecidability here places us on deconstructive terrain, that is, in Gayatri Spivak's favorite phrasing *the critique of a structure one cannot but inhabit* or, as Drucilla Cornell would prefer, the radically open thinking of the limit. I cannot think of a better definition of an ethical relation to the academic apparatus inhabited by Murdocks and by ourselves. Much could be said about the ethical foundation of canon expansions, disciplinary and transdisciplinary revisions, institutional reforms, and curricular changes in the light of Murdock's story, but for now the lessons learned from Borges will offer us a tool to critique the provincial universalism of Anglo American ethical theory.

The Unhappy Marriage of Moral Philosophy and Literary Theory

Much of the work produced in recent years on the relationship between ethics and literature has responded to two major concerns: on the one hand, the possible or desirable role of literature as a source for ethical theory (Nussbaum, *Love's*; B. Williams; McIntyre) and, on the other, the contribution of ethically informed perspectives to the understanding of literature (Nussbaum, *Love's*; Booth; Parker; Newton). Philosophers in search of alternative models of ethical agency have found much from which to profit in the examination of literature, especially of prose fiction. Likewise, ethically oriented critics have added a new dimension to their interpretive task by incorporating the philosophical tradition of ethical inquiry, especially the Kantian and post-Kantian. However, on both sides of the disciplinary divide the dialogue with literary theory in the past couple of decades has been, to say the least, problematic. Viewed with suspicion by both moral philosophers and ethical critics, "theory" has often been cast as responsible for the bracketing of ethical concerns in literary studies. My argument is that this unhappy marriage between ethics and literary theory is best understood when referred back to a neocolonial "international division of intellectual labor," an asymmetrical and hierarchical distribution of cognitive positions among different countries and regions of the globe. That phenomenon is, by definition, best observed and lived in a language other than English, even thought it is best combatted, in some circumstances at least, in this very language.

Throughout the 1990s a number of Anglo American studies championed a presumed return with a vengeance of ethical literary criticism. It was the liberal and conservative wings of U.S. philosophy prematurely celebrating a victory over deconstruction after the "De Man affair."[8] After being obscured by a host of methods oblivious to ethical concerns, we were told, the inquiry into the ethical powers of literature had become again a central concern for literary studies. Leona Toker found "the reasons for the temporary eclipse of ethical criticism in the second half of the twentieth century" (xi) in "the widespread disillusionment with the traditional moral values—in the wake of the Nazi crimes, or those of the Gulag, or the unhealed wounds and unanswered questions of Vietnam" (xiii). Introducing a chapter on the "resurgence" of ethical criticism entitled "the return of the repressed," David Parker noted "the virtual absence of explicit ethical interest in contemporary literary discourse" (4), a vacuum filled by moral philosophers whose work testified that "literary studies can no longer ignore the ethical without yielding up a once central part of its intellectual responsibility and constituency to other disciplines" (4). Martha Nussbaum, herself one of the philosophers quoted by Parker, identified an "absence, from literary theory, of the organizing questions of moral philosophy, and of moral philosophy's sense of urgency about these questions" (*Love's* 170).

Of the conflation presupposed by many of these texts between the ethical dimension of literary studies, whether present or absent, and the concerns of moral philosophy, especially in the forms canonical in U.S. philosophy departments, I will attempt to say something later. For now let me underscore that the examples of a narrative of decline and a (more or less successful and widespread) return of the ethical could be multiplied (Booth 25–7). As the reader will have inferred from my tone, I view such narratives with a good deal of skepticism. From Marx, Nietzsche, and Freud, all of them thinkers of the return, let us retain the notion that a return is never a simple emerging back from absence into presence, that what returns may in fact have been there all along, or that the return may be another name for the subject becoming something else.

Deconstruction in particular and post-phenomenological thought in general[9] occupied a central position in those apocalyptic narratives about the place of ethics in literary studies: "recent critical theory has, of course, placed in question the idea of the constitutive subject of language by subordinating selfhood to linguistic structure, and this theoretical position makes the study of ethical attitudes difficult, to say the least" (Siebers 2). Siebers does not demonstrate the point, but the reader is led to assume that the displacement of the sovereign humanist subject and its inscription in a textual/political/libidinal field that exceeds it (which is the better informed translation of his gross generalization of the terms "subordinating selfhood to linguistic structure") has caused an apocalyptic demise of the ethical. The obvious question that imposed istself was, of course, when exactly that realm of prelapsarian ethical paradise assumed by Siebers ever existed. If one can no longer think of "responsibility" and "moral decision" in the terms one once did, it follows that a new theoretical barbarism has replaced our good old ethics. The rhetoric surrounding literary theory's supposed abandonment of the ethical tended to construe the problem by assigning to universalist humanism and its offspring in moral philosophy an exclusive monopoly on ethics. Moral philosophy did so at the price of ignoring the powerful ethical motifs raised by post-phenomenological thought and transdisciplinary endeavors such as psychoanalysis, feminism, Marxism, and race studies. It turns out, of course, that the definition of what qualifies as an ethically valenced inquiry is considerably overdetermined by national boundaries. Much of the ambiguity surrounding the phenomenon stems from a rift between, on the one hand, what has come to be called "critical theory"—the fundamental epistemological claims of which are predicated on modern continental philosophy—and, on the other, the considerable resistance it has raised in the U.S. literary and, especially, philosophical establishments.[10]

My discussion of the ethical implications of the international division of labor draws upon a dialogue with two of today's most erudite humanist critics: Wayne Booth and Martha Nussbaum. In addition to the appeals to ethics coming from traditional strongholds of right-wing custodians of "Western values" (a phenomenon serious enough to deserve a separate analysis and a careful critique, which themselves constitute one of our ethical tasks)[11] the position represented by Booth and Nussbaum is the one that most often makes reference to ethics. This is a liberal brand of humanism, philosophical or literary, that has confronted, with varying degrees of good faith and success, the challenges presented by poststructuralist, deconstructive critical theory. Liberal humanism often presents itself as the only ethically valenced alternative to the conservative hysteria about the demise of "Western values." In the eyes of humanists, contemporary theory has been "oblivious" to ethics. That picture is to be doubted, since despite the fact that both Booth and Nussbaum elegantly handle massive amounts of literary and philosophical information, neither of them gives us great signs of having read post–World War II European thought very carefully. My goal here is to interrogate them from the standpoint of an international intellectual market characterized by a heavy dissymmetry among its agents, a perspective that their (rather provincial) brand of universalist liberalism is perhaps precluded from carrying out. On the agenda is a rethinking of the concept of the universal in an age in which that concept has been spectacularly voided and contested.

However one views the role of ethics in literary studies, a prominent position must be accorded to Wayne Booth's *The Company We Keep*, a crucial work in what has been construed as a resurgence in ethical criticism. Booth holds the seemingly contradictory claims that ethical criticism "fell on hard times"—"it goes unmentioned in most discussions among professional critics" (25)—*and* that "just about everybody on our scene is an 'ethical' critic" (67), in the sense that aesthetic and epistemological stances will always include, if implicitly, ethical choices. Booth's challenge to the Kantian separation between moral and aesthetic philosophy thus echoes Hegel's, who had showed how an "ought to" lurked behind every "is" in the Kantian definitions of the beautiful and the sublime.

Booth's work deplores the lack of explicit clarification of the values underlying specialized aesthetic analyses—hence his contention that ethics most goes often "goes unmentioned." In his attempt to fill this gap Booth makes a compelling case for the humanist project of enlightenment through letters: "a Conversation Celebrating the Many Ways in Which Narratives Can Be Good for You—with Side-Glances at How to Avoid Their Powers for Harm" (ix), as he defines it. Taking distance from the prescriptivism of much moral philosophy and aligning himself with an entire tradition that has dissolved the commonly accepted equivalence between the *moral* and the *ethical*, Booth shows how the reflection on the encounter between a text's or an implied author's ethos and that of the reader cannot be subsumed under a set of norms. "[P]ostponing most questions about good and bad *morality*, in every ordinary sense," Booth stresses that "*ethical* distinctions do not depend on choices between traditional *moral* virtues" (179). Aware that moral condemnations common in earlier ethical criticism, from Plato to Leavis, "gave ethical criticism a bad name," Booth poses the question: "Can we hope to find a criticism that can respect variety and offer *knowledge* about why some fictions are worth more than others?" (36). An attempt to ground the latter claim, that is, that indeed some fictions *are* worth more than others, could only dispense with an implicit morality by resorting to an investigation of historical processes through which values *have been assigned* to those fictions. Otherwise, if one takes those values to be intrinsic, either "potentially" or "actually" present—as Booth attempts to distinguish when faced with the problem (89)—how can one possibly "respect variety" other than by refusing to take one's ethical position to its necessary logical conclusion, the advocacy of those values *over* others that are "worth less" than they are? Booth touches on questions long ago addressed and resolved in the sociology of art, in Sartrism, in the poststructuralist critique of Sartrism, and in the full range of contemporary offspring of those debates, including Barbara Herrstein Smith's radical critique of the concept of value. As he has not seriously devoted time to reading any of those traditions, Booth cannot but approach the problem and then immediately step back, fall back upon his unreflexive, provincial-universalistic morality.

Booth's dilemma reflects a relationship of overdetermination: Readers who have grappled with Booth's admirable work have noticed a subterranean dialogue with contemporary theory, even if it is only at times explicitly foregrounded—as, for example, in the reassessment of Rabelais in the light of feminism (383–418). His challenge is to maintain some insights of contemporary theory, say, on the historical variability of meaning, or the impossibility of a transcendental measure of value, and thus keep at bay all moralism, while at the same time holding on to the notion of literature as a unique provider of a "submersion in other minds" (142), a force that could provoke a "range of effects on the 'character' or 'person' or 'self'" (8), namely "the Good" or "the Harm" alluded to in his preface. Wayne Booth's *The Company We Keep* is then a painstaking effort to define what this "Good" and "Harm" would consist of, in an attempt to accept variability of interpretations (which Booth defends in the name of "pluralism") while refusing to shift the ground from intrinsic value to social valuation. Booth accomplishes the task with the help of number of exercises in *reductio ad absurdum*, such the contrast between *King Lear* and an issue of *Hustler*, or a Yeats poem and an improvised joke in verse. After morally overcoming these strawmen, great literature emerges unscathed, reassured of its morally edifying function. Shakespeare was indeed superior to all this stuff for his undeniable human and ethical teachings. A word about the Marxist, feminist, New Historicist, and queer earthquakes in Shakespeare scholarship, already quite visible in the late 1980s when Booth published his treaty? Nowhere to be seen in his prose, pages of which are wasted jabbing at literary theory for its "disregard of evidence"!

Booth's is a pedagogical model for the understanding of literature, in the broader sense that the ethical moment is placed in the "effect" exerted by the text upon a human subject. One can see how this model is at odds with the antihumanist strain of contemporary criticism, which conceives of literature as a linguistic, cultural, and historical construct, the value of which can only be determined through a more agnostic, distanced perspective vis-à-vis any given content in the text. The need to walk the tight rope between his acknowledgment of formal and historical contingencies and his humanist commitment leads Booth incessantly to hammer home the book's main pluralist point: What is good here is not good there, it may be good for you but not for me, any virtue pushed too hard may destroy the others, too much of any value (be it irony, formal openness, what not) may be harmful rather than good, etc.

(49–79). The bulk of *Company* is devoted to coming to terms with divergent responses to texts, and therefore these texts' various ethical dimensions in each situation. Booth does as good a job as anyone in making room for all the determinations weighing upon that evaluative act—those arising from the reader, from textual ambiguities, from the interpretive community in which the encounter takes place, etc. The entire third chapter, "The 'Logic' of Evaluative Criticism," strives for that middle ground, the sensible gray area that would allow the critic to avoid "Universal Syllogisms" (this work is good because it possesses X; therefore all works that possess X . . .), while not renouncing the claim of an intrinsic ethical value of literature, of some works of literature over others, and of some methods of reading those works over others. The goal is to avoid the "risks" of too much "closure" and too much "openness." The misgivings of ethical criticism are then liable to being explained by its special temptation to "overgeneralize" (51), a middle-of-the-road solution for a pluralism that remains equating the ethical with an inherent value which, however variable, still always transcends the conflicts of social valuation. In other words, the most thorough, extensive, and elegant treaty on ethical criticism of literature recently to come of the US academy is, in strictly philosophical terms, pre-Nietzschean.

The minute one poses the problem as one of overgeneralization the ground is set for the conscientious moderate to search for the reasonable compromise. Despite his claims (350), we are before a moderate and conservative— not a radical—pluralism. Speaking of contemporary criticism, Booth affirms that theory's emphasis on "the variety of interpretations tells us little about the actual value of the works" (84). Booth is so wrong about the literary theory that he has not read that in fact any perusal of contemporary criticism would show that the ethical issues he acknowledges as present in theory—say, the study of questions pertaining to race, class, and gender—have all evolved in dialogue with the "formalist dissection" of "texts" that Booth disqualifies as ideologically neutral (422). As any beginning comparative literature graduate student knows, "poststructuralist" and "deconstructive" thought have exerted wide influence in the development of gender, race, and class scholarship since the 1970s, even though the news has taken 30 years to reach some quarters. Booth mistakes theory's emphasis on the social variability of interpretation to mean an obscuring of the question of value. His confusion happens because he clings to a more Romantic, essentialist notion that works of art possess value as an inherent property, an eternal essence. By refusing to consider seriously the argument on contingent, historically variable processes of value assignation, Booth must discard all relating of culture to ethics as "subjectivist" (73). By doing so he disregards another bibliography, a range of philosophical and anthropological reflection on culture and positionality.

The attacks on "subjectivism" and "relativism" from the standpoint of humanist ethics are well-known, and Booth rehearses them in his work: "[a] complete equivalence in the competence of all interpreters is clearly entailed by the claim that works do not *possess* or *exercise* inherent value, but are only *valued*" (85). His is another version of what Barbara Herrnstein Smith has satirically termed the egalitarian fallacy, "the recurrent anxiety/charge/claim . . . that, unless one judgment can be said or shown to be more 'valid' than another, then all judgments must be 'equal' or 'equally valid'" (98). Barbara Herrnstein Smith's choice of words is felicitous, for what is at stake is truly an *anxiety* in the Freudian sense. If one does the research, one will see that "postmodernists" and "deconstructionists" have very rarely argued in strictly relativistic terms. Conservatives have found themselves threatened by those discourses or, in most cases, have deftly used and manipulated the ghost of relativism in order to impose an absolutist agenda.

There is nothing egalitarian, therefore, about the *egalitarian fallacy*. This is a narrative typical of Anglo American ethical theory, one that proposes that if I do not agree with you that all value comes from God or from Reason, then it follows that in my universe everything equals everything else, that I cannot differentiate *Hamlet* from *Hustler*. The Robinson Crusoe–type of fantasy that moves the egalitarian fallacy mirrors the structure of anxiety, for it fears something that remains unknown to it (Freud, *Inhibitions,* 60–89). Take, for example, the following comment by Wayne Booth: "It is a bit harder to believe . . . that if a person in our culture who is completely inexperienced in literature sees no value in, say, Faulkner's novels, his or her opinion is as pertinent to our discourse about Faulkner as the opinions of experienced readers" (85). The fallacy is that, of course, a "person" "completely inexperienced in literature" would not belong to the same "our culture" as "experienced readers." Those hypothetical readerly claims would, therefore, by definition not be as pertinent to "our discourse" (one should always ask, deconstruction and Marxism have taught us, what enunciative instance, what kind of interest, what kind of *game* hides behind a first-person plural). In fact it is *precisely because* not all judgments are equal that values are never intrinsic, self-identical, but rather articulated through conflictive social interactions. It is exactly because valuations are not only *not* equally valid epistemically but also not on equal footing within power relations that they are never interchangeable. One or the other is never a matter of indifference, contrary to the essentialist anxiety that if valuation has been shifted away from a dormant immanence to a network of social relations all values have somehow become equal to all others.[12]

The central metaphor of Booth's work is that of friendship, in what is roughly an Aristotelian model of the text-reader encounter: "my chief responsibility to myself as storyteller is fulfilled when I choose to create an implied author who qualifies as my friend" (129). The relationship is predicated on a number of actions construed by a certain philosophical tradition as "human": texts "invite," "tolerate," or "reject" a given response; they create a reciprocal or hierarchic relationship with the reader; they are "reserved" or "intimate," etc. (169–98). Booth anthropomorphizes the text in order to make of it an ethical agent. In that there is nothing original, to be sure, in Booth, of course, as he is following a venerable and long tradition. Only insofar as texts have somehow become "human" does Booth find it possible to respond to them ethically. Despite all the talk about narrators and implied authors, what is at stake here is an author-centered and ultimately unidirectional model (Newton 65). This explains Booth's emphasis on "assent," "surrender," "succumbing" as preconditions for the encounter with fiction. Instead of the ethical constituting a possibility of questioning the attributes ideologically assigned to human nature, those attributes themselves are made to engulf the ethical encounter. As opposed to the tradition of ethical thought that culminates in the work of Emmanuel Levinas, for whom the ethical encounter—the response to the call of the other—is prior to any anthropological content one could construe, to any possible definition of "the human," Booth implicitly aligns himself with the tradition that subordinates ethics to a humanist anthropology. Of course he had no idea he was doing this, for he was speaking of ethics, in the late 1980s, without giving any signs of having bothered to read Emmanuel Levinas's ouevre, arguably the twentieth century's greatest in the realm of ethics. Instead of locating ethics at the text's foundation, Booth's model eliminates all alterity from it by, curiously enough, refusing to read the thinker of ethics's relation to alterity. Instead of opening the possibility that the text *interrupt* one's identity with oneself, including one's self-assurance about "human nature," Booth turns the text into another "human." What it is that one assumes to be the content of that "human" remains, naturally, unquestioned. The anthropomorphization of the text serves the clear purpose of eliminating its alterity. Hence the necessity of the friendship model. Get rid of the ontological anthropocentric premise, and the ethics falls apart.

Assumptions about human nature also govern much of what moral philosophers have said about literature. Martha Nussbaum's neo-Aristotelianism looks to literature for new ways of posing the ethical question: How should one live? (*Love's* 168–94). For Nussbaum, literature is a privileged space in which to renew ethical inquiry while preserving the complexity of particular situations and the role of emotions and affects. As the autobiographical moments of *Love's Knowledge* make clear, Nussbaum had to work against the grain of mainstream American philosophy in order to establish literature as a legitimate field of philosophical inquiry. Confronting a moral philosophy dominated by utilitarianism and Kantianism, "both positions that were, for good internal reasons, hostile to literature" (13), Nussbaum had to critique the dominant approach to ancient philosophy that did not take "the ethical contribution of literary works . . . to be a part of Greek ethical thought as such—but, at most, a part of the background of 'popular thought' against which the great thinkers worked" (14). Elaborating an alternative to this position has meant, for Nussbaum, the crafting of an ethical stance much more attentive to particulars than mainstream, normative moral philosophy would admit. Since my purpose here is to foreground the international division of intellectual labor, I will simply refer the reader to Nussbaum's elegant analysis of Greek literature, Henry James, Beckett, etc.,[13] and focus instead on her perception of contemporary literary theory and on her edited volume on patriotism and cosmopolitanism. I will also have in mind, though not engaging it directly, Nussbaum's universalist defense of liberal education in *Cultivating Humanity*.

Much like Booth's, Nussbaum's intervention in the debate is framed by the perception of a "pressure of the current thought that to discuss a text's ethical or social content is somehow to neglect 'textuality,' . . . ; and of the related, though more extreme, thought that texts do not refer to human life at all, but only to other texts and to themselves" (170). The supporting evidence offered by Nussbaum of this "pressure of current thought" does not cite any critical theorist but refers to an article by Arthur Danto which makes the same claim, again without any serious engagement with contemporary theory. It may seem incredible, but American moral philosophers have repeatedly allowed themselves to say, in print, the utmost insanities about "literary theory" without having seriously read *any* literary theorist at all. And this coming from people who speak in the name of rigor, reason, and ethics!

The accusation that critical theory has disregarded "human" concerns simply does not hold water, for much of its thrust has been exactly to delimit the historical and geographic scope of the notion of "the human," its by-no-means universal applicability, its rather regional and circumscribed philosophical history. One cannot possibly mistake the critique of humanism for a presumed disregard for "human" concerns. Continental theory's critique of humanism has taken, precisely, the form of an inquiry into the conditions of possibility under which a human essence has been imagined. This can hardly be taken as a dismissal of the problem of the "human," as far as I can see it. When Michel Foucault showed that man is a recent invention (*Order* 250–387), coextensive with the emergence of the domains of life (when biology takes the place of natural history), language (when linguistics replaces general grammar), and labor (when political economy succeeds the analysis of wealth), his contention is that the realm of "the human" was not one of an unchanging universal essence but a very particular construct of a historically situated culture. Likewise, when Jacques Derrida deconstructively probed into post-war humanism in France, the emphasis was on the fact that "although the theme of history is quite present in the discourse of the period, there is little practice of the history of concepts. For example, the history of the concept of man is never examined" ("The Ends" 116). The same naturalized, taken-for-granted approach to notions such as "man" or "history" that Derrida critiques here (and he clearly had Sartre in mind) is what we find at the basis of Nussbaum's anxious attacks on critical theory's "abandonment" of human or moral concerns. The only difference is that the Sartrist position critiqued by Derrida in 1968 was already far more nuanced and sophisticated than the defense of the "human" that U.S. moral philosophers want to pass for genuine thinking in the 1990s into the twenty-first century.

To be sure, Nussbaum does admit exceptions to her picture of a textualist literary theory hostile to "human" concerns: "clearly, feminist criticism and Marxist criticism are major exceptions to the situation described here. But they are, in their difference from and frequent opposition to what surrounds them, exceptions that prove the rule" (*Love's* 171). If it were not troublesome enough to identify immense clusters of subfields of contemporary theory like feminism or Marxism as "exceptions" to anything, it would suffice to underscore that the multifaceted polemics in which feminists and Marxists have been involved cannot be construed as involving the presence of ethical concerns on one side and their absence on the other. Based on what presumably their exceptionality consists of, one could easily show that race studies, queer theory, and postcolonial criticism, to mention only three obvious examples, also partake of the very same ethical impulse. One would thus not be far from concluding that what Nussbaum refers to as ethical "exceptions" in contemporary literary criticism is nothing but the field of contemporary literary criticism itself!

Related in a number of ways to Nussbaum's work in ethical theory is her call for an educational cosmopolitanism that would instruct children to follow Diogenes and the Stoics in thinking of themselves first of all as "citizens of the world" rather than as members of any ethnic or national group. The "worthy moral ideals of justice and equality" are best served, Nussbaum argues, by "the cosmopolitan, the person whose allegiance is to the worldwide community of human beings" ("Patriotism" 4). Much of Nussbaum's emphasis is pedagogical, as she goes on to argue that students in the United States must "learn to recognize humanity wherever they encounter it, undeterred by traits that are strange to them, and be eager to understand humanity in all its strange guises" (9). First of all, today more than ever one can only welcome all attempts at a cosmopolitan pedagogy. Certainly, making "the imaginative leap into the life of the other" (132), striving for a "state of things in which all of the differences will be nonhierarchically understood" (138), and making "all human beings part of our community of dialogue and concern," (9) are noble goals, but the trouble begins when one asks in whose terms the dialogue will occur. For it is far from obvious that there is a universal, neutral language in which this dialogue could be conducted.

In fact, Nussbaum's argument itself shows how much in the liberal cosmopolitan's benevolence is composed of unexamined ethnocentric assumptions. Her starting point is Rabindranath Tagore's novel *The Home and the World*, where a cosmopolitan landlord, who supposedly "transcends" divisions of race, gender, and class, is finally defeated by the political forces that Nussbaum identifies with "nationalism and ethnocentrism" ("Patriotism" 5). I know next to nothing about the colonial history of India, its long and storied struggle against British colonialism, the India-Pakistan partition, and their 50-something-year-old existences as independent nations. But I do know enough to be very suspicious of anyone who divides camps neatly like that in a postcolonial context. In dividing the camps in this fashion, Nussbaum ignores the extent to which what she calls "reasonable and principled cosmopolitanism," represented by the *landlord* Nikhil, may be carrying the traces of a particular brand of humanist liberalism, one that often is embraced by colonial and postcolonial elites, and bears the unmistakable mark of *one class*. More consideration of the politics embodied by humanist liberalism in colonial situations, such as the one found in the work of the subaltern studies group, would have given Nussbaum extensive evidence that "there is an affinity between the imperialist subject and the subject of humanism" (Spivak, "Subaltern" 202).[14] This link is based, I hasten to add, not on any contingency or correctable lapse in the implementation of the humanist project, but rather on its very foundation, so that it would make no sense to differentiate between its universal "essence" and flawed actualization. Hence the falsity of the claim that the decline of Tagore's ideal "now threatens the very existence of a secular and tolerant indigenous state" (16). Likewise, it is misleading to move from that example to saying that "Americans have frequently supported the principle of *Bande Mataram* ["Hail Motherland," the slogan of the nationalist movement in Tagore's novel], giving the fact of being American a special salience" (3). Nussbaum's argument assumes that it makes no difference to be a nationalist in a colonized country or in an imperial world power. The argument proceeds as though each given "Motherland's" position within the international hierarchy were a matter of complete indifference. Again, this comes from a scholar who has accused literary theorist in general and deconstruction in particular of sponsoring a dangerous "disregard for evidence"!

Nussbaum's applying of the word "ethnocentric" equally to U.S. disregard for other cultures and to a nationalist movement in India—whatever may be latter's limitations, which I am as incompetent as Nussbaum to judge in scholarly fashion—masks the crucial fact that one of these "ethnocentrisms" partakes in the hierarchical distribution of power among nations that made the other "ethnocentrism" possible, inevitable, and perhaps indeed necessary after all. Again, a whole Marxist and postcolonial bibliography on the merits and limits of nationalism in (neo)colonial situations begs inclusion, but Nussbaum does not show any signs of familiarity with it. To put it differently, and moving the discussion to a world region I know better, does Nussbaum's cosmopolitanism make room for the difference between the U.S. nationalism that justified the ten-year-long onslaught of the Nicaraguan Revolution in the name of national security and, on the other hand, Nicaragua's defensive nationalism against foreign aggression? It does not seem like it. As Judith Butler argued in her comment on Nussbaum's piece: "what constitutes the community that might qualify as a legitimate community that might debate and agree upon this universality? If that very community is constituted through racist exclusions, how shall we trust it to the deliberate on the question of racist speech?" (49). Unfortunately, the reply by Nussbaum—a scholar who has written so extensively on ethics—chooses to focus only on the commentators who had presented unthreatening objections, and ignores Butler's powerful critique, the only one that really addressed the *grounds* of Nussbaum's quite local and provincial, mid-American brand of "universalism."

Nussbaum's benevolent First World liberalism proposes a "global dialogue" and stresses that "we need knowledge not only of the geography and ecology of other nations . . . but also a great deal about their people, so that in talking with them we may be capable of respecting their traditions and commitments" (12), but she never considers the potential contradiction: What if "respect" for "other traditions and commitments" demands that one renounces the project of a global dialogue in the terms in which it has been posed? What if the definition of "human personhood" as "the possession of practical reason and other basic moral capacities" (133) clashes against a notion of humanity elaborated by groups who have endured one catastrophe after another and have been led by experience to define "human personhood" as, say, "the possession of the infinite capacity to inflict pain"? What is the language in which the negotiation between these two definitions of humanity can take place? Certainly it is not that of U.S. American, Ivy League moral philosophy.

When exemplifying how cosmopolitanism does not preclude a commitment to one's particular situation, Nussbaum takes the case of mother tongues:

> A useful analogy is one's native language. I love the English language. And although I have some knowledge of some other languages, whatever I express of myself in the world I express in English. If I were to try to equalize my command of even five or six languages and do a little writing in each, I would write poorly. But this doesn't mean that I think English is intrinsically superior to other languages. I recognize that all human beings have an innate linguistic capacity, and that any person might have learned any language; which language one learns is in that sense morally irrelevant. ("Reply" 136)

The passage is intended as an argument for the noncontradiction between commitment to universalism and embeddedness in the particular, but it says considerably more than that. Nussbaum's choice of the English language as her example of a particular is revealing, for English is rapidly becoming a particular that can lay claim to a quasi-universality in several fields. In this sense, her argument suffers from oblivion to everything that makes the various particulars not only different but also hierarchically organized among themselves. For Nussbaum's point loses its force when one considers that her option for monolingualism in English implicitly assumes that the same option is open to speakers of all other particular languages. And here is the fallacy of universalist humanism. Monolingualism in Quechua is not an option available to the intellectual from the Peruvian hills, much like monolingualism in Maya is not a possibility to the Guatemalan or Southern Mexican intellectual. It is not an option *even* to Hungarians or Brazilians who wish to argue *their* conceptions of universality in any international forum.

If it is obviously true that languages are morally irrelevant in the banal sense that no language is intrinsically superior to any other, it is never *politically* irrelevant which language one speaks, for only in the hegemonic languages is it structurally possible to ignore this political determination over the struggle around morals. Gayatri Spivak has made this point most compellingly: "it is only in the hegemonic languages that the benevolent do not take the limits of their often uninstructed good will into account. That phenomenon becomes hardest to fight because the individuals involved in it are genuinely benevolent and you are identified as a trouble-maker" ("Politics" 191). To illustrate the importance of Spivak's point here, you may try to imagine the above-quoted passage from Nussbaum, when she exemplified her embeddedness in the particular by speaking of her relation with the English language. Try to picture that same statement uttered in languages as diverse and apart in their history as Spanish, Portuguese, Guaraní, or Bengali. You will probably reach the conclusion that only in English can one utter that without sounding completely comical. Something intrinsic to the phonology, lexicon, or syntax of English? Of course not. Just an effect of a highly unequal division of labor among world languages, one that makes a certain particular kind of universalist blindness possible in only *one* of those languages. If one wants to do serious intellectual work today, English is the *worst* language in which to be monolingual, in spite of the fact that it is the language where, for most fields, the largest amount of information circulates and key battles are fought. It is probably the only language in the world in which one can be monolingual and still be a scholar in the humanities and the social sciences.

Voiding the Universal in the Age of Endless War

With the critiques of Nussbaum and Booth I do not intend to deliver attacks on first-rate scholars from whom I have learned a great deal. My goal is, rather, to highlight the limits of a well-meaning and reasonably sophisticated First World–type liberalism in dealing with ethical questions in an international context. The current crisis of universality—dramatically emblematized by the carnage *on and since* September 11—has left universalist humanist ethics on the verge of its complete voiding into catachresis. This rhetorical figure, revived by deconstruction in recent decades, designates those metaphors for which "no *historically* adequate referent can be advanced" (Spivak, "Scattered," 281). For example, "humanity," "progress," and "democracy" have now, more than ever, a purely catachrestic existence. They have become metaphors of a referent that has increasingly ceased to exist even as a plausible fantasy. The dissolution of those metaphors continues to happen over and beyond the fact that moral and analytic philosophy go on with their businesses as if those generalizations indeed had a real referent, as if they designated real historical processes.

On the other hand, when disenfranchised groups set out to critique existing notions of universality they cannot but engage in what Judith Butler has called a "performative contradiction: claiming to be covered by that universal, they thereby expose the contradictory character of the previous conventional formulations of the universal" ("Universality" 48). No real democratic expansion of rights can ever take place without shaking and unsettling a previouly held notion of universality. Butler's words, written before the U.S. bombing of Afghanistan and the invasion and occupation of Iraq, resonate even more eerily and urgently today, when appeals to absolutist notions such as "freedom," "secularism," and "democracy" have justified atrocities and acts of war on a planetary scale. When the first version of this essay was written, it was still possible and perhaps even forgivable for a liberal to insist on maintaining a closed, dogmatic, universalist insistence on certain concepts such as "reason," "democracy," and "Western rationality." After getting a taste of how universals—even the nicest ones, such as "freedom" and "democracy"—can be appropriated and manipulated by the most criminal war machine, liberal humanists ***had better*** understand that they have some lessons to learn from deconstruction.

As Zygmunt Bauman has argued, the birth of a modern morality that conceived of itself as universal was inseparable from the assumption of a "civilizing mission" of the "most advanced" nations (39–43). In other words, Kant and Napoleon go rather well together. The ultra formalization of Kantian language should not obscure its roots in the experience of colonialism. It was only from the standpoint of the comparability, however biased, among all humans—inagurated by the voyages and expeditions of modern colonialism—that the transcedental Kantian subject became imaginable. Universality in philosophy was, in short, a legitimate offspring of the colonial hierarchization and comparison of human beings. The critique of the universal— begun by Freud, Nietzsche, and Marx, continued by Frankfurt, poststructuralist, and deconstructionist schools of thought—has unveiled a constitutive paradox of all ethics since Kant, namely the requirement that in order to qualify as such, ethics has to take the form of a universal imperative embodied in a free individual choice, a singular and uncoerced embrace of this imperative. But the individual acceptance of the imperative would, insofar as it is truly individual and uncoerced, be in contradiction with its universal applicability. The paradox of a free acceptance of a universal law was the oxymoronic way out of the dilemma between the postulate of an innate human rationality, on the one hand, and the need for a legislative philosophical elite to promote and guard the morality of actions, on the other (Bauman 16–28). Variations on this aporia underlie moral philosophers' and moralistic critics' claims that deconstruction and other branches of post-phenomenological thought "disregard ethical questions." For these critics the ethical is to be found in the treatment of the content of moral values (the peroration over how moral it is to do X or avoid Y), whereas deconstruction shows that it is the *formal* structure of a demand, the other's *call* to responsiveness that makes ethics possible, prior to and constitutive of the definitions one may ascribe to good or evil, desirable or undesirable modes of valuation or behavior.

One could perhaps hypothesize that the tradition of benevolent, naively universalist managerial liberalism is now witnessing the beginnings of its disappearance, accelerated by the fury with which Christian, Zionist, and Islamic brands of fundamentalism threaten to submerge the world in an endless war. In a context such as the one we live in, would the first task of ethical theories elaborated in the dominant nations and cultures not be the inclusion of their own position of privilege into the conceptual horizon to be analyzed? This would certainly open up avenues of inquiry that could provide them at least with a glimpse into the ways in which their own universalism may in fact be a rather particular province, the "village of the liberal managerial class" (Pinsky 87). How to formulate universal imperatives in a time when the most vigilant and critical brands of philosophical thought have convincingly unveiled the *particular* allegiances of the available notions of *universality*? How to reconstruct conceptual universality when all major universals have been sequestered by the war machine? If one is aware that all major tropes of ethical theory have collapsed into catachresis, how can one still fight for justice, for what is *humane*, for what is right? If those words have been really irrevocably stolen and abused, must one renounce them? Can one rewrite them? If such a thing is possible, what is the protocol for that rewriting? If another discourse on value and justice is possible, may it step forth, for the humanist/universalist ethics of the U.S. philosophical apparatus has failed miserably. Deconstruction fares way better in this task, although much of what follows will be a critique of one of Jacques Derrida's major attempts to respond to that call. I begin with a word on why Derrida's work radically transforms what we understand as justice.

Chapter 3

Specters of Walter Benjamin

Mourning, Labor, and Violence in Jacques Derrida

Labor and Mourning

> *"The truth will not escape us," reads one of Keller's epigrams. He thus formulates the concept of truth with which these presentations take issue.*
>
> —*Benjamin,* Arcades, *463*[1]

In order to understand the relationship between Marxism and deconstruction one could go back to *Specters of Marx* (1993), where Derrida writes that "deconstruction has never had any sense or interest . . . except as a radicalization . . . *in the tradition* of a certain Marxism, in a certain *spirit of Marxism*" (92). More than most names in contemporary philosophy, Derrida has always been haunted by a demand coming from Marx's text or formulated on its behalf. An important moment of this clash is *Positions* (1972), where Derrida defends and explains his protocols of reading to two interviewers, Jean-Louis Houdebine and Guy Scarpetta, who corner him with questions regarding his relationship to Marx's work and the Marxist tradition, a relationship that was, at that moment, for Derrida, still the object of a promise. Houdebine's and Scarpetta's interventions push Derrida into choosing between: 1. A declaration of complicity with the Marxist tradition and the recognition of a kinship between the deconstruction of phonologocentrism and the critique of idealism; or else: 2. A clarification of what it was that separated Derrida from the Marxist project, preferably accompanied by an argument concerning how the operation of *la différance* was irreducible to what the interviewers called the materialist "position taking" [*prise de position*].

In 1971 Derrida was an upcoming star philosopher, and already author of three important books: *Grammatology, Speech and Phenomena,* and *Writing and Difference*. Now imagine the tough either-or situation with which he was confronted in the interview: If you do not declare total complicity and full interiority vis-à-vis a powerful and consolidated tradition such as our own, the Marxist one, you have to admit that you *are somewhere else,* and therefore liable to being interpellated on behalf of this tradition and being asked to position yourself vis-à-vis its illustrious body of thought. Either you admit you are saying the same thing we have been saying all along, or we will ask you to make explicit where exactly you differ from us. Once one accepts that framing of the debate, one is setting oneself up to admit, sooner or later, that either social being determines consciousness or is determined by it.

To choose either option, to accept that dichotomous framing of the debate between Marxism and *what was then only being born* under the name of deconstruction would have meant, for Derrida, to renounce the project altogether. Houdebine, Scarpetta, and Maoists in general were tough people to debate, and they quite explicitly put that skill to work in order to minimize the political damage that deconstruction could do to the already depleted post-'68 French Marxism. *Positions* was, in a way, a book about how not choosing could be, agonistically, the only radical choice, the only one that truly maintained the future as an open promise. The interview surely shows the imprint of May 1968 on the dialogue between the French Left and the various philosophical and literary voices that were then beginning to labor on the theme of difference (Derrida, but also Deleuze, Barthes, Kristeva). Important in making possible the encounter between Marxism and philosophies of difference, *Tel Quel* magazine acted as a bridge between sectors of the organized Left and intellectuals with various genealogical connections to structuralism, such as Phillipe Sollers, Roland Barthes, and Julia Kristeva, authors whose complicity with the Derridean project was quite apparent (Derrida had already published "Dissemination," his essay on Sollers).[2] In that context the corner into which Houdebine and Scarpetta attempted to drive Derrida was cruel: Make explicit a visible antagonism between your project (and voices closely associated to it) and the materialist horizon guiding us or else accept that the deconstruction of logocentrism and of metaphysics is part of materialism, and perhaps nothing but one more chapter in the age-old materialist struggle against idealism.

Both options were, of course, bad choices, and Derrida's response was an attempt, agonistic but quite impressive in its ethic, to make explicit the irreducible nature of the experience of the undecidable, while making of this operation something other than a simple eulogy of indecision.

Houdebine and Scarpetta's "are-you-for-or-against-Marxism" game allows Derrida to elaborate the radical difference between undecidability and indecision. Undecidability is then a concept from the beginning indebted to the Marxist tradition, even if in negative fashion. The tradition provided an interpellation, a call that Derrida took quite seriously. He first responded by demonstrating his willingness to discuss the multiple protocols of reading through which the complexity of Marx's text might be approached. By doing so he was, of course, deferring the game and gaining time. Hurried by his interlocutors' urgency when it came to Marx and Marxism, Derrida was slowly forced to admit: "why not say it bluntly: I have not yet found any [reading protocols] that satisfy me" (63). His book on Marx, published more than 20 years later, was an attempt to develop them, but in 1971 there was a clear split between Derrida's search for satisfactory protocols of reading and the Marxists' call for position taking.

The decisionism of the Maoists made them unable to recognize political importance in the temporal aporia that Derrida was beginning to map out around the concept of decision. If all decisions were rigorously and unambiguously reducible to a deductive operation—for such and such "reasons," I took this "decision"—they would necessarily cancel themselves as such. They would not be decisions but at best mere applications of pre-established rules. The fact that these rules are prior to the moment of decision (as they must be, otherwise they would not be rules) ends up irreversibly installing an aporia at the very heart of all decision. It was after the publication of *Positions* that Derrida mapped out a *constitutive undecidability proper to decision as such.* The ethics that guided his responses to Houdebine and Scarpetta, however, already showed signs of some reflection on that problem. *Positions* is an *avant la lettre* response to those who later associated the practice of deconstruction with a relativistic and rhetorical "postmodernism." Derrida's work understands the thematic of the undecidable as the constitutive ground of every decision, that is to say as a *determined relationship* never to be confounded with (the praise of) *indeterminacy.* Undecidability has nothing to do with a willy-nilly, pseudo-postmodern eulogy of intermination:

> The undecidable is not merely the oscillation or the tension between two decisions. Undecidable—this is the experience of that which, though foreign and heterogeneous to the order of the calculable and the rule, must [*doit*] nonetheless—it is of duty [*devoir*] that one must speak— deliver itself over to the impossible decision while taking account of law and rules. A decision that would not go through the test and ordeal of the undecidable

> would not be a free decision; it would only be the programmable application or the continuous unfolding of a calculable process. (Derrida, *Force*, 252)

Published two decades after *Positions* and originally presented at a colloquium on "Deconstruction and the Possibility of Justice" at the Cardozo Law School (1989), *Force of Law* elaborated the thematic of the undecidable first debated with his Marxist interlocutors in 1971: "the memory of the undecidability must keep a living trace that forever marks a decision as such . . . the undecidable remains caught, lodged, as a ghost at least, but an essential ghost, in every decision, in every event of decision" (253). *Force of Law* will also occupy me in the second half of this chapter, as it is there that Derrida engages, in most sustained but also in most equivocal fashion, the oeuvre of Walter Benjamin. For now, let me stress that the mapping of decision here yields the image of a moment, an action always inhabited by an *essential ghost* (Derridean oxymoron par excellence) that announces the interplay between spirit and specter, *Geist* and *Gespenst*, around which Derrida would later organize his reading of Marx. How can a ghost be essential if the ghostly is the suspension of every essence? How does decision, even after it has been taken, continue to be haunted by the undecidable?

For Derrida every true decision has to face, at one moment, the strictly undecidable. A decision that does not host the trace of the undecidable would be nothing more than the unfolding of mere calculation, of a pedestrian and predictable application of predetermined rules that make of the action, in fact, something *other* that a true decision. For deconstruction, the essence of decision is the undecidable. The challenge facing deconstructive reading is to map that terrain beyond all calculation while acknowledging that *undecidability is never the end of the matter*, for there always remains responsibility for everything that, at the heart of decision, "cannot be fully rationalized and therefore justified in advance" (Cornell, *Philosophy*, 157). Often attacked in the name of a thematic of responsibility, Derrida's concept of undecidability is in fact a full engagement with the question of responsibility. "We cannot be excused from our role in history because we could not know so as to be reassured that we were 'right' in advance." (Cornell 169). In other words, responsibility exists because there is undecidability inhabiting every decision.[3] Framed by an engagement with *Positions*, *Force of Law*, and *Specters of Marx*, my own essay interrogates the status of one particular ghost that haunts Derrida's thinking on decision, that of Walter Benjamin, *the* thinker of tough decisions if there ever was one.

The title of Derrida's *Specters of Marx* should certainly be read as a double genitive. As objective genitive, it alludes to the spectral field mobilized by Marx, that is, all of the many ghosts that he sets in motion in his text. They are legion indeed, from the famous "a specter is haunting Europe"(54) that opens *Communist Manifesto* (1848), to the dance of flying tables invoked to explain commodities' "metaphysical subtleties and theological niceties" (163) in the key first chapter of *Capital* (1867), devoted to the theory of commodity fetishism. Ghosts also appear in Marx's historiographic reflection on the "tradition of the dead generations" that "weighs like a nightmare on the minds of the living" (146) in *The Eighteenth Brumaire* (1851). When one thinks of ghosts in Marx's text one should mention all of the ghosts taken apart by Marx: Stirner and Bauer's ghosts of religion (as if religion were the origin and primary cause of the contradictions of the real world), Bakunin's ghosts of the state (as if the state were the cause rather than the product of domination), Malthus's demographic ghosts (as if population growth rather than private appropriation of collective production were the cause of social inequality), and Adam Smith's and Ricardo's ghostly notion of "value of labor" (ghostly insofar as it confounds "labor" with "labor power"). Religion, the state, the people, and "the price of labor," are denounced by Marx as myths, ghosts, specters (*Gespensten*), products of the blindness of idealism, anarchism, Malthusianism, and political economy to see the roots of things. Each one of these four currents of thought, whatever its particular merits, still insisted on seeing origins where a closer and less ideological look revealed mere effects. Marx's critique of them is first and foremost a dismantling of their ghosts.

But *Specters of Marx* should also be read as a subjective genitive, alluding to Marx insofar as *he himself returns as a ghost*. But would not the act of returning as such be nothing more than an instance of the very structure of spectrality? Is there a return that is not necessarily spectral? There is an uncanny irony in the fact that Marx is the modern thinker most obsessed with ghosts and specters while also being the one who presents himself today in the most spectral fashion. Marx's signature, now more than ever, puts into play an infernal proliferation of reminiscences that cannot but question the triumphant chorus of neoliberal and militarized globalization. Understood as a subjective genitive, the phrase has taken on special cultural relevance since 1989, after the defeat of communism in Eastern Europe and the self-congratulatory orgy with which an intense bombardment of media messages went on to celebrate the "death of Marx."

In an attempt to respond to that steamroller, a disoriented group of Marxists and allies got together at the University of California, Riverside, in 1991 for the colloquium *Whither Marxism?* where Derrida presented a draft of *Specters of Marx*. The colloquium generated an eponymously titled volume edited by Bernd Magnus and Stephen Cullenberg that dialogued with Derrida's monograph.[4] It is somewhat allegorical that the chosen title makes use of "whither," an archaic synthetic interrogative pronoun preferentially replaced, in most dialects of contemporary English, with the more contemporary form "where (to)." The papers replicate this archaism, as if the deliberately anachronistic lexical item were a symptom of a problematic stuck in time. As the heart of the problem lay in the very teleological structure of the "where to"(determination of a destination, of a *telos,* of a fixed horizon), conference participants offered answers to a question that seemed to have become anachronistic. Derrida's long intervention was the only one, it seems to me, that provided enough elements to think through, simultaneously, the *whither* and the *whence* of Marx. If the name of a thinker acquires ghostly overtones, if that thinker has in a way *become* a ghost, where is that ghost coming from? Spectrality, Derrida argued, presupposed a permanent hesitation between that which returns, seeking restitution for the past, and that which announces the future: "before knowing whether one can differentiate between the specter of the past and the specter of the future, of the past present and the future present, one must perhaps ask oneself whether the spectrality effect does not consist in undoing this opposition" (40). In interrogating the subjective form of the genitive, Derrida confronts a Benjaminian theme: the task of inheritance as an imperative that interpellates us from the past.

In its Benjaminian sense, *past* is a noun that should be understood as the name of a pending struggle, as an ineluctable claim of the unresolved, as something to be redeemed. By returning to the name "Marx," Derrida cannot but evoke a past that continues to be repressed, lost amidst the triumphant discourses of globalization and security. Marxist tradition's truly subversive past is not, of course, that of the Stalinist states or their "proletarian heroes" mummified in Moscow (those, in museum-fied form, are able and are allowed to enjoy a long and harmless afterlife). The subversive past is, rather, everything that in the Marxist tradition was always inseparable from a certain promise that does not wait, a certain demand for an impossible revolution, one that is all the more urgent the more impossible it is. What the media's exorcism of Marx's ghost attempts to eliminate and bury, then, is Marx's *messianic* force, precisely what Derrida's return to Marx, under unmistakable Benjaminian inspiration, attempted to rescue.

In the neoliberal mass media conjuring of Marx and of Marxism that dominated the 1990s, Derrida noted a perverse operation between constative and performative uses of language. The operation included organized exorcism around a statement—"Marx is dead"—that presented itself as the flat retelling of a fact. The constative form, nevertheless, masked the performative that was its true motor—"May Marx die," "let us kill Marx." The Derridean operation was to unveil the performative beneath the presumed neutrality of the constative. The euphoria accompanying the announcement of the "news" of Marx's death was in fact performing that which it pretended to be reporting. The constative statement of the good news was hiding its performative pragmatics. The constative, Derrida noted, "certifies the death but here it is in order to inflict it. This is a familiar tactic. The constative form tends to reassure"(48). In this operation of masking the performative motor of the constative, Derrida argued that Western media were simply performing what Freud's *Mourning and Melancholia* called the "triumphant phase of mourning." In that still rather Romantic piece Freud associated the triumphant mode of mourning with mania, that is, the regime in which the ego triumphs over something that remains permanently hidden from it. In the triumphant phase of mourning work, denial takes the form of a loud, arrogant, festive rhetoric that attempts to exorcise the unsettling power of a ghost that remains lingering around.

Derrida dedicated his second chapter to dismantling Francis Fukuyama's thesis on "the end of history," and thus carrying out the task ten years before the 9/11 attacks gave that idea the burial it deserved. Already in 1991 Derrida saw that the so-called end of history was merely "a new gospel, the noisiest, the most mediatized [*médiatique*], the most *successful* one on the subject of the death of Marxism" (56). Derrida insisted on the need to remember the fact known to any philosophy student, the ignorance of which made possible all the apocalyptic celebration of Fukuyama's presumed novelty in the early 1990s: Modern philosophical practice as such, at least since Hegel, has been nothing but the staging of its own end, a reflection on its own end, and a discussion of its own possible death. In other words, Fukuyama's pretentiously prophetic "good news" (the phrase with which Fukuyama neoevangelically designated the "definitive victory of capitalism and liberal democracy") had arrived late to the end. It was announcing a novelty that had had an existence as a theme in Europe for at least 50 years: "All these themes of the end (end of history, end of man, figure of the 'last man,' entry into a certain post-Marxism, and so forth) were, already at the beginning of the '60s, part of the elementary culture of the philosophers of my generation" (*Specters* 69). The man bringing the news arrived late, a delay made all the more visible by his insistence on its supposed apocalyptic novelty.

Only in U.S. America's ossified and bureaucratic philosophical "tradition"[5] was it possible for someone to be taken seriously while presenting, in the 1990s, an involuntary parody of 1930s Kojèvian end of history, one that proclaimed postwar America as the embodiment of Hegel's universal state of recognition. Fukuyama's caricature depended primarily on a brutal simplification of "the fulfillment of history" thesis with which Kojève had crowned his reading of Hegel in the 1930s. By caricaturing Kojève, Fukuyama produced an apocalyptic parody, one that believed to have conjured up all ghosts in order to proclaim the end of history as pure presence, as something we were witnessing there and then. For Fukuyama, the self-congratulatory end of history was the moment of definitive victory of capital. While it was a grotesque parody of a Kojève "who deserved better" (*Specters* 56), it was a parody that did not stop being dangerous and influential until September 11 definitively buried it. During the ten years that separate the heyday of Fukuyama's announcement and the attacks of 9/11, Western media and dominant political culture firmly believed, defended, and propagated a particular form of denial embodied in a ghostly tale about "the end of history." Derrida's vigilant voice was the first powerful critique of that tale.

Having dispatched Fukuyama and the chorus on the "death of Marx," Derrida goes on to theorize spectrality as the force of an insistent repetition. One should here be reminded that Derrida's work on repetition bears clear traces of extensive engagement with the Freudian *Wiederholung*, "repetition" understood as the incessant inscription of a past that remains unresolved. Derrida captures the connection between spectrality and repetition beautifully with the French word *le revenant,* the ghost, a noun that is nothing but the progressive form of the verb *revenir,* to return. The ghost is that which returns, the one whose essence resides in returning itself. The specter is for Derrida the embodiment of the law of iterability. This is why it is by definition impossible "to distinguish between the future-to-come and the coming-back of a specter"(38). Specters, much like vampires, are never coming for the first time. They are always returning.

In order to understand the spectral, Derrida chooses the most illustrious ghost of Western literature, the one who haunts the rotten kingdom of Denmark and imposes upon the king's son the mandate of avenging his death, of "giving him justice." Hamlet is, no doubt, one of the most paradigmatic literary figures of mourning. While being the paradigm of mourning for literature, he is also the paradigm of literature as mourning. In *Hamlet,* the theme of the specter is linked with the theme of justice to come, of the urgent promise that resists all postponing. Every urgent call for justice is, then, the result of a demand coming from a specter. There is no imperative of justice that does not imply, in one way or another, a settling of accounts with the past. In this sense, Hamlet is a protoBenjaminian figure, and it was Derrida's encounter with Marx's text that made that lineage visible.[6]

Derrida shares with Marx the idea that if the theme is ghosts, Shakespeare is not one source among others. Hamlet is, for our modernity, the prototypical figure of the mournful heir. He is the figure that reminds us that in fact all heirs, by definition, are in mourning, as Derrida never tires of insisting. Inheritance and mourning represent both a "having it out with the past" and a necessary condition for all future action. At the heart of every act of inheriting lies an undecidable play between past and future. This is, in fact, the origin of Hamlet's uneasiness. It is certainly not a matter that the prince is in some way "undecided." Hamlet has *made* a decision and he knows quite clearly what he wants: He wants to avenge the death of his father. The problem is that he knows that the justice to come, the justice without which the present will continue to drag on in an unendurable nightmare of sameness, is irreducible to any act of revenge, punishment, or retribution. It is a terrible misreading to think that Hamlet "can't make up his mind." The play makes it very clear that he has. The problem is that the choice is imploded and rendered sterile by the very motives that led the prince to make it. In the process, we learn, along with the prince, that revenge is not justice, that revenge does not bring us an inch closer to justice.

When exploring Hamlet's beautiful, untranslatable phrase, *time is out of joint,* Derrida runs into a problem that had occupied Heidegger: If the foundation of all law is an economics of restitution (punishment, retribution, compensation), "can one not yearn for a justice that one day, a day no longer belonging to history, a quasi-messianic day, would finally be removed from the fatality of vengeance?"(*Specters* 21). Could one aspire for a time in which time *were not* out of joint? Is the disjointedness, the unhingedness, of time something of its very essence or is it a lack that is accidental to the nature of time, a lack that can be corrected or filled some day? Can one hope to put time back into its hinges, into its joints?

In the *Anaximander Fragment,* Heidegger attempts to wrest the concept of justice from the economic logic of restitution, from those who insist in confusing the just (*das Gerechte*) with the avenged (*das Gerächte*). Heidegger skillfully manipulates the homophony between the two words and implicitly shows how easy it is to confuse them. The forgetting of the question of Being (the irredeemable and constantly reproduced Fall that Heidegger is constantly hammering us with) was coextensive, for him, with the confusion between justice and revenge, beautifully captured in the homophonous nouns formed after the two past participles in German. For Heidegger, the irreducibility of justice to vengeance is a constitutive soil to which all jurisprudence must remain blind, unable to circumscribe the ground that makes it possible. The discourse of law, as such, comes into being by forgetting the difference between restitution and justice. Law necessarily forgets that restitution can never be confused with justice. So if Heidegger translates Anaximander's *dike* as "justice," with the aim of conceptualizing Being as presence, as the proper hinging of agreement, Derrida's fundamental inversion consists in postulating the very state of the present as something *out of joint,* the very fallenness of time as the condition of possibility, as the basis, as the foundation for all justice as such. For Derrida, justice *as such* always means *justice to come.* It is of the very nature of justice to have an essentially futural character. If Heidegger calls our attention to the anthropomorphic reduction of the concept of justice to a system of restitutions and debts, Derrida insists on the question: Would the fundamental condition of all justice not be the very disjunction and discord of the present with itself? Would the very imagining of a future state of justice not depend upon understanding the present as something *out of joint?*

Marxists would insist on placing the question of the abolition of class at the very heart of any concept of justice. From a Marxist point of view every present is necessarily disjointed, as no present will ever be fully visible to itself. Full visibility would only happen in "redeemed humankind," a future state of things that has *hypothetical* but heuristic existence in Marxist theory. In the historical present of class struggle and social differences, that is to say in our present, time will not be fully visible to itself. As Benjamin insisted against Keller, in the fallen time of class struggle, truth can indeed run away from us. In the present of class differences there is no justice possible, only systems of restitutions. The inevitability of thinking from the point of view of class indicates, therefore, the unthinkable, unrepresentable nature of justice. Because there is class difference, justice is aporetic, impossible, futural, perennially promised, and never simply present amongst us.

Justice is thus not to be confounded with the law. While one can (and should) always deconstruct the law, justice as such is that which cannot be subject to deconstruction, as it *doesn't take place* in language, it announces a sheer *atopos.* More than a positive content, justice is for Derrida the name of a limit: that which can never, will never, lend itself to deconstruction.[7] In differentiating law and justice, Derrida's work runs into Walter Benjamin, the thinker who had the revolutionary audacity to discern the legacy of mourning for the defeated as the only force capable of maintaining the future as an open promise. For Benjamin, as is well known, only a full confrontation with the imperative of mourning left by the miserable past can lead us to discern a true justice beyond the law. The remembrance of enslaved ancestors is the best inspiration for a democratic, radically open future.

One of the merits of the reading that Fredric Jameson dedicates to Derrida's *Specters of Marx* is to note that the reference to Benjamin—or rather the buzz, the frequently unnamed specter of Benjamin in that book—displaces the Heideggerian problematic and vocabulary somewhat (Jameson, "Marx's" 83). The status and degree of such a displacement is not easy to define, as it would imply revisiting Heidegger's linking of authenticity *(Eingentlichkeit)* with Being-unto-death.[8] This abyssal link between authenticity and death in Heidegger has not yet been sufficiently explored, much less insofar as it informs Derrida's practice. If in Heidegger Being-unto-death offers the very possibility of genuine, "authentic" experience of Being (what Heidegger circumscribes in *Being and Time* as the experience of Being-as-a-whole, *Ganzsein*), Derrida proposes a reversal in that mourning *for the other* is affirmed as foundational with respect to all Being-unto-death. Whereas Heidegger's premise in the formalization of the concept of Being-unto-death is that "death is in every case mine" (*Being* 240), Derrida's emphasis is symmetrically opposed: The *death of the other* is the "always already" *(dèjá toujours)*, it is the event that has inevitably, by definition, arrived and interpellated me as a legacy, a task, and an inheritance, as the beginning and the condition of possibility for everything. This is, for Derrida, the truly important moment.

American legal philosopher Drucilla Cornell beautifully captures this uniqueness of Derrida vis-à-vis the Heideggerian tradition that inspires him: "we do not directly know the death of the Other. We only know the Other's absence. The Other's death, in other words, is only there for us as *her* absence. This is why Derrida says that death does not *literally* exist, *for us,* only mourning exists" (*Philosophy* 72). Derrida establishes the imperative of mourning as unavoidable, irreducible, and prior to any Being-unto-death that one could formalize. The problem with the Heideggerian concept is that it implicitly prioritizes an ego: After all, "death is always mine." Derrida, in shifting the emphasis to a theory of mourning, implicitly demonstrates the egological limits of the analytic of *Dasein,* no matter what merits Heidegger's critique of psychologism and anthropologism may have in their own contexts. The emphasis on mourning for the *other* as opposed to the Heideggerian Being-unto-death shows clear signs of Derrida's engagement with the ethical philosophy of Emmanuel Levinas, and is in part what would lead Derrida into Benjamin.

If Jameson's reading of *Specters of Marx* notes that at a certain moment in Derrida's work Benjamin comes to displace the centrality of Heidegger, there is also a narrative to be told about how Benjamin comes to displace *Lukács* in *Jameson's* work. It is largely under Benjamin's impact that the Lukácsian orthodoxy of Jameson's early days evolves into the more complex and culturally sensitive forms that allowed the emergence of theories such as that of the postmodern. In matters of cultural theory there is, certainly, a radical incompatibility between Benjamin and Lukács: For Lukács failure, mourning or experience could never be historically relevant categories. They were not legitimate concepts to be interrogated, but simple ready-made contents about which all one could discuss was how to represent them. Benjamin developed a different position altogether: Prior to the representation of experience, there is a battle, Benjamin says, to define what will be understood by "experience," what the access to it will mean for whom, what the forms of narrating it will be. Those are the battles in which one must intervene, not the facile Lukácsian battle over what kind of *content* should be represented. Lukács renounces the theoretical struggle over the concepts of representation and experience and goes on to discuss a formula for what should be represented and how. This is a discussion in which Benjamin is much less interested, especially when taken to its logical conclusion by party apparatchiks. The rift between Benjamin and Lukács separates the Jameson of *Marxism and Form* (1971), still anchored in the reconstruction of a Marxist tradition, from the Benjaminian, heterodox, for more agnostic Jameson of *The Seeds of Time* (1994).

Inspired by Benjamin, Derrida's *Specters of Marx* reclaimed the notion of "the messianic," a word that for readers of Benjamin resonates with questions related to urgency in history, promising, catastrophe, and with the attempt to rescue left-wing politics from the conformism of social democracy. Derrida attempts to differentiate the adjectival form from the noun, given all that "messianism" suggests in terms of movements and identities that believe they know what it is that they await (as the noun usually implies that one is pretty certain regarding who is arriving).[9] In calling for a "New International"—a puzzling entity insofar as it insists on not being a party although its name brings the *memory* of a party—Derrida wants to maintain the recourse to the adjective as an experience without making any concessions to messianism as an identity group. To what extent those two things are separable is certainly a legitimate question to pose to Derrida, much like Derrida interrogates Marx for always attempting to separate spirits from specters.

Much like Derrida wants to separate the experience of the messianic from the identity trap of messianism, Marx was always trying to separate *Geist* from *Gespenst*. For the Marx of *The Eighteenth Brumaire,* the spirit of past revolutions should always be distinguished from their mere "specter," their mere farcical repetition. In a true revolution, Marx argues, the content always exceeds the phraseology, unlike these farces where too much language contrasts with too little action. But here Derrida reminds us that Marx knew better than anyone that the work of mourning is interminable, that the burden of past generations will inevitably weigh like a nightmare on the minds of the living. This implies that all real revolutions will inherit dead words from the past, no matter how radical they are. In other words, the historical unfolding of the spirit is always contaminated by specters. The theory of the revolution faces, then, an unresolvable dilemma, a nucleus of undecidability at its very heart. The lexical dissemination in Marx's text represents a symptom of this crisis in the theory of revolution. Much like *espíritu, l'esprit,* and *spirit, Geist* also can mean "specter," "ghost," "apparition." In order to differentiate spirits from specters, Marx resorts to a word that can never quite decide if it means "spirit" or "specter." The theory of the revolution depends upon strict control over the difference between *Geist* and *Gespenst,* literally impossible to establish. The coherence of the theory of the revolution depends, then, upon controlling rhetorical effects that are, in the end, uncontrollable. It was the merit of Derrida's reading to unveil that aporia without making any concessions to those who would rush into proclaiming "the death of Marx."

Mourning and Violence

> *The law's concern with justice is only apparent, whereas in truth the law is concerned with self-preservation. In particular, with defending its existence against its own guilt.*
>
> —*Walter Benjamin, "The Right to Use Force"*

Prior to *Specters of Marx,* where his presence is somewhat spectral, Benjamin had occupied Derrida's attention in at least two important texts: "Des tours de Babel" (1980), devoted to the theme of translation, and *Force of Law* (1990), which proposed a reading of Benjamin's "Critique of Violence" (1921). I focus here on *Force of Law* because of its importance as a moment where Heidegger and Benjamin meet in Derrida's work. The task is not easy, as to the proverbial difficulty of paraphrasing Benjamin's enigmatic essays one should add the arduous task of paraphrasing Derrida's paraphrases. It is not easy to separate Derrida's reading of Benjamin from what Benjamin wrote himself. As we accomplish the task some problems emerge in Derrida's interpretation. In order to make them visible we will alternately resort to and bracket the considerable critical fortune of these two essays, which includes, first and foremost, a key book of American critical legal studies, Drucilla Cornell's *The Philosophy of the Limit.* Unfortunately I will have to bracket a considerable secondary bibliography on

Benjamin that has addressed related issues, for these have been dealt with mostly in discussions of other pieces such as "On Language in General and Language of Man," "The Task of the Translator," and "On the Concept of History."[10]

Benjamin's "Critique of Violence" is a text structured around a number of dichotomies. The text begins by mentioning the relation of violence to the fields of law and justice. Obviously these two areas cannot be confused for Benjamin. Law is one thing, justice quite another. In the relation between violence and the field of law, Benjamin proposes, the most "elemental" relationship is the one established between ends and means. As one separates means from ends, violence should be sought in the former, not the latter. That is where all the disagreement lies, as people tend to agree that they do not seek a violent society as an end. The first dichotomy is then the following: If the debate around violence is violence as a means, the question imposes itself, in each case, whether or not violence is a means to achieve just or unjust ends. But to reduce the question to this would be to avoid answering it, Benjamin argues, since reflection on violence would be reduced to a "criterion for the cases of its uses." All reflection, in other words, would be exhausted in the judgment of which ends are legitimate and which ones are not. A more exact criterion is necessary, Benjamin says, in order to discriminate among means.

The absence of a criterion to think about means themselves is one of the insufficiencies of legal philosophy. For natural law, violence is the product of nature and only condemnable when used for unjust ends. The opposite dead-end street is the one inhabited by positive law, which is only able to think through the legality of means, never the justice of ends. If natural law attempts to "justify the means" through the fairness of its ends, positive law attempts "to guarantee the justice of the ends through the justification of the means" (278). One school starts from the premise of the naturalness of violence, and based upon that it reduces the justice of the means to the justice of the ends. It reduces the just to the adjusted. The other school dedicates itself purely to judging the justice of the means and evaluating them according to ends that have been defined beforehand. It reduces the just to the legal. "For if positive law is blind to the absoluteness of ends, natural law is equally so to the contingency of means" (279).

The work of the critic is to find, therefore, a "standpoint outside positive legal philosophy but also outside natural law" (279) In order to accomplish this, it is necessary to reject the "dogma" that legal ends cannot be maintained if the search for natural ends finds recourse in violence. In other words, avoid the illusion that legality is by definition deprived of violence, or that it is the opposite of violence. Legality is often the most violent thing there is. Benjamin deconstructs the "dogma" remembering the legal uses of violence, including the moments in which the state renounces, partially, its monopoly on the legal use of violence. One of these cases is the right to strike.

What is a strike? Can we count the rejection of work as an act of violence? Doubtlessly, Benjamin proposes, as long as we read it from the standpoint of those who have recourse to it. There is an antithetical relationship between the reading of the state, which permits strikes but maintains the power to declare them illegal, and the reading of those who utilize the strike and therefore cannot but see it as the right to use violence/force *(Gewalt)* to reach certain ends. Derrida's rigorous paraphrase neglects to extract the full implication of the fact that for Benjamin the strike represents at once both violence and nonviolence. There is, for Benjamin, a certain lack in the language that attempts to name the violence that takes place in a strike. The strike will always be, should always be, read in both ways simultaneously, *before* the distinction between the implicit violence of the *act of striking* and the explicit violence of the *general revolutionary strike*. The latter is, for Benjamin, a derivative and a posterior dichotomy.

This is then the first reduction of Derrida's paraphrase: The internal fracture inherent to the concept of violence handled by Benjamin disappears, an internal fracture emblematized in the moment when the strike becomes praxis. Derrida indeed maps various fractures in the Benjaminian text, with ineluctable conclusions; but the fracture internal to the concept of violence seems to me to be the important axis missing in Derrida's reading. Let us go on keeping in mind the important point: For Benjamin, the strike is the moment when the distinction between violence and nonviolence becomes undecidable. The nature of the act is then already irreducibly split according to the social position of the subject. Read from the perspective of the factory worker, the strike has always been violent. Derrida's omission of this moment of the constitutive split in Benjamin's text, in a certain way, allows for the collapse of Benjamin into Heidegger and the characterization of "Critique of Violence" as a text "too Heideggerian" (*Force* 298). We will see what "Heideggerian" could possibly mean in these contexts, that of Benjamin's essay from 1921, and that of Derrida's text, delivered in 1989.

Derrida insists that it is impossible to separate clearly between the strike and the general revolutionary strike. He does so with so much emphasis that at times he seems to assume that Benjamin didn't know that. Derrida insists on this point precisely as he omits the antagonism that makes the inseparability of the two inevitable in Benjamin: the nature of the strike is always already *violent* and *nonviolent,* oscillating according to the social position of the subject experiencing it. The split is attributed by Benjamin to an objective contradiction in the foundation of law, as opposed to a mere logical contradiction in the law. This is, then, a matter of a remainder: a difference unnamable in language presides over the nature of the act taken as exemplary of the problem of violence. Derrida keeps reminding us that it is difficult to separate the "common" strike from the general revolutionary strike. But the truly important thing in Benjamin's text goes unnoticed: It is impossible to attribute a positive content to violence because there is no universally comprehensible language capable of speaking about it. Why not? Because at the very moment when the state *renounces* temporarily its monopoly on violence, workers *cannot but* see the act they are resorting to as an act of violence. Since there is no universal language that names violence consensually, it may always be seen *elsewhere.*

"Critique of Violence" does not replicate a presumed Heideggerianism (as if one could simply speak of something being "Heideggerian" in 1921, six years before *Being and Time,* when Heidegger did not exist as a philosophical voice), but it does carry echoes of the Romantic eulogy of the prelapsarian notion of "name" elaborated by Benjamin in his essay on "Language as Such and the Language of Man" (1916). In there Benjamin thematizes the return to a moment prior to the originary split. The essay on language does so by leaping back over the "abyss of chatter of bourgeois signs" toward the fullness of the name, the intensity of the word that pre-dates the separation between language and the world. The essay on violence does so by showing that— due to the contradictory, antagonistic, split character of society—the state's renouncing of its monopoly on violence cannot but trigger the workers' very *entrance* into the realm of violence even if when looked at from the outside their action does not look violent at all.

Whereas it is true that this constitutive split of the concept of violence appears in Benjamin as a sort of prelapsarian moment—and therefore perhaps shares some *thematic* coincidences with what Heidegger would do *later*—only by a brutal simplification can one note this merely thematic coincidence without exploring the conceptual and intellectual difference: For Benjamin it is the concept of workers' struggle that will give you the definitive insight into the nature of violence. I differ with Derrida on "Critique of Violence" precisely as I continue to read Benjamin *in a certain spirit* of *Force of Law.* Let us maintain the notion of the irreducibility of justice to law—carefully crafted by Derrida—as we understand the fact that Derrida's reading of Benjamin is lawful and it is legal. It is fine and *rechtig. É legal.* But it is not just, not nearly approaching the justice it deservedly should be doing to Benjamin. Even though Derrida's works repeatedly frustrate the full encounter with Benjamin, he is, in many respects, the great Benjaminian philosopher of our times, notwithstanding the impact and influence that separate him from what Benjamin was able to achieve in his life.

The next point in Benjamin's "Critique of Violence" is the separation between law-preserving violence and law-making violence—*die rechtserhaltende Gewalt* and *die rechtsetzungende Gewalt.*[11] It is against the strike, which *the state does not initially characterize as violent but that has always already been a violent act for the worker,* that the state may introduce legalized violence as an instrument to preserve the law. The enigmatic character of Benjamin's text derives, partially, from the fact that his dense sentences mix together the two distinct moments of thought. On the one hand, there is the split between revolutionary law-making violence and the law-preserving violence that operates within an existing legal structure. On the other hand, as the condition of possibility of this split, there is the fracture that occurs within the notion of violence itself, the simultaneous characterization of the strike as being necessarily violent, when read from the perspective of the worker, and nonviolent, when read from the perspective of the state. In other words, there is, on the one hand, the dichotomy between violence-as-origin-of-law and violence-as-daily-reproduction-of-law. But that dichotomy is made possible by the inherently split character, the antagonistically duplicitous nature of violence itself.

Although impure and unstable, although subject to intersections, the separation between law-making violence and law-preserving violence is irreducible in Benjaminian thought. As Derrida notes, this dichotomy cannot be confounded with the difference between the violence of the strike (for the worker) and the (episodic, occasional, but always possible) state violence against the strike to defend existing legality. If it is clear that the state, when it intervenes, does so to maintain a law, it is not always the case that the strike necessarily has the goal of installing another law. Not, at least, until it becomes a general revolutionary strike. And given that the strike in and of itself is not seen by bosses and the state as an act of violence, why would the state have recourse to violence to suppress it? Because of *fear,* Benjamin claims, that the strike could eventually become a general revolutionary strike and inaugurate another legality. Law-preserving violence operates, therefore, as the anticipation of a virtual, possible, future violence, that presumably could arrive to defeat the existing law and install another legality. There is no essential reason to think that the violence of the strike will look to the installation of another law. But for the state the preservation of the law is too dear a task. It makes use, beforehand, of violence.

But does law-making violence equal revolutionary violence? Would the *rechtsetzungende Gewalt* always be revolutionary? Not at all, Benjamin says. Proof of that is a form of violence that for Benjamin is never an example among others: military violence, which is not revolutionary but establishes a new legality. Militarism is, in fact, the subordination of citizens to the law; it arrives whenever it is necessary to maintain existing legality. On the other hand, however, militarism is the "compulsory, universal use of violence as a means for state ends" (284). These ends inevitably include the establishment of new legalities. For this reason, there is something "inherently law-making" in military violence, even when displayed to preserve the existing law. The privileged example of the inseparability between law-making and law-preserving violence is military violence, that kind of violence that is explicitly in charge of preserving the existing law, but that cannot but continuously disrespect it, on its way to setting up a new law altogether.

It is here that Benjamin's essay reaches a great insight. When, in primitive legal systems, the death penalty is established for crimes against property, it is not merely preserving a law. It is, at that moment, imposing another law. For Benjamin, the paradigm for the impossibility of neatly separating law-preserving violence and law-making violence is the *establishment of the death penalty to punish attacks against property.* In the same way that the (possible, promised) general revolutionary strike is law-making, so also is, for Benjamin, military violence, allegorized in the violence that legally kills those convicted of crime against property. The establishment of the death penalty for property crimes is here the very allegory for the arrival of the law. The next question that Benjamin draws from this insight is: Once this punishment is established by the state apparatus, will all legal violence have the goal of preserving the law? And will every attempt at a new legality come from revolutionary forces, from possible general strikes? Not at all, Benjamin answers. The state has developed an apparatus where the difference between law-making and law-preserving violence *is permanently suspended.* That apparatus is called the police.

The police are for Benjamin the apparatus that simultaneously preserves legality and makes new legalities. If law-making violence "is required to prove its worth in victory," and law-preserving violence "is subject to the restrictions that it may not set itself new ends," police violence is, for Benjamin, "emancipated from both conditions." It does not have either to prove its worth as a victorious force or to resign itself to operating within the existing legal system. In "countless cases" its violence operates where "no clear legal situation exists." Such cases are so countless that they define the very essence of police violence, if police violence may possess an essence—Benjamin defines it as "formless [*gestaltlos*], nowhere tangible, all-pervasive, ghostly" (286) in other words, in fashion notably similar to Derrida's account of the specter in

Specters of Marx. If police use violence for legal ends, they do so with the simultaneous authority to decide, within broad limits, the nature of these ends.

For Benjamin, the police represent the *legalized* violence that, nevertheless, is not contained within any *legality*. It is the violence of the law, the very voice of the law, but isn't circumscribed by it. It has the function of preserving the law, but does so, in "countless cases," *outside* of the existing law, installing another law. The apparatus charged with enforcing the law cannot do so without consistently violating its limits. The police's operation of preserving the law cannot but constantly dwell outside of the law. *The preservation of the law is its outside.* This is what we could call Benjamin's deconstructive moment, anticipating the work of *la différance* such as theorized by Derrida. The distinction between law-preserving and law-making violence is subject to deconstruction because the preservation of a law never operates fully within legality. The preservation of the law is by definition, quite frequently, *illegal*. Not only unjust, but also illegal.

The decadence of an institution occurs, according to Benjamin, when it forgets the violent origin from which it emerged. Drucilla Cornell captures this well when she insists that for deconstruction as well as for Benjamin "what is 'rotten' in a legal system is precisely the erasure of its own mystical foundation of authority so that the system can dress itself up as justice" (*Philosophy* 167). Parliament, argues Benjamin, has not remained conscious of the revolutionary forces to which it owes its existence. In other words, it is the forgetting of originary violence that allows for the most brutal forms of present violence. Not seeing what Drucilla Cornell saw— namely that deconstruction and Benjamin are in full agreement on that point—Derrida refers to Benjamin's essay's presumed membership in a "anti-parliamentarian and anti-*Aufklärung* 'wave'" (*Force* 259) in Weimar Germany, in what is certainly one of the most unfortunate generalizations of all of Derrida's work. Naturally, Benjamin's "Critique of Violence," before being part of a wave, is part of a subterranean tradition, a lineage devoted to carrying out a critique of forgetting. One cannot associate Benjamin's statement about parliament's amnesiac character with a supposed "anti-parliamentarian" position of Benjamin's essay. Benjamin clearly grants that the blooming of a parliament is desirable and gratifying, as he calls it. Benjamin's is not an attack on parliament, then, but simply a reminder: It is naive to believe that parliament is the antithesis of violence. It can never be a pure stance of nonviolence, since it already is, by definition, the space where the *worst form of violence* occurs: the forgetting of the originary violence. That is where we start: Benjamin's "Critique of Violence" is one of his great contributions to the critique of forgetting, even as he forgot that one must also carry out the Nietzschean task of critiquing memory, too.

For a Walter Benjamin who was quickly becoming familiar with Freud, *forgetting* was a word that already appeared with the overtones it had acquired in psychoanalysis (and that would later be so decisive for Derrida's thought). Given the neurotic *repression* of the memory of violence, of the originary revolutionary violence that gave us some of the institutions we have, could one ask whether or not a nonviolent resolution of conflict is possible? Assuming the question can be posed, what is the answer? Benjamin's is paradoxical as always. Personal relationships confirm, Benjamin hints, that the choice of nonviolence comes from the fear of mutual disadvantages that might arise in violent confrontation. In social conflicts, typically, the consequences of violence are not visible, beforehand, to the social actors who might resort to it. Hence Benjamin's dichotomy, no longer between the violence of the strike and the antistrike violence of the state, but between the two types of strikes he inherits from Georges Sorel, namely the political strike and the general proletarian strike. Contrasting with the political strike, the general proletarian strike posits the task of destroying all state power. The political strike, after the material victory (salary raise, paid vacation, etc.), posits the return to work. The general proletarian strike, the one that destroys state power, places itself outside of all legality. And here the paradoxical conclusion drawn by Benjamin while reading Sorel is confirmed in the experience of many labor activists around the world: The general revolutionary strike is, precisely because it proposes another legality, the truly nonviolent strike. The more revolutionary and general the strike is, the less violent it will be. In other words, the notion of revolution and the destruction of the state apparatus are not associated, in Benjamin, with violence, but rather with a utopian moment of nonviolence.

Benjamin's conclusion is that the nonviolent resolution of conflicts is only possible insofar as violence is not excluded beforehand. In order to clarify this apparent paradox, he returns to the dichotomy established at the beginning between natural law and positive law. If natural law attempts to justify the ends through the justice of the means, "positive law attempts to 'guarantee' the justness of the ends through the justification of the means" ("Critique" 278). Natural law reduces the just to the adjusted, confounds justice with necessity. Positive law reduces the just to the legal, confounds justice with law. Both maintain the reference to a presumed necessary relationship between the justness of the ends and the justification of the means. But what would happen if we envisioned a form of violence that, using justified means, represented an irreconcilable conflict with the justice of the ends? What happens if we completely decouple the justice of ends from the justification of means? What happens, suggests Benjamin, if we think of violence in a way completely irreducible to the dialectic between ends and means? What if we mess up the premise of a dialectic relationship between these terms?

In order to define this space, Benjamin resorts to an adjective that frequently appears in his early work to name the unnamable. In contrast to the legal violence that Benjamin calls merely mythical, the violence that is completely outside of the dialectic between ends and means is *divine* violence. Benjamin says: "if mythical violence is lawmaking, divine violence is law-destroying." (297). Only the banality of mythical violence, Benjamin claims, is recognizable on a daily basis to men. Divine violence is the name of a sheer promise. Divine violence is, for Benjamin, "annihilating" and "sovereign," *waltende* in German, almost a homophone for Benjamin's first name, a phonological coincidence that Derrida chooses to highlight at the opening of his essay.

In paraphrasing this passage, Derrida states the following: "Next there is the distinction between the founding violence that makes law—it is named 'mythic' (implicit meaning: Greek, it seems to me)—and the destructive violence that annihilates law (*Rechtsvernichtend*)—named 'divine' (implicit meaning: Jewish, it seems to me)." (*Force* 265) Derrida adds the phrase "it seems to me" almost as a disclaimer: The words "Greek" and "Jewish" *do not appear* in Benjamin's essay in the context of mythical and divine violence, nor in any other context. Certainly, Benjamin exemplifies mythical violence with the narration of the Greek myth of Niobe. It also true that he exemplifies the nonmythic, the "unmediated" kind of violence with a reading of the biblical story of Korah. But the leap from that to the conversion of these narratives in national or ethnic attributes is an operation that takes place in Derrida, not in Benjamin. Nothing authorizes that operation. Of Niobe Benjamin says that "violence bursts upon [her] from the uncertain, ambiguous sphere of life." The horrifying experience of the character (whose children are slain by Apollo's arrows) establishes the myth, the story, the theatricality of violence. But nothing authorizes Benjamin's reader to oppose the Niobe tale to the Korah story as one would oppose "Greek" to "Jewish."[12] What happens when one raises a singular anecdote to the status of national allegory?

Faithful to the teachings of Derrida, I do not answer that question before considering the text's context of production and circulation. The second part of *Force of Law* is presented at the University of California, in 1990, in a colloquium entitled, "Nazism and the Final Solution." The colloquium is on the theme of the Final Solution, but Derrida reads

Benjamin's essay from 1921. By choosing his object anachronistically vis-à-vis the theme of the conference, he forces himself to be guided by only one possible question: "what would Benjamin have thought, or at least what thought of Benjamin is virtually formed or articulated in this essay (and can be anticipated?) on the subject of the 'final solution'?" (260). I confess that it was the first time that I ever encountered, in an essay by Derrida, the proleptic conditional construction: What would x have thought of z? What does this text anticipate about this other phenomenon that took place 20 years later? The question that guided Derrida's text was blatantly external to Benjamin's text, this coming, of course, from the thinker who has most often taught us to formulate questions rigorously internal to the texts being read. His justification for casting Benjamin's essay in the colloquium reads:

> I believe this uneasy, enigmatic, terribly equivocal text is haunted . . . by the theme of radical destruction, extermination, total annihilation, and first of all the annihilation of the law, if not of justice; and among those rights, human rights, at least such as these can be interpreted within a tradition of natural law of the Greek type or the "Aufklärung" type. I purposely say that this text is haunted by the themes of exterminating violence. (259)

Let us take a closer look at the confusion between annihilation and violence that provides the link between Derrida's first and second sentences. Benjamin's text indeed posits revolution as the annihilation of all law (in *this* sense the text speaks of destruction). As we have seen, however, for Benjamin the moment of the end of all law *has nothing to do with violence,* it is in fact *the utopian moment of nonviolence* as such. Benjamin insists on the axiom: the more revolutionary, the less violent. Derrida's association of revolution with violence goes against Benjamin's text and ignores his theorization of the inherently split nature of violence. While speaking of the moment of destruction, Derrida adds the phrase "annihilation of the law, if not of justice," as though the latter could have been Benjamin's theme. As we know after reading Benjamin's piece, it would have been impossible for him to ask if the annihilation of the law could disseminate itself to the point of threatening justice. That kind of contiguity between the two is unthinkable for Benjamin because for him the promise of justice implies the destruction of the law, destruction that, let us recall again, is not a synonym but rather the opposite of violence. Derrida's classification of Benjamin as part of an antiparliamentary "wave" illogically and anachronistically rotating around Heidegger prevents him from fully seeing the utopian moment of nonviolence in Benjamin's early essay. This is most ironic, as that is the very anticipation of Derrida's inquiries into undeconstructible justice, promise, or the gift.

Among the "limited but determined affinities" he sees between "Benjamin's text and certain texts by Carl Schmidt and even by Heidegger," Derrida counts "the hostility to parliamentary democracy, even to democracy as such, not only because of the hostility to the *Aufklärung,* but because of a certain interpretation of the *pólemos,* of war, violence, and language" (261). Even when granting that Heideggerian *Destruktion* cannot be confused with the "concept of 'destruction' that was also at the center of Benjaminian thought" (261) (as if one could so confidently speak of a "center" to Benjamin's thought, by the way), Derrida proposes that "one may well ask oneself what such an obsessive thematic might signify, what it prepares or anticipates between the two wars." (261) This is where Derrida's essay really loses rigor and resorts to generalizations. For Derrida, Heidegger's *Destruktion* and Benjamin's divine violence are part of the same "thematic" and this thematic is "obsessive," a curious claim as the notion is far from being ubiquitous in Benjamin. If we were to list Benjamin's "obsessions," nouns such as allegory, mourning, skulls, experience, daydreaming, interruption, redemption, montage, toys, and collecting would all deserve mention way before the notion of "destruction," which is, as we have seen, a notion associated in the 1921 essay with the moment of divine violence, a form of "sovereign" *(waltende)* violence that accomplishes one very particular destruction, that of the law. Destruction is miles away from being either contiguous or synonymous with violence for Benjamin, and at times Derrida's essay proceeds as if he did not know that. Given the vast and well deserved importance of *Force of Law* for a whole range of juridical and interdisciplinary debates on law and justice, existing theory would certainly profit immensely from a Derrida *revisiting* of the issues raised in *Force of Law,* accompanied by an acknowledgement of the limits of the earlier essay.

To crown the misunderstanding, Derrida resorts to the conditional perfect to define what Benjamin *would have thought* of the Final Solution. In three of the four of those hypotheses, I quote only the beginning of Derrida's sentence:

> [Benjamin]would probably have taken the "Final Solution" to be the extreme consequence of a logic of Nazism that . . . corresponded to a multiple radicalization:
>
> 1. The radicalization of evil linked to the fall of communication, representation, information . . .
>
> 2. The totalitarian radicalization of a logic of the state . . .

> 3. The radical but also fatal corruption of parliamentary and representative democracy by a modern police force that is inseparable from it.
>
> 4. A radicalization and total extension of the mythical, of mythic violence . . . (294–5)

It is astounding, but one could not make a more exact list of all the things that for Benjamin Nazism *was not.* I will omit the reasons that led Benjamin to think of Nazism as *none of those things,* but suffice it to say that he never equated Nazism with mythical violence or with the mythical as such, much less with a presumed corruption of democracy.

What Benjamin *thought* about Nazism is written, published, translated into several languages, and available for whoever would like to read it, in various places but most especially in his testamentary "On the Concept of History," a piece omitted by Derrida in an 80-page essay on the space in which Benjamin *would have constructed* his discourse on Nazism and the Final Solution. One might retort that Derrida was reading another text by Benjamin, in circumscribed fashion. True enough, but if the essay where Benjamin *did write* about what Nazism *indeed was for him*—in a quite literal sense the end of his life—then the anachronistic nature of the question that Derrida poses to "Critique of Violence" becomes all the more unpardonable. I say unpardonable as I read Derrida, the thinker who has taught us that precisely because it is unpardonable we *must* pardon while we continue attempting to read Derrida carefully, as he brings *Force of Law* to a close with the following speculation:

> Benjamin would perhaps have judged as vain and without pertinence, in any case without a pertinence commensurable to the event, any juridical trial of Nazism and of its responsibilities, any judgmental apparatus, any historiography still homogenous with the space in which Nazism developed up to and including the final solution. (296)

This scandalous hypothesis is literally irremissible to any text that Benjamin ever signed, before or after 1921. What is it in Benjamin's thought and work that authorizes one to speculate he would have found "vain and without pertinence" a juridical trial of Nazism? After this absurd point of departure, how can one claim that "this text, like many others by Benjamin, is still too Heideggerian, too messianico-Marxist or archeoschatological for me" (298), when in fact it is the one doing the reading who is guilty of a gross Heideggerianization of the essay? Derrida's closing is appropriate when he affirms that this is a "task and a responsibility the theme of which I have not been able to read in either Benjaminian 'destruction' or Heideggerian *Destruktion*" (298).

It would not be unfair, I believe, to say that Derrida has not been able to read this theme because he has not taken to its ultimate consequences the promising critique of Heideggerian Being-unto-death carried out from the point of view of a theory of mourning in *Specters of Marx*. The golden opportunity to accomplish that was given to Derrida when he confronted the twentieth century's most radical reflections on mourning, those of Walter Benjamin. But in that most auspicious encounter Derrida fails, and the roots of this failure again can be described bluntly: Derrida is still unable to see Benjaminian mourning and melancholia in their irreducibility vis-à-vis the tired, guilty, and sacrificial Heideggerian thematic of Being-unto-death. Again, he sees it, but the thinking is trained to proceed as though he had not.

Derrida's mischaracterization of Benjamin's "Critique of Violence" takes place by reference to another essay where Derrida resorts to national and racial allegorizations in the very title: "Interpretations at War: Kant, the Jew, the German," presented in Jerusalem in 1988, during the first Intifada against the Israeli occupation. A summary of the argument was distributed before the discussion and entitled by Derrida "The Jewish-German Psyche: Hermann Cohen y Franz Rosenzweig." In that piece Derrida again portrays early twentieth-century figures—this time not Benjamin, but Cohen and Rosenzweig— as thinkers who "anticipate Heidegger" or "what some have described as the encounter with Heidegger's teaching during the years immediately following the war." Derrida casts Rosenzweig and Cohen as predecessors of a thematic that would later ripen and blossom with the work of Heidegger. Postulating a between-the-wars "Jewish-German Psyche" Derrida reads Cohen, Rosenzweig, and Benjamin from the standpoint of Heidegger or at least insofar as they implicitly dialogue with, replicate, or "anticipate" Heidegger. In addition to being Heidegger-centric, Derrida's phrasing here is again—much like his reading of Benjamin's 1921 essay vis-à-vis the "Final Solution"—organicist and teleological.

"Interpretations at War" is a reading of Cohen and Rosenzweig, two early twentieth-century non-Zionist Jewish thinkers. In fact, it would not be unfair to call Rosenzweig "anti-Zionist," as he was explicitly hostile to the project of an Israeli state.[13] Derrida presents his reading of those two thinkers as part of a conference in Jerusalem in which no Palestinians have been allowed to participate. Derrida mentions the fact in his introduction, along with the manifestation of his "concern" to the organizers, Wolfgang Iser and Sanford Budick. He goes on to take part in the conference anyway, and opens by condemning the violence of terrorism and the violence of the occupying forces. He also reaffirms his friendship toward Palestinians and Israelis. All very symmetrical, as if we were dealing with two comparable forms of violence.

But is there not something the exclusion of which makes possible Derrida's reading? Is it accidental that the Palestinian had not been able to enter to the delivery of the piece where Derrida so eloquently related "the German" to "the Jew"? Could that fact be accidental if we recall that "Interpretations at War" is the essay alluded to in *Force of Law,* at the moment when Derrida *dreamt* he had seen the words *Greek* and *Jewish* in a 1921 essay by Walter Benjamin? Wouldn't the Palestinian be today the silenced and excluded ghost inhabiting Derrida's discourse? S/he may very well be the constitutive outside of the Jew and the Greek such as they are invoked by Derrida in his reading of a text where these words don't appear. The impossibility of naming this figure, this unrepresented nationality, this outside of the state may indeed have something to do with Derrida's inability to read Benjamin beyond Heidegger or yet with his inability to read the powerful refusal of Zionism in Benjamin's thought.

The goal here is neither to proselytize with the dispossession of Palestinian land nor to take a cheap shot at Derrida, a thinker whom we must continue to read with utmost attention and care. In fact, precisely *because* Jacques Derrida's work is ineluctable and indispensable, the omissions and errors he commits should be especially instructive for all of us (not only in philosophy, but also in critical thinking in the humanities as a whole). Reading Jacques Derrida, an entire generation realized that the rhetorical and the political were interlocked in ways not yet clearly understood or particularly well theorized. Inspired by him I have tried to relate his own shortcomings with Walter Benjamin to a certain tendency to subsume Weimar Germany (and particularly Benjamin's work) under the mark left by Heidegger on Derrida. In the process I mapped the context in which Derrida's encounters with Benjamin (do not) take place, including the justification of the concept of Jewish-German Psyche at a conference in Jerusalem where Palestinians were not welcome. Clearly, one does not want to make much of the extratextual context, most especially in a complex situation such as that of Jerusalem. But it is impossible not to see the symptomatic link between the surroundings of the conference and what Derrida fails to read in Benjamin.

The relation between Derrida's misreading of Benjamin and his reference to two presumably symmetrical forms of violence in the occupied territories becomes clear when we recall that one of the key errors in his paraphrase of "Critique of Violence" is the silence on Benjamin's point on the eminently *illegal and law-making* nature of military violence. For Benjamin military and police violence *suspends* the distinction between law-preserving and law-making violence. To put the contrast as bluntly as possible: In "Critique of Violence" Benjamin alludes to the police as the permanently illegal redrawing of the borders of legality itself. While forgetting this important point amidst the nebulous Heideggerian "wave" of Weimar Germany, Derrida refers to his interpretation of the Jewish-German Psyche developed in "Interpretations at War," a piece that opens by condemning "both" forms of violence, as if the violence of the occupation forces were one form of violence among others, as if Benjamin had not reminded us that it is the prototypical image of illegality laying down the law according to which all forms of violence will be judged.

Since the publication of Derrida's *Force of Law* and "Interpretations at War," the concentration of all legal violence in the hands of one empire has escalated to a level that neither he nor anyone else could have imagined. Regardless of the fact that a closer look at Benjamin's 1921 essay could have given Derrida a better read of 1988 Jerusalem, Benjamin's essay—especially in its insistence on military violence as a complete suspension of the difference between preservation and creation of law—has now acquired renewed relevance and interest that no one could have predicted. As we watch the conversion of Empire into a war machine that operates outside of all legal precedence and creates new laws with each repressive act, again Jerusalem is not one city among others, and the Palestinian population is not one victim among others. The difference between *owning your land* and *having it occupied* is way too irreducible a difference, and "Interpretations at War" does not do justice to that irreducibility, much like *Force of Law* had not done justice to the irreducibility of the notion of revolution-as-nonviolence in Benjamin. The analogy is not impertinent. Neither of those acts of unjustice is, in my opinion, less internal to Derrida's text than the other. Both are quite fair interpellations to pose to Derrida's essay. They certainly are questions more internal to Derrida's text than the "Final Solution" could ever have been to Benjamin's 1921 piece.

In recent years, Derrida's voice has assumed a leading role in organizing the debate amongst cosmopolitans. For Derrida and for so many other leading intellectuals of our times (these rather *violent* times) cosmopolitans of all lands must today more than ever stick together, so that the fundamental values of multilateralism and hospitality prevail in world politics ("Cosmopolitanism"). As Derrida has argued in different forums, Apartheid should be maintained as the *last* name of racism and the momentous victory against it should never be forgotten("Le derniers"). Forgiveness and responsibility are now, more than ever and much as Derrida has taught, *political* categories that will only be ignored in the First World at a considerable price for the entire planet. Along with

Derrida one must now, more than ever, insist on reflection and research—of a philosophical nature—on the concept of *justice,* as irreducible to and completely distinct from the category of law. One must certainly continue to follow Derrida's footsteps in rethinking through the conditions of possibility for the university as one of the truly urgent tasks. For all who live and work in Europe especially, it is now imperative to engage Derrida, Giorgio Agamben, Jürgen Habermas, and other thinkers anchored on the values of peace and multilateralism as they attempt to think through a balanced European response to the current war machine developed in the United States.

For all of us fortunate enough to live in Derrida's time, around the sheer luminosity of his philosophical effort, we must not only attempt to proceed in that infinite task of engaging and rereading his work. We must not only think through these immediate problems in ways that ethically and politically would do justice to the insights of that work. From Derrida many have learned not only how to read but also how to write. In that process one of the key lessons has been that urgency may never be an excuse for hurry. Thus we must also remind *him,* the writer who has in a way taught so many of us how to read, that something in the order of a *task, a promise,* remains for deconstruction: a definitive encounter with the radical critique of capitalism and of militarism in the philosophy of Walter Benjamin. This task, for Derrida, remains as open as ever.

Chapter 4

Transculturation and Civil War

The Origins of the Novel in Colombia

Introduction: Statehood, Literature, and Transculturation

Latin American literary criticism has moved beyond a number of paradigms that until recently held positions of dominance in the field. Among these paradigms we could count the biographical (based on the search for links between life and work), the genetic (based on notions such as sources and influences, usually found in previous European authors), and the stylistic-historiographical (based on the study of a succession of literary movements such as Realism and Romanticism). Without necessarily discarding the contributions of those methods, much recent criticism on nineteenth-century Latin American literature (Viñas; Rama, *Ciudad*; Ramos, *Divergent*; Montaldo, *De pronto* and "Transculturación"; Molloy; Ludmer; Sommer; Franco, *Plotting*) has been guided by a different set of questions: the role of literature in the constitution of a lettered and conservative postcolonial status quo; literature's relationship with processes of modernization, specialization, and professionalization; literature's tense and contradictory responses to the autonomization of art as well as its vexed appropriation of a popular voice. The question of the *nation* has been one of the most recurrent of these problems. The hypothesis handled by the newer generation of critics is that the relationship between literature and nationhood must never be assumed as given, but should rather be interrogated from the point of view of its mutual construction.

In the case of Colombia, the question regarding the nation has always been a central one in literary criticism and in other humanistic disciplines. Endowed with an absolutely singular process of state building, Colombia, more than other countries, cannot afford to presuppose "literature" and "nation" to be concepts with clear and unequivocal referents. Precisely because Colombia has lived an uneven process of national unification—one that has been considerably more truncated and belated than those of other Latin American countries—it is imperative that the relationship between nation and literature not be posed as one in which the meaning of these terms are given in advance. The intersection between them takes extremely different forms in each one of the semi-autonomous regions that comprise nineteenth-century Colombia. This chapter will make an argument about the constitution of Colombia's literary canons, an expression that must be maintained in its plural form, as it designates different realities on the Caribbean Coast, in the Andean Center-East, in the Cauca Valley, and in Antioquia. Drawing upon historians of Colombian society such as Marco Palacios and Frank Safford, upon literary essayists such as Germán Colmenares and Alvaro Pineda Botero, and cultural historians such as Jaime Jaramillo Uribe, this chapter proposes a genealogical argument about nineteenth-century Colombian literature through a reading of four of its early novels. For reasons that have to do with the particularities of Colombian regionalism, I have elected texts foundational for the prose fiction of those four regions: *Ingermina* (1844), by Juan José Nieto, *Manuela* (1856), by Eugenio Díaz Castro, *María* (1867), by Jorge Isaacs, and *Frutos de mi tierra* (1898), by Tomás Carrasquilla.

This essay was initially conceived as a reading of the topos of impossible love such as allegorized in *María*, by Jorge Isaacs. My purpose was to move from that close reading of the text to the question of its consolidation as the national Colombian novel and the country's privileged literary allegory. As I worked, it became clear that one cannot make an argument about the canonization of Isaacs's novel without also looking at the various traditions that coexisted, in nineteenth-century Colombia, with that of the Cauca Valley out of which emerged *María*. The canon of nineteenth-century Colombian literature has an essentially *retrospective* nature, as the national tradition only gets unified belatedly, in the twentieth century. In the decades that preceded and followed the publication of *María*, the signifier "Colombia" designated a plurality of contradictory and region-specific armed projects, not a unified and referable political entity. As late as 1930—and to a certain extent afterward—Colombian citizens still identified themselves primarily with a region, more than with the nation, and with a political party, more than a social class (Palacios, *Estado*, 138).[1] In other words, when we speak of nineteenth-century Colombian literature it is imperative to avoid the idea of a "national spirit" expressing itself in fiction. Texts like *María* underwent, rather, processes of canonization that retrospectively constructed fables of national identity. To analyze these processes requires not only a study of the texts but also a synchronic look at all traditions being gestated in conflict-ridden nineteenth-century Colombia.

María imagines the nation negatively, as an unrealized allegory. To understand this allegory one must avoid taking Isaacs's novel as a European transplant that one could simply judge as a more or less accomplished imitation. This has been the procedure of a number of critics who chose not to read it in its Colombian context.[2] It is more productive to see the novel as a piece in a web of synchronic regional traditions that coexisted within a fragmented society characterized by a strong localism. It is paramount to avoid the retrospective illusion that through Isaacs's pages one could witness the embryo of a unified Colombian subject. Much of the hagiographic criticism of Isaacs's works falls in this retrospective illusion, one that is part and parcel of idealist conceptions of nationality, conservative or liberal. I will attempt to bypass this retrospective mirage with a reading strategy that combines attention to Isaacs's text with a study of the other three great literary traditions that coexisted, with a considerable degree of autonomy, with that of the Cauca Valley in nineteenth-century Colombia: the Coast, the Andes, and Antioquia.

In Weberian terms, the history of nineteenth-century Colombia is the history of a sequence of conflicts in which none of the contending actors acquires a lasting monopoly over the legal use of violence, an impasse that ends up disseminating violence itself. In fact, Colombia is an extreme instance of the tautology to which a certain Weberian sociology has made recourse in attempting to explain contradictory Latin American entrances into modernity: The absence of state consolidation is explained by the impossibility of constitution of said monopoly on violence, which, in its turn, is retroactively explained by the feebleness of the state. In the shadow of a state unable to guarantee political stability, scattered populations of peasants find themselves trapped in the bipartisan system, and only survive in areas left behind by the expansion of large land property. These are social spaces not yet organically incorporated into international trade and upon which the cities, of course, did not yet exercise hegemonic control. In the 90 years that separate the independence from the dawn of the twentieth century, Colombia underwent four national civil wars (1876–77, 1885–86, 1895, 1899–1902) and countless regional conflicts, in a history of precarious relations of "a shaky national state with the individual, the Church, and the provinces" (Palacios, *Entre la legitimidad*, 15).[3]

As opposed to countries like Brazil and Argentina—where the entrance of British and later North American capital was a key mediator in the post-independence processes of modernization—Colombia remained throughout the nineteenth century an agrarian country without major insertion in the international market. The arrival of the Liberal party to power in 1849, albeit accompanied by significant changes such as the abolition of slavery (1851), the end of state monopoly on tobacco (1850), and the constitutional guarantee of freedom of press and of religion (1853), did not produce an intra-elite pact that could ensure governability of the kind witnessed in Argentina after Rosas's defeat at the Caseros Battle.[4] In 1854 the fission between two rival fractions of the Liberal party reached its limit: the *draconianos,* representing primarily artisans and military subjects ("men in *ruanas* and men in uniform"), staged a rebellion headed by Gal. Melo against the constitutionalist *gólgotas* (the "doctors"). The latter, counting on the inestimable help of conservatives, defeated the rebellion in a few months. That was the "greatest war operation yet seen in the nation's capital" (Sánchez 384). It represented a profound break in Bogotá's political and intellectual field. That was the background upon which provincial writer Eugenio Díaz-Castro, the author of *Manuela,* made his intervention in the capital's intellectual circles.

Toward 1870 "there emerged in Colombia the first systematic critiques of the liberal idea of the state" (Jaramillo Uribe 201). In the same decade the right to lay education, such as guaranteed by the constitution of 1863 (one of the world's most liberal at its time), became an excuse and a battle horse for the conservative backlash that unleashed a bloody civil war of national proportions. The clash was not only between two antagonistic national projects, neither of which, needless to say, managed to impose itself completely upon the other. It was also a conflict between two different understandings of the national past. For liberals, it was a matter of overcoming Hispanism and embracing the Anglo-Saxon civilizing project. For conservatives, the goal was to establish a continuity between the Republican present and the colonial past based on religion as a unifying thread. Literature—that is the poetic, dramatic, and narrative writing then produced by statesmen and later designated as "literary"—positioned itself in unique fashion within those conflicts. Unlike Argentine narrative, whose origins can be traced back to a liberal and modernizing cultural war waged from exile against Rosas, and unlike Brazilian literature, whose origins hark back to a national project relatively stable within a monarchic-conservative order, the Colombian narrative traditions gestated between 1840 and the early twentieth century maintain a *catachrestic* relationship with the nation, as these novels did not coincide with the consolidation of national pacts but rather attempted to explain their failure.

The reference to the nation inhabits these novels, then, in particularly spectral and phantasmic fashion, as they weave metaphors of a referent—the nation—that did not quite have a literal existence in reality. They are never reducible to a finished, coherent project such as the Sarmiento variety of liberalism that became hegemonic in Argentina, or the idealist-conservative allegories of José de Alencar that consolidated the Brazilian Romantic novel. The Colombian texts, however diverse and differentiated, do have something in common vis-à-vis the rest of Latin America's foundational Romanticism: They seem to be texts that hesitate, that consider contradictory hypotheses, that never fully settle around a conclusive project. This is, no doubt, related to the fact that they are national novels of regions that have not yet formed a nation. Their privileged trope is the catachresis, the metaphor of a nonexistent referent.

One of my assumptions here is that *María*'s nationalization is made possible by its essentially catachrestic character, that is to say, its position as a narrative that weaves a metaphor of something that does not fully exist, something isomorphic with the fragmented nation to which the novel alludes. Hence the fact that *María* is the member of a group, that is, a genus within the species (a novel foundational of the literary tradition of one of the country's major regions, the Cauca Valley) and at the same time the name of the *entire* species, a novel that unlike *Ingermina,* from the Coast, or *Manuela,* from the Andes, or *Frutos de mi tierra,* from Antioquia, is able to become a national canonical novel and a privileged literary metaphor of the impossibility of consolidating the national project. *María* does have a specificity, then, as it is the name of one piece in the whole while also naming the entire fragment itself. *María* is, in Colombia, a genus and a species. It is at the same time a regional novel like many others and yet the only regional novel that became the national novel. Our analysis will, then, examine each piece separately, but knowing that one particular fragment possesses the key to the void that holds all the fragments together.[5]

Ingermina, or the Diasporic Origins of the Caribbean Novel

You argue that you have left us in peace, it is true, but this is an unworthy, despicable peace, purchased at the costly price of our independence and sustained by the abjection of slavery.

—*Catarpa, in Juan José Nieto's* Ingermina

The Atlantic Coast of Colombia that witnessed the birth of writer and statesman Juan José Nieto in 1804 had inherited from colonial times a slave-based economy and a key fortress and port in Caribbean history, the city of Cartagena. It was the Coast that saw the establishment of the first *palenques,* maroon communities that came to emblematize black struggles for freedom. That was also, curiously enough, the area where it was possible to see both free blacks and peasant Indians aligned with royalist armed groups. These two opposing phenomena testify to the same fact, namely that the young independent state did not incorporate those populations into a national project that they could recognize as their own. Even though the complete replacement of slavery with wage-earning labor was not concluded until the latter half of the nineteenth century, the *manumisión* law passed in 1821 included free birth for blacks and the gathering of a fund of indemnization. The same Juan José Nieto who would author *Ingermina* and later govern the province of Cartagena was an active participant in one of the boards in charge of *manumisiones.* This unique, incipiently monetarized transition away from slavery made possible on the Colombian Coast something unthinkable in other areas of strong black concentration, such as Brazil or Cuba: The early constitution of a free class of Afro-descendants who accede to degrees of control over the land was not common in other latitudes, except as a collective act of resistance and war, such as the Brazilian and Cuban maroon communities. The coast's social structure contrasted with the significantly more rigid slave system of the gold- and sugar-producing area of the Cauca Valley, where the high concentration of land remained fairly intact until the twentieth century. Already in the 1776–8 census, free blacks and mulattoes represented three-fifths of the population of Cartagena, and slaves were fewer than 10 percent. In any case this allowed for the constitution of a small black lettered class in the Coast out of which a writer of the stature of Calendario Obeso could emerge.

Calendario Obeso was a poet, grammarian, and playwright. He was a translator of Shakespeare, Goethe, Byron, Victor Hugo, Longfellow, and the author of manuals on arithmetic and language, a figure whose importance is still to be established by Colombian and Latin American criticism. He was a foundational, pioneering black voice in literature—precisely, to be sure, the voice that Nieto chose to elide by locating his novel in 1530s Cartagena, at the moment when the Spaniards conquered the kingdom. If *Ingermina* was a foundational landmark for the Colombian novel, the novelty of Calendario Obeso's *Cantos populares de mi tierra,* published 33 years later, was no smaller. Obeso was the bastard son of a lawyer and a washerwoman, and was born in what is today the UNESCO patrimony of Santa Cruz de Mompox. He received a fellowship from the Military School and was also a student of engineering and law in Bogotá, before returning to Mompox. He later worked as a teacher in La Mojana and as a municipal treasurer in Magangué before arriving in Santa

Marta, where a "love passion sent him to jail" (Burgos Cantor 12). He wrote the novel *La familia Pigmalión* (of which no contemporary edition exists) and a *Spanish Grammar*; he later retuned to Bogotá, where he produced good part of his work, including the drama *Secundino el zapatero* (an early and incipient critique of the lettered city), an *Intimate Life*, a *Miscellaneous*, and a compilation of writings in prose and verse entitled *Lecturas para ti*.

Lecturas para ti contains some of his most accomplished compositions, such as "Sotto Voce," a pan-Colombian lyric poem composed in melancholic *silvas* (a classic Spanish poetic form that intersperses 7- and 11-syllable verses, most famously cultivated in Latin America by patrician and founding father Andrés Bello). The rhythm of Obeso's "Sotto Voce" is reminiscent of the lightly elegiac tone of early sixteenth-century Peninsular poet Garcilaso de la Vega, who brought (along with his friend Juan Boscán) the Petrarcan 11-syllable verse into Spain. Another Calendario Obeso composition in classic *silvas* is "Un día tras otro," dedicated to the barroque thematic of anguish facing the passing of time. The cruel and implacable woman appears in Obeso's poetry depicted both in the swaying rhythm of the *silva* and in the faster tempo of popular, shorter-verse forms, as in "Canto del Boga ausente," "Cuento a mi esposa," and "Canción del pescador."[6]

In a wide range of erudite and popular dictions, Obeso's *Cantos* nostalgically evoked origins lost and dialogued with Romantic sentimental poetry. He left a unique register of racial, regional, and national politics of his time. As witnesses and subjects of an uneven, harshly negotiated, and precarious access of nineteenth-century black men to poetry, Obeso's texts insistently interpellated whiteness in tones that ranged from interracial alliance to proud affirmation of freedom and difference. In Obeso's lyric poetry the affirmation of self insistently recalls the image of *another*, be it a woman of whom one doubts, or be it a white man posed as an inverted mirror through which the poetic voice reflects upon his socially subordinate but firm and proud position. Partisan or racial politics in Obeso's writing included a firm pacifist ending to a *serenata* song, where he countered the possibility of civil conflict with "want war? / with the city?/ I don't move / from my here ranch / if you intend / to climb up on top / look for ladder / on another spot" (Obeso, *Cantos*, 53).[7] Obeso's social critique later matured in the dramatic poem *Lucha de la vida*, where a sequence of social types, "students, lost women, ministers, soldiers, priests, thieves, murderers, unfaithful wives, go-betweens" (Prescott 68), composed a caustic and sarcastic tableau that functions as the background for Gabriel, a young idealist black poet and alter ego of Obeso. Two years after the publication of *Lucha de la vida* (1882), Obeso fired a pistol against his own body and reportedly agonized for days before expiring. The designation of the episode as "suicide" or not varies according to who narrates it. The same Coast that produced the pioneering black poetic voice of Calendario Obeso also produced the exiled author of *Ingermina,* the radical liberal Juan José Nieto.

Juan José Nieto (1804–66) belongs to that generation of liberal politicians who lived between the long period of colonial hegemony of Cartagena and the rise of Baranquilla in the 1870s to the status of most important port city in the region. A disciple of Santander in his youth, Nieto was an autodidact who acceded to print with a *Geography of the province of Cartagena* (1839). He later got elected provincial deputy and took part in the "Revolution of the Supremes" in the 1840s. Caught by conservative Gal. Mosquera, he left Colombia for exile in Kingston, Jamaica until 1847. In Jamaica he wrote, in addition to *Ingermina,* two other novels, *Resina* and *Los moriscos,* before his return to Cartagena. Having achieved the post of chamber deputy and later governor of the province, he was overturned and later reconducted by a Constitutional Assembly of the self-declared independent state of Bolívar.

In the name of Bolívar state he celebrated a curious treaty with the same Gal. Mosquera who had sent him to exile, and who was now waging war, from the Cauca Valley, against the hegemonic Granada Conference led by conservative president Mariano Ospina. This cartographically impossible treaty declared the unification of Bolívar and the Cauca Valley, under the name of United States of New Granada, a territory in two pieces, constituted over and above the Antioquia region, which geographically separates them. As president of Bolívar, Nieto still won battles in Santa Marta and Barranquilla, but his legacy would ultimately be one of defeat. The Mosquera follower González Carazo was responsible for Nieto's definitive defeat in the military world. A few decades earlier, as a writer, Juan José Nieto had composed an elegant account of how a subject, a tradition, and a lineage find themselves forced to deal with defeat. Nieto extracted from the tragedy of the Calamar people a powerful image of that piece of the nation that was exiled with him in Jamaica.

The history of the publication and (non)circulation of *Ingermina* (1844) contrasts with the world success of Jorge Isaacs's *María.* Between *Ingermina*'s first edition, done at Rafael de Córdova Press at the expense of friends of the author and the second edition (1998), carried out under the auspices of the Bolívar governorship, 154 years passed during which the novel did not circulate. The marginal history of *Ingermina* is not a contingency or a mere reflection of the Coast's subordinate position vis-à-vis the canon that began to take national shape a few decades later. The disqualification of novels such as or Nieto's *Ingermina, Los moriscos,* and

Resina (the latter two never republished) has already left a few traces beyond the silence devoted to it by the classics of Colombian literary criticism like José J. Ortega's *Historia de la literatura colombiana*. This silence is not a contingent or accidental event but rather is articulated with Colombian political history in interesting and surprising ways.

Luis María Sánchez López's *Diccionario de autores colombianos* (1978) incorrectly names Cartagena (and not Loma de la Puerta, in the Atlantic Province) as Nieto's place of birth. Beyond the characterization of Nieto "as soldier, playwright, and novelist" it does not offer us anything other than a description of *Ingermina* as "Colombia's first novel of violence" (325). In almost the entire secondary bibliography, the adjective "first" is followed by a derogatory judgment based on an ideal of what a "mature" novel would look like. Antonio Cursio Altamar defined *Ingermina* and *Los moriscos* as "formless embryos of a novel, endowed with all the shortcomings of Romanticism and deprived of its imaginative spirit" (65). Donald McGrady refers to *Ingermina* as a *novelita* or "the babbling of a novel" that brings with itself all the "defects later manifest throughout the development of this genre in Colombia" (63, 33). According to McGrady, Nieto's merit was the early exposure of shortcomings that would later become *real* defects of the Colombian Novel. In the 30 essays compiled in the indispensable *Manual de literatura colombiana* (1988), Juan José Nieto receives two very marginal mentions, both in passages dedicated to other authors. Highly valuable reconstitutions of the nineteenth-century Colombian canon such as Raymond Williams's and Álvaro Pineda Botero's, have not altered that value judgment significantly. The latter defines *Ingermina* as a "naive narrative, full of pre-Cervantine literary topics, already passé for nineteenth-century Spain." For Pineda Botero, *Ingermina* is, moreover, a text that sinned in "leaving out the black race," which according to the critic should have been depicted in the novel, as it takes place in 1533–37, and the "introduction of black slaves in New Granada began right after the conquest" (105). Pineda Botero concludes his analysis (his condemnation) of the novel with the conclusion that by using the historical novel Nieto "rewrote history to fulfill the needs of his own present" (108) without telling us what, in that case, would differentiate *Ingermina* from any other historical novel.

Raymond Williams devotes a careful, region-specific look at nineteenth-century Colombian literature and makes interesting observations regarding *Ingermina* as a paradigm of a historical and archivist gaze particularly acute on the Coast, but his analysis ultimately attempts to reduce *Ingermina* to an opposition between the "oral" and the "written" (*Colombian* 93–100). More recently, in his prologue to the well-designed third edition of *Ingermina*, published by EAFIT in Medellín (2001), Germán Espinosa mentions Nieto's donation of a copy of the novel to the National Library in 1856. In that copy, one can read a dedication written by a careful author that takes the time to remind his readers that the publication has been carried out in "a press not of the Spanish language" and that he therefore hopes they will "dissimulate" the work's faults. Nieto writes from the standpoint of translation, already marked by the English language that he was just beginning to learn. His writings display the clear concerns of an exile addressing a distant or absent motherland. As would become frequent in Latin America, the imagination of that virtual home took, in Nieto's work, the form of a visit to the past, understood as a fountain of narratives, emblems, and allegories. As a national allegory, Nieto's *Ingermina* shares more with some Mexican foundational tales than with the early stories of other Colombian regions. In Nieto's narrative, national allegory is extracted from the image of a defeated and enslaved indigenous nation. *Ingermina* brings us back to the invasion and conquest of the proud kingdom of Calamar, and its conversion into the colonial Cartagena of the New Granada Vicerroyalty. Against this historical background, Nieto relates a story of love, war, and resistance.

Nieto opens his novel with a "Brief Historical Note" where a nonfictional, authorial voice portrays a preconquest, happy society, the "most numerous, the strongest, and the most civilized" of its surroundings. Adopting a sort of protoethnographic tone, Nieto describes the Calamares' complex polygamic system, in which women are distributed among friends during the patriarch's travels and the ensuing children are assumed as legitimate of the house. Nieto dedicates special attention to the Calamares' mourning practices, which include "the right to speak well or badly of the deceased one: his/her memory belonged to the people" (41). Nieto's text also focuses on a fascinating "supper of the dead," a "banquet held in presence of the corpse, attended by all of the dwellers of the house and their friends. One ate while weeping or pretending to weep, and supposing alive the corpse to which one was ultimately saying good-bye"(41). Calamar culture is poligamic, impersonal, and collectivist. It cultivates a certain ethos of anonymity. Nieto's account offers us the image of a people made up of "strong, sagacious, and determinate" subjects, although the text also reminds us that they "participated in the bad faith that has generally characterized the Indians" (42).

Only on a superficial level, however, does *Ingermina* narrate the conflict between the Spaniards and the Indians. Rather, it assumes that conflict as a background, and proceeds to narrate the superposition of two other conflicts. On the one hand, Nieto relates the tension between the Calamares who are willing to negotiate in subservience and those more radically in revolt against colonialism. The interesting point about this conflict is that both groups act in good faith, and thereby contradict Nieto's own authorial comments about "Indians" in his "historical note." On the other hand, the novel relates the antagonism that opposes the criminal Spaniards and the virtuous Spaniards. The antagonism between quietism and kamikaze struggle that splits the Calamares is of the order of the survival tactics, that is to say of pragmatics. The antagonism between virtue and dishonesty that separates the Spaniards (an antagonism that unites all Calamares and makes them side with the "good" Iberians) is of the order of ethical essence. The superposition of these two conflicts makes possible the novel's rhetorical operation: to present the colonial order as inevitable (the text never envisions an outside to that order) and at the same time to depict the indigenous resistance as just and justified, albeit doomed to failure.

The story begins before the conquest, with an account of a rebellion among the Calamares. They rise and defeat their tyrannical leader Marcoya and replace him with well-liked Ostarón. "In order to avoid popular fury to be unleashed upon the Cacique's family" (59) Ostarón takes "the widow to his home, along with Ingermina, then a 4-year-old child" (60). Ingermina is thus raised by Ostarón with his son Catarpa, in an ambiguity identical to the one that haunts the relationship between María and Efraín in Isaacs's novel. They are not really siblings, not really cousins, and never really lovers as the text insists in anticipating and frustrating. María-Efraín and Catarpa-Ingermina are two instances of incestuous mysteries announced and reserved for the future in Colombian literature. In *Ingermina,* this reserve is interrupted with the success of the colonial invasion, softened in the novel by the altruist portrait of the colonizing Heredia brothers, one of whom eventually seduces Ingermina. The antagonism between the Calamares who resist and those who progressively adapt begins to set Catarpa apart from Ingermina. The former find his compatriots to have "humiliated themselves at the feet of the victorious, without the slightest sign of receiving subordination with repugnance" (61), while Ingermina is surrounded by the attention, courtship, and pedagogical labor of Alonso de Heredia. In contrast with Catarpa, Ingermina begins to find the "almost savage manners of her co-citizens to be inferior and even shocking" (69). With a certain air of inevitabililty, the Calamar princess slides toward the Hispanic cultural field and Alonso Heredia's area of influence, shared with Alonso's brother Pedro, the future administrator of Cartagena. After the Calamares are defeated in the war of conquest, Catarpa's bravery is publicly acknowledged by the Heredias, the "magnanimous" colonizers, who confer on him the status of prisoner of honor following his capture without violence. Over time, Catarpa's fearless character changes and he is incorporated into the antagonism that structures the second half of the novel, the one that opposes the magnanimous colonization of the Heredias' and the bloody colonization of Badillo and Peralta.

As the first Colombian literary figure seduced by a Spaniard and his culture—as the first to become a *translator*—Ingermina shares more, in fact, with Mexico's Malinche than with the other Colombian heroines, those of Isaacs, Díaz Castro, or Carrasquilla. The limit of that resemblance is the fact that in Ingermina one sees no traces of the trauma and guilt that accompany the Mexican legend.[8] The Malinche-type negativity is not absent from the text, but it is concentrated in another character, Catarpa, the last Calamar to be captured, and who only in jail is convinced to obey the Spanish rule by Alonso de Heredia's respectful persuasion. Ingermina's *malinchismo* go as far as her falling in love with the colonizer. However, there are no traces of guilt, betrayal, or translation. The otherness that separates the colonizer from the native woman is in fact erased at the end of the novel, when we are presented with Ingermina's labyrinthine Spanish origin. Retrospectively, Ingermina appears no longer as a native who converted (a Malinche) but rather an Iberian who returned, in circular fashion, to a point of origin. By doing so Ingermina implicitly renames her half brother Catarpa as the true *other* of the novel, the character who is really alien to the intra-Spaniard antagonism that eventually becomes the focus of the text.

Contrary to what many critical accounts have suggested, *Ingermina* is not a text "deprived of logical progression" or "full of loose cables" (McGrady 33). It is, in fact, one of the most rigorously constructed novels of nineteenth-century Latin America. Both the first and the second parts have eight chapters. Each part narrates a sequence of events that evolve out of basic antagonisms, the intra-Calamar tension between adaptation and rebellion, and the intra-Spaniard antagonism between bloody colonization and magnanimous transculturation. The first part narrates Moncoya's tyranny over the Calamares, the subsequent kingdom of peace under Ostarón, and the Spanish invasion, which triggers a brave reaction and then a "wise" and "mature" submission of the Calamares to the clever and moderate leadership of the Heredia brothers (who have to face Catarpa's fierce opposition for no longer than 25 percent of the novel). The second half narrates the intra-Spaniard antagonism, with the arrival of a new provincial magistrate, Badillo, who incarcerates the Heredias and imposes a reign of terror.

The central antagonism is intra-Iberian, but the indigenous population cannot be indifferent to it: The final resolution in favor of the Heredias is ultimately a product of struggles by Ingermina (who "bathes Alonso in tears" when visiting him in prison) and Catarpa (who, since his capture, begins to mention an unnamed "wife," a phantasmic substitute for Ingermina, who is now promised to the magnanimous Spanish other). The indigenous population, in its totality, "understands" that Heredia's victory is the condition of their survival. The alliance between the good Spaniards and the Calamar population is consolidated. This is curiously coincident with the appearance of Catarpa's "wife," and also coincident with a subtle rhetorical shift in the novel: The narrator begins to designate Catarpa as Ingermina's "brother." In other words, the second part of the novel narrates the dissolution of the intra-indigenous conflict between rebellion and adaptation, within the intra-Iberian conflict between good and evil. The motor of that quietist and conservative collapse is the ghost of incest, which operates in a manner not dissimilar to Latin America's most famous semi-incestuous romance, the *María* that Jorge Isaacs would publish a couple of decades later.

Each part of *Ingermina*'s two halves concludes with an afterword that narrates a tale told in first person. At the end of the first half we encounter Hernán Velázquez, and at the end of the novel Gámbaro and Armósala. Both are narratives in which a miserable wretch recounts, in flashback, an as-of-yet ignored source of the story. Around the two central antagonisms, linearly narrated in the two parts that lead to each of these stories, both flashbacks weave *movements,* in the musical sense of the term: variations that progressively let the theme be envisioned in all its complexity. At the end of the first part, before the illegitimate magistrate Badillo's usurpation of power, Alonso de Heredia and Ingermina's honeymoon-like expedition to the jungle is interrupted by the arrival of a tramp who narrates, much like a Byzantine narrator, a sequence of tragic events. Hernán Velázquez is a Valencian citizen who becomes a Muslim for the love of a woman, and then after the end of the armistice between Christians and Muslims is overtaken by patriotic Spanish furor and convinces his father-in-law to convert into Christianity and follow him. After a brief period of happiness with his wife and father-in-law, she dies and Velázquez, disillusioned, leaves for America, where he participates in the conquest of a kingdom close to the Calamares, but is ultimately forgotten on the beach with the Indians. Over time adapted to the indigenous society, he marries Tálmara, the daughter of his protector Contarmá. But happiness eludes him here as well, as the Calamar kingdom suffers the tyranny of Moncoya, who kidnaps his wife and daughter, the latter being no one but Ingermina herself. The Spaniards find him at this moment of defeat, when he already considers Tálmora and Ingermina to be dead. In a typical novelistic miracle they meet up with him as he is being reunited with his wife and children while visiting the political prisoners of Badillo's tyranny.

This is crucial insofar as it reveals that the girl named Ingermina, saved by a magnanimous Cacique (Oscorón) from a tyrant (Montoya) is in fact the daughter of a Spaniard (Velázquez). We are led completely to reinterpret the entire first half of the novel, which recounts Alonso de Heredia's seduction of Ingermina and her progressive abandonment of a love promise made to Catarpa by both families *on her behalf.* Here Ingermina departs from the Mexican Malinche paradigm for good. More than the surrender to an invader, Ingermina's move becomes a reencounter with lost origins. The emblem of the Calamar essence was a hybrid figure all along. Hybrid, yet a reversal of the Mexican Malinche myth: Her conception was the product of the "indianization" of a defeated Spaniard, lost in picaresque peripetia and led to fall in love with an indigenous woman and build a Calamar family. This defeated, beat-up Spaniard, a victim of colonization himself, would ultimately depend on the Heredia victory over the Calamar leaders in order to see his wife and daughter again. From Spanish Christian to Muslim, from Muslim back to Christian, from that to Calamar, only finally to reencounter his own Hispanism: Velázquez is a kind of emblem of transculturation, deployed in Nieto's novel as a tool to dissolve the political antagonism between colonizers and colonized in the bleach of the moral antagonism between good and evil.

That dissolution achieves full cycle when a story parallel to Velázquez's appears at the end of the novel. Gámbaro, also a miserable character—this time a true Calamar—appears after the text has narrated Badillo's usurpation; the incarceration of Heredia, Ingermina, and Catarpa; and the heroes' subsequent escape in a maritime adventure just before being deported as slaves to Santo Domingo. They eventually triumph over Badillo with the help of a priest who denounces the tyrant to the king and thus seals the national allegory: moderate Calamares plus virtuous Spaniards plus humanitarian clergy. The mediating presence of the church resolves the moral antagonism that splits the Spanish field in favor of the heroes. The arrival of Gámbaro, the reminiscing Indian, endows the allegory with its final axis, in a tale placed in perfectly symmetrical position vis-à-vis the closing of the first part, which had revealed Irgermina's origins.

Gámbaro, in his turn, is the son of the Cacique of the province of Turbaco, and he has been promised to the elder daughter of the Cacique of neighboring Zipacúa. However, he falls in love with the younger daughter, Armósola, who has been promised to someone else, the villain Combacóa. Gámbaro's love for Armósola is requited, and they flee together, only to witness the outbreak of a war between the two kingdoms—caused by the mistaken perception that Gámbaro's father, the tribal leader, had been complicitous with their escape. After the two kingdoms make Gámbaro a prisoner and declare a peace accord based on his sacrifice, he manages to flee from prison with the help of a woman, in time to save his father as well as his father-in-law, the virtuous Zipacúa leader, from a trap set up by the villain, Combacóa, who operates moved by jealousy. After saving the same father who had disinherited him for disobedience and the same father-in-law who believed him to be a traitor, Gámbaro is granted his freedom and, after many more adventures, during which he becomes convinced that Armósola had died, he finally reencounters her thanks to the "virtuous" colonization of the Heredias, and the pardon they grant on the last Calamar warriors.

Gámbaro appears at the end, much like a ghost, to embrace Catarpa, now knowing he was his brother-in-law: Gámbaro is the brother of the unnamed "wife" that accompanies Catarpa since Ingermina's romance with Alonso de Heredia. The couples are reunited, and the last remaining villain, Peralta (a representative of Badillo's former fraudulent and corrupt scheme), is condemned in a legal trial, pardoned by the new virtuous magistrate, and then lynched by the Calamares, who do not join the pact of compassion and take revenge on Peralta for old punishments. Roundly closed, the fable leaves us with a picture of the colonial coexistence, liberal and tolerant, between the Heredia hegemony and the subjugated but eventually vindicated Calamares.

The absence of *Ingermina* in the national canon is neither a mere lack of attention of the literary institution nor a mere accident: There are good reasons to suppose that *Ingermina* is a sort of antinational allegory. As such it was not canonizable within the positive project of state construction. That is to say *Ingermina* is illegible for nineteenth-century Colombia, liberal or conservative. Written in exile by a humanitarian liberal who yearns for a nonexisting motherland, the novel depicts action that took place in an enslaved nation. Although the magnanimous conqueror is the book's great hero, the only *national,* collective identification allowed to the readers are the defeated Calamares forced to cope with life under colonialism. In fact, this remained Nieto's primary identification, at least in the early years when he composed his novelistic work. In his prologue to *Los moriscos* (again focused on a defeated collectivity, this time the Muslim exiles in post-1492 Spain), Nieto wrote: "also expelled from my country by that surplus of force so common during political commotion, it was natural for me to identify with the Moors as I followed my plume" (qtd. McGrady 31). Besieged by political commotions that left an imprint of urgency in his text, Nieto's pages display a remarkable desire to find in the past an emblem analogous to his exile in Jamaica in the 1840s. The reasons for the appearance of a lack of a "truly national vision" in *Ingermina* was perhaps not that Nieto was "more concerned with defining a regional identity for the Coast" (Williams, *Colombian,* 96) but rather because the source for his text was the image of a defeated and enslaved nation that could allegorize his own predicament and that of his political project, already shown to be defeated and not viable in the 1840s. In other words, Nieto's humanitarian liberalism occupied an impossible position in Colombia at that moment. Not only was he exiled in Jamaica, but he did not fit the limits of what was speakable in Colombian political language.

According to the verist, mimetic objection of some critics, Nieto sinned by not depicting the African populations that were just arriving in Colombia at the time when the novel's action is set (1533–37). Still his allegory seems to me a powerful one. The failure of Nieto's ideological project—to recuperate colonization from the point of view of humanitarian liberalism *and at the same time to recover* the dignity of the defeated—is not deprived of a certain moment of truth: the depiction of the clear subjection of a population by another, where the colonized, however, maintained considerable ability to articulate and negotiate independently. This accounts, at least partially, for the fact that all of the novel's truly important elections and cultural legacy *resided in the members of the defeated community that survived.* In this sense, then, the novel is a rather able allegory of the Coast, where the dominated populations have an immense presence in the shaping of popular and erudite cultures. The constitution of a truly national allegory would have required, naturally, that Nieto break with the limits of his humanitarian liberalism and that he radicalize the critique of the conquest. It is not a minor merit that *Ingermina* made visible that aporia, one that haunts even the most progressive forces of nineteenth-century Colombian liberalism. This aporia could only be emblematized in the 1840s as the diasporic story of a Caribbean subject who takes to its limit the liberalism of his time in his Afro-Anglophone exile in Jamaica. It is not far fetched to suggest that now, 160 years later, when the impossibility of a national pact in Colombia continues to produce devastating human consequences, Nieto's tragedy finds its most clear and ominous legibility.

Manuela, or the Andean Novel of Manners as Ethnographic Fable

In warm lands people are far more relaxed than people in cold lands, and thus there are more than a few citizens, among the shoeless ones, who actually understand their rights.

—*E. D. Castro,* Manuela

Eugenio Díaz Castro (1804–65) was born and raised on a farm outside of Soacha and did his studies in Bogotá before returning to agricultural labor, first on the savannah and then at a sugar mill closeby. In *El Mosaico,* Colombia's most influential nineteenth-century literary periodical (1858–72) and vehicle for the emerging narrative, Díaz Castro published the first chapters of *Manuela* and some of the tales of manners that made him famous. Treated in criticism through a number of optical metaphors— "tableaus," "pictures," "brush-strokes," "vivid paintings" are a few of the most recurring—Díaz Castro's image harks back to a legendary description made by José María Vergara y Vergara (mediator of the novel's publication in *El Mosaico*) of Díaz's arrival in his house in 1858, dressed in a *ruana* (a heavy poncho, an attire associated with provincialism) and carrying the manuscript of *Manuela* (Vergara y Vergara 443). Díaz was, for Bogotá's lettered élite, a kind of privileged ethnographic witness of the provincial world. From that appropriation it was one step to uncritical acclaims of Díaz as a "genuinely peasant writer" (Sánchez López 141) and his literary production as "born and inspired in the direct painting of life" (Reyes 193).

In one of the most lucid pieces written on *Manuela,* Colombian historian Germán Colmenares points out that at the early stages of the novel's canonization, elements such as Díaz's garments and his limited formal education played a mythical role. These topoi became part and parcel of the legitimation of his writing as direct testimony, "almost as if it was an ethnographic curiosity" (Colmenares 252). This legend underwrites the eulogy of *costumbrismo* in Colombian criticism, where the trend is usually associated with the consolidation of a national narrative in the mid-nineteenth century. Written by a provincial subject who arrives to the city already mature (but unpublished) at 50 years of age and joins the intellectual field then coalescing in Bogotá, *Manuela* is a novel that treats the uselessness and artificiality of the knowledge brought by a *cachaco* (Bogotá citizen) to a provincial village. It is a particularly hybrid, "transculturating," and foundational novel. Taking place in, and harking back to, the provincial sugar mills, the novel assumes an implied reader and a rhetoric that are essentially Bogotan. More than a "kiss of death" (Williams, *Colombian,* 57),[9] Vergara y Vergara's description of Díaz's *ruana,* hat, and peasant manners was in fact Díaz's ticket of entrance to *costumbrismo* as the first Colombian narrator with enough legitimacy also to speak as a native informant. The novel presents itself as a *machine of translation between these two cultural codes.*

As is usually the case, much criticism has been devoted to the mapping of what is depicted in the novel (a parish in the Bogotá savannahs, the village of Ambalema, the sugar mill in the "warm lands"), the appreciation of the author's faithfulness to it or the richness of the details with which he evokes it. Beyond these maps, rhetorical criticism inquires into the gaze brought by the one who arrives at that reality, the place from which the novel speaks, and the social and cultural discourses that inform it. When analyzed from that perspective *Manuela* displays the signs of Díaz Castro's attempt belatedly to enter the *costumbrista* fraction of the Bogotá intellectual field. Congregated around *El Mosaico,* those intellectuals claimed a lettered heritage that harked back to eighteenth-century chronicler Rodríguez Freyle, and already possessed a solid history in Bogotá. There are good reasons to believe, in fact, that the very concept of "lettered city"—in Angel Rama's sense of a remarkable colonial-state apparatus for the production and reproduction of writing and power—was, at the moment of its elaboration in Rama's work, influenced by the city of Bogotá as its privileged paradigm.[10]

Home to a considerable tradition in political writing, in historical chronicle, and in jurisprudence, among other genres, mid-nineteenth-century Bogotá lacked a narrative canon, and particularly it lacked a novelistic canon. Fiction had not gone beyond the epidermic tableau of manners. From the province there came this strangely-dressed unpublished mature writer, with a novel of hundreds of pages and 31 chapters full of descriptions, alternative plots, and discussions involving dozens of characters. It starts with Demosthenes, a Bogotá citizen, journeying back from the United States to Colombia and settling in a small town. As he continually fails to understand his provincial surroundings, Manuela, as the figure of impossible *love,* comes to impose herself as the very center of the novel, until everything is tragically interrupted with her death, exactly on the morning of her announced wedding, July 20, national independence day in Colombia. Between the urban gentleman's arrival in the village and Manuela's death, one finds a sort of Borgesian encyclopedia of nineteenth-century Bogotá: the Enlightenment, the

Church, moderate and radical liberals at war, constitutions, conflicts, pacts, Scott, Zorrilla, Sue, Voltaire, Montesquieu, the Bible, modern sciences, women's right to vote, the right (limited to heterosexuals) to domestic partnerships rather than marriage, provincial bosses, the colonial heritage of the colonial municipal councils *(cabildos)*, the popular St. John parties against the lettered July 20 celebrations, waltzes versus bambucos,[11] the subjection of the Indian, the life of peasants and landowners, Hispanism, Anglophilia, and a vast gallery of female characters who underwrite discourses that range from pious Catholicism to feminisms and socialisms surprisingly radical for their moment and their surroundings.

The story begins with a common event in nineteenth-century Hispanic literature from both sides of the Atlantic, the arrival of a modern subject in the province. Demosthenes is a Bogotá liberal of the *gólgota* (lettered liberal) fraction who since his stay in the United States has been fascinated with railways, democracy, and new Anglo American science. Upon return in Colombia we are taken to his arrival in a rural parish of the province of Cundinamarca. Demosthenes' name is "an allegory of the view liberals had of the law (*demos*: people; *sthenos*: force)" (Rojas 259). It needs to be added, of course, that Díaz's use is ironic, in the sense that the people's force is precisely what Demosthenes most ignores. The visitor is hosted by pension owner Doña Patrocinio and her daughter Manuela, a heroine with whom Demosthenes shares the virtue and honesty of *costumbrista* heroes, and from whom he is separated by his clumsy misreading of social dynamic in the parish. In the antagonistic field we find the liberal don Tadeo (of the *draconiana*, rough down-and-dirty fraction), who is the very image of clientelism, as a man who has accumulated power in the province by controlling the population through lies, blackmail, and economic extortion.

Witnessing a population divided between *tadeístas* and *manuelistas* (as the young woman begins to exert political leadership and becomes an emblem of the virtuous alliance between conservatives and moderate liberals), Demosthenes finds his privileged dialogue partners to be Manuela and the priest, with whom he disagrees on everything but in whose interlocution he finds, as a good liberal, a point of support precisely in disagreement. The conversations with them repeatedly give Demosthenes proof of how distant his constitutionalist and modernizing beliefs really are from the concrete social reality of the province. Celia, Demosthenes' fiancée in Bogotá remains throughout the novel a spectral figure, one that only reappears at the end. Manuela has been promised to Dámaso, a peasant whom she is supposed to marry. Throughout the novel, however, the meetings of Demosthenes and Manuela are haunted by bottled eroticism constantly announced and postponed. At one point Demosthenes speaks of the "ecstasy of contemplating your seductive forms, and dissolve in the fire of your gaze" (286). The voyeuristic invitation made by the text is for us to expect something to happen between them, the unadapted liberal (promised to a capital city girl), and the vivacious provincial woman (promised to a peasant). We expect it, but it never happens. Each one remains within an intraclass and intraregion couple, as an abyss impossible to overcome exists between the two cultures.

With his peroration caricaturesquely abstract and distant from reality, Demosthenes repeatedly misunderstands his surroundings. Upon his arrival and acquaintance with Rosa—a genuine provincial woman and worker at the pension where he arrives—Demosthenes indulges himself in a nostalgic speech on the wonders of American hotel services, while receiving his first lesson in Colombian regionalism. To make it worse, he finds that the currency he brings, the *condores* ("gold coins in the value of two and half pesos," as he explains to Rosa) do not entitle him to expecting water or food ready as he wishes, and that "in these lands one carries food with oneself" (11). In chapter 1 Rosa prepares dinner for him, introduces him to the wise manners of the people, and speaks to him about the villain don Tadeo. The house belonging to Manuela and her mother, where he takes definitive shelter, is described by Demosthenes in chapter 2 as a "busy house" that "stands out because of its variety store" *(establecimiento de venta)*, a vague class marker that does not align Manuela automatically either with landowners or with the poor, whose speech and garments the novel caricatures. Rosa will reappear singing and dancing the bambuco in chapter 23, when Demosthenes again reacts scandalized to a popular, and primarily Afro-Colombian, habit, that of "dancing a little angel," that is, gathering festively around a dead infant (called *angelito* as s/he is presumed to have died without sin). In chapters 25 and 27, which describe Rosa's death after the St. John parties, Demosthenes remembers the first gesture of hospitality that he had received and had not known how to appreciate. He eventually would raise a monument in honor of Rosa in the cemetery.

These retrospective insights into the arrogance of his cosmopolitanism do not make of Demosthenes, however, a Bildungsroman-type character, as his learning is never synthesized. In chapter 4 he meets Manuela and learns that, unlike a city man, a provincial woman is not scandalized at the idea of going to the river to bathe accompanied by a man.[12] In chapter 7 he learns that his knowledge of botany and zoology does not serve him much in an expedition to the mountain. In chapter 9, which depicts a dance in the village, Demosthenes takes a while, but finally seems to learn that *bambuco* music has a cultural solvency in the parish that is unmatched by waltz or polka, and that it is ultimately ridiculous to impose the latter on others in the name of progress. So on ad infinitum, he learns isolated facts but repeats the same error in the following chapter, all the way to the disastrous ending, when the villain comes back to burn down the church where the heroine was to marry. The final disaster is a product of Demosthenes' naive belief in the separability between juridical system and political power, as he foolishly thought that justice would take care of don Tadeo in spite of his dominant economic position. The critics who have pointed out a repetitive structure in the novel are correct, but one needs to add that it is not a contingent error or a failure attributable to hasty execution or faulty technique. The roots of the sterile repetition resided, for moderate Díaz's enlightened conservatism, in liberalism's incapacity to understand the guts of the country that it attempted to modernize. The agonizing design of repetition is the very theme of the novel, and it parallels the theme of the impossibility of crossing class and regional lines that separate Demosthenes from Manuela.

Manuela is a kind of monstrous novel in the etymological sense of the term; that is, it implodes limits, borders, and typologies proper to a genre. It incorporates into that genre a vast extension of hitherto excluded matter. Much like José Mármol's *Amalia,* one of Argentina's foundational texts, *Manuela* is not structured according to the progressive, dialectical, Bildungsroman-esque temporality of the modern novel. It follows, rather, an episodic, segmented, and discontinous temporality, one that is periodically marked by extradiegetic interruptions such as political pamphlets, philosophical or scientific digression, description of manners, letters, diaries. This is a kind of excessive, chaotic temporality common in nineteenth-century Latin American novels *(Amalia, Enriquillo, El fistol del diablo)* and usually resolved by the deus ex machina of death.

Much like Rosa in chapters 1, 7, and 25, the appearance of other secondary characters is segmented in two or three parts: Don Blas, conservative owner of the Retiro sugar mill and his daughter Clotilde (with whom at first Demosthenes foolishly believes himself to be in love, one of many snafus of his in matters of the heart); *taita* Dimas, the old black man whose guiltless concubinage with Melchora is a reason for Demosthenes to be in shock again; and the liberal don Cosme, the owner of our Lady of Solitude sugar mill. Along with Don Cosme we are introduced to his daughter Juanita, whose dialogues with Clotilde give us the first feminist sparks in the Colombian novel: "there is a school that thinks that we women should do our own July 20 [Independence Day,

I.A.] and present ourselves to the world in red hats and with full enjoyment of our political rights" (50).

The thread running through the story is clear: Little by little Demosthenes becomes aware of the criminal nature of the local political bossing, the peak of which is represented by the incarceration of Manuela and Dámaso under false accusations. Their innocence is eventually proven by documentation intercepted in the mail that criminalizes don Tadeo, the regional caudillo. The interception of that mail takes places in chapter 19, "Mailmen," which also brings us the longest stylization of black popular speech in the novel. Following the unmasking reported by mailmen, don Tadeo is arrested. He later flees prison, helped by mercenaries who carried signs of support for him (and caricaturesque signs of hatred for land-owning classes). Demosthenes, always naive, continues to act in ignorance of the criminalized local bossing, and in the belief that the juridical system will prevail over crime. The news about don Tadeo's correspondence with his accomplices reaches Demosthenes and confirms that one of don Tadeo's goals was to induce jealousy in Manuela's fiancée Dámaso, given Manuela's proximity to the Bogotan intellectual. The threat that jealousy will become a political weapon leads Demosthenes to return to Bogotá to see the pale Celia, while Manuela prepares to marry Dámaso. The dialogue between Manuela and Demosthenes when he receives the invitation to the wedding is a categorical demonstration that the key love story in the text is the unrealized one that bounds the two of them:

> —Dámaso came over right after you'd left. Didn't you see him in the street?
>
> —No, Demósthenes answered agitated. What did he come for?
>
> —Don't be so . . . What would he come for?—answered Manuela's eyes, but her lips said: he came to speak with my mom and myself about . . . about the wedding, replied Manuela, blushing.
>
> —What about it?
>
> —He came so we'd set a date.
>
> —And you did?
>
> —Yes, July 20.
>
> —Anniversary of Independence, said Demosthenes jokingly.
>
> —Day of my patron saint Librada.

> —I take joy in that, for I believe that you'll find happiness, and your happiness is as dear to me as if it were mine.
>
> —Thank you, don Demosthenes. Please prepare your feet for the dance.
>
> —Oh, Manuela, in no other party would I dance with more pleasure . . . there is a mixture of candor and malice in you that maintains in perpetual ecstasy all of your . . . friends. (398–9)

The wedding is set for the last chapter, in a ceremony that was to include also the religious legalization of Melchora and *taita* Dimas's long concubinate. With the priest's and Demosthenes' blessings (the latter seeing his fiancée restored to her pale position), the three couples were to celebrate, if not a genuinely multiclass, national allegory (as a union between Manuela and Demosthenes could have represented), then at least the consolidation of a pact of *regional hegemony,* binding moderate liberals and conservatives against the political bossing associated by Díaz with the *draconiano* liberalism embodied by criminal boss don Tadeo.

In fact, the social pact that the novel has in mind in its dreams is clear; the novel is set up in such as way that *the only possible happy ending was a restoration of the pact responsible for the 1854 rise to arms* by both liberals and conservatives against Gal. Melo. This alliance between the two major Colombian political forces is emblematized in the novel in the union of liberals such as Cosme and Demosthenes with conservatives such as Manuela and the priest. The novel sees this coalition as a requisite for the establishment of the stable order to which it aspires. The pact presupposes, of course, the silencing and isolation of another political fraction, the *draconiano* liberals, opposed to the lettered fraction of liberalism, *gólgotas.* Díaz portrays the cosmopolitan, lettered liberals as out of touch with the country, but ultimately noble, honest, and decent. The draconians, on the contrary, are portrayed as barbarism itself. The pact imagined by the author, like all pacts, assumes particular inclusions and exclusions: in the particular case of *Manuela,* the model for Díaz Castro was the image of a more inclusive national pact that could split the liberal camp.

But the pact, and this is the fundamental piece of the puzzle, *never takes place.* The day of Manuela and Dámaso's wedding is made to coincide with the national independence of Colombia, July 20. That day was also to be Dimas and Melchora's religious ceremony to legalize and celebrate their lifelong concubinate. Prior to the collective ceremony, "a man very similar to don Tadeo" was seen "walking toward the square" (405). A few moments later Don Blas's house and the church are set ablaze, in a fire that ends up killing Manuela. The priest manages to declare Dámaso and Manuela husband and wife, before she expires in his arms (thereby making the *symbolic* pact just sealed with Dámaso crumb into an *allegory*, a temporal image of the failure of the symbol-to-be).

The novel suggests that the preparation of the wedding was damaged by Demosthenes' naive belief in the juridical system. The villain Tadeo continues to operate after his escape and commits the murder that prevents the symbolic July 20 wedding. The alliance dreamt by the novel (between conservatives of all stripes and *lettered, nonradical* liberals) failed to translate its moral and cultural superiority into a stable and brotherly political order. To the critique of liberalism, that Díaz portrays as half criminal (don Tadeo, the draconians) and half naive (Demosthenes, the *gólgotas*), *Manuela* adds an implicit critique of the conservatism with which its author was aligned: Although reasonable, decent, and fair, the novel's conservative characters are unable to translate their cultural and moral hegemony into the legal and political realms, that is to say they are unable to go from the ideal into the actual. Though for different reasons, everyone fails.

Manuela portrays, then, the powerlessness of the liberal vs. conservative antagonism to translate into partisan state politics the real, constitutive social antagonisms in nineteenth-century Colombia: "there is a thickness in manners that political preaching cannot penetrate" (Colmenares 260).[13] This is the novel's important political insight: Whereas at the level of ideology there is a plurality of perspectives represented, at the level of social practice there is an abyss between *all these positions* and the real processes of oppression partially masked by them. These processes are understood quite well by the poor, as indicated in the dialogue where *taita* Dimas shows Demosthenes how empty his premises about equality of rights really are in provincial 1850s Colombia (219). Only on the surface is *Manuela*'s central antagonism the one opposing liberals and conservative, enlightened Bogotans and backward provincial subjects, or future versus past. The essential, decisive antagonism is the rift between the *entire* political structure (both the council controlled by villain Tadeo and the naive constitutionalist beliefs of Demosthenes) and social reality itself, the latter remaining untranslatable by the former, immune to the operations of transculturation attempted by partisan politics. It is politics as such that fails.

The novel depicts a certain failure of the political structure to translate the movement of the real social reality. Díaz Castro composes an allegory of the powerlessness proper to the central political antagonism in Colombia, between liberals and conservatives, that does not seem to account for the real pluralism of social reality. Much like Eugenío Díaz Castro's

Manuela, Jorge Isaacs's *María* is also an allegory concocted around the image of a failed love, interrupted by death. As opposed to *Manuela,* however, *María* does not refer the failure of transculturation to a split between the political cultural field and the social reality that it attempts to represent, but rather to far more ethereal and mysterious reasons, as we will see.

María as Regional and National Novel, or the Genus as the Name of the Species

The poet, novelist, playwright, soldier, statesman, and ethnographer Jorge Isaacs was born in Cali in a family of trading farmers. His father was a Jewish Briton from Jamaica, and his mother was a *criolla* (a Hispanic American of European descent) and daughter to a Catalan official. Isaacs was raised on the farm before he was sent to study in Bogotá at age 11. Halfway through the 1850s, back in the Cauca Valley, and having returned to a family who faced economic decadence, Isaacs volunteered as a soldier in conservative forces against Melo (1854) and Mosquera (1860–1). Already close to sheer ruin when *El Mosaico* started publishing Eugenio Díaz Castro's *Manuela* in installments, Jorge Isaacs came back to Bogotá and presented a sample of his poetry in a literary reading held at the house of no one less than José María Samper, the great liberal thinker of nineteenth-century Colombia, author of an *Ensayo sobre las revoluciones políticas y condición social de las repúblicas colombianas.*[14] By all accounts Isaacs made a powerful impression that night. When he read those poems he was deadly harassed by poverty and had become "a doubtful conservative"(Licona 158). *María,* the most successful Colombian novel ever, was written between that melancholy literary meeting and the election of Isaacs to the Chamber in 1866, precisely during the period that witnessed his transition to liberalism, a political position that he would embrace for good during the following decade.

That was the beginning of a 25-year period in which Isaacs struggled with meager means and occasionally against extreme poverty. In that long cycle he was Colombia's council in Chile (1871–2), a liberal soldier in the Battle of the Chancos (1876), municipal officer for education, secretary of state in the Cauca Valley government (1877–8), and revolutionary leader of the sovereign state of Antioquia, quickly defeated by federalist troops after 40 days (1880). This was his last state adventure before being "repatriated" to the Cauca Valley, expelled from the Chamber, and then hired by the Nuñez liberal government as the secretary for the scientific committee in charge of studying the indigenous languages of the Santa Marta area. The committee failed but Isaacs concluded his work and presented his *Study on the Indigenous Tribes of the Magdalena State, former province of Santa Marta,* a text with anthropological premises, discreet Darwin quotes, and translation exercises seasoned with spicy sexually charged sentences that horrified the conservative thinker Miguel Antonio Caro. It was Caro, the country's great philological authority, who imposed upon Isaacs's study an angry condemnation, not deprived of the anti-Semitism of which Isaacs seems to have been spared during his moments of economic prosperity.[15]

In addition to *María* and the *Estudio,* Isaacs left a considerable body of poetry, the historiographic essay *La revolución radical en Antioquia,* and a drama in four acts, *Paulina Lamberti.* In his youth he started two novels that promised to be rather more complex than *María.* They were to offer a panorama of the recent history of his Cauca, told through a liberal prism that Isaacs was beginning to handle quite skeptically toward the end of his life. Of each of these novels, *Fania* and *Alma negra (Camilo),* only a few pages remain. From the young man who published *María* at 30 to the 50-something who dies having witnessed and participated in the failure of the liberal project, there is an abyss of maturation and radicalization that makes us suppose that these are Colombia's most important nonexistent novels. Jorge Isaacs, retired to Ibagué and isolated by his victorious enemies, died in 1895.

The Cauca Valley, from independence until the conflict of 1876–77, had a social structure far more rigid and hierarchical than that on the coast. Within the overall nineteenth-century Colombian picture of "unequal and disconnected regions," the Greater Cauca was "extremely diverse in its racial base, its traditions and idiosyncrasies, its ecosystems and productive bases. In the south, the agricultural *altiplanos* of Pasto, Túquerres, and Ipiales presented an ethnic, social, and cultural picture where the indigenous influence was strong, unlike the zones of clear dichotomy between white landowners and black or mulatto populations" (Palacios, *Entre,* 19–20). *María* depicts a world marked by this dichotomy, at the same time as it helps consolidate it culturally.

In his flavorful book on Isaacs, Colombian writer Germán Arciniegas offers us a definitive allegory of the continental power of the story. In a small town in the pampas of Argentina, thousands of miles away from Isaacs's hometown, Arciniegas asks "the first person I caught sight of" why the store at the main square was named "el Cauca," and hears an answer full of surprise and indignation: "but don't you know that is the land of María?" (94). Arciniegas, profound connoisseur of his native

Colombia and of Isaacs's work, resigns himself to watching his interlocutor walk away, probably pitying his cultural illiteracy. Widely read in editions produced domestically in Mexico (already in 1868), Argentina (1879), and exported continent-wide from those countries, from Bogotá, or even from Spain (beginning in 1883), *María* is, in the ampleness of its reception, the most Spanish American of all novels, an almost instantaneous classic with early representations in the school system, in painting, and in cinema.

"What is a classic?" Julio Ramos once asked. A classic is a text whose "conditions of production have become effaced in the process of its canonization and the passage of time" (*Divergent* 252). The classic text thus becomes an "immediate cypher" in which discordant zones of culture "recognize its identity." Ramos's inquiry starts from Martí's "Nuestra América," but it is just as applicable to *María,* not only due to its continental canonization but also because much like the Martí essay, *María* begins to be confused with the reality that it presumably describes. Therefore, to an ample sector of readers, "sentimental, colorful, romantic, harmonious" are not simply rhetorical figures found in Isaacs's work, but rather ontological attributes of the Cauca itself. Most interpretations that attempt to trace *María* back to its historical, cultural soil struggle against the same paradox: They refer to a history and a culture that have been considerably shaped by the novel's fabulation itself. This is, then, a classic: a text that, facing the critic's attempt to circumscribe its conditions of possibility, reflects back at him/her a false base, a product of its own game of mirrors. The critic realizes that what looked like a step toward the outside was in fact a doubling of the text itself. The critic understands that no reading will be forever exempt of the peril of infinite regression.

Contrary to Latin American nineteenth-century novels that compose complex arguments around the figure of a woman (Díaz Castro's *Manuela,* José Mármol's *Amalia,* José de Alencar's *Lucíola* and *Senhora*), *María* is, plotwise, minimalist. It reduces all to one story line, the unrealized love of María and Efraín. There are no parallel plotlines in the strict sense.[16] The secondary characters are no more than part of the landscape for this love. It is a novel that is easier to summarize than most in the Latin American canon: Salomón early loses his wife Sarah, and hands their daughter Ester over to a relative, who renames and baptizes her María. María is raised with her cousin Efraín, who narrates the story in his old days. The two cousins fall in love, live a brief pseudo-idyll, and face separation due to Efraín's trip to England, much-needed as part of elite self-fashioning in the nineteenth century. Efraín's trip is, of course, understood as temporary and preparatory of the wedding. Efraín returns sooner than expected after receiving news of María's recurring illness, but not soon enough to see her alive.

The critics who devoted time to listing all the things that Isaacs copied from European Romanticism have not pointed out this curious originality of his: None among the great European romantic novels represent the impossibility of love in this odd manner that we see in *María,* that of an *interdict without a prohibition.* Efraín and María's love does not face any of the obstacles typical of romantic taboos (family prohibition, class difference, enmity between social groups, etc.). It is, rather, a love haunted by *untimeliness.* There is no secret surrounding it: Love is announced before Efraín's first study travel to Bogotá. It begins with the novel itself. After Efraín's return it is consolidated and watered by their group reading of Chateaubriand's *Atala.* The love is revealed to the family when Efraín's trip to England is inevitable. With the blessings of his natural parents (under whom María was also raised) he accedes to being a good boy and waiting to marry María upon his return.

The first manifestation of María's epilepsy occurs before Efraín's departure, and the reader gets a chance to evaluate Efraín's moderation: He must learn to contain his love and his reaction within medical restrictions so as not to overwhelm María. He may literally kill her. This task of Efraín's temporalizes love as *calculation.* He must restrict his sincerity with his lover to preserve her for tomorrow. In this sense Efraín is the least romantic of characters. María's definitive crisis takes place in the middle of Efraín's travels, forcing him to come back. His arrival begins to be lived by the reader with anticipation and urgency, and allows the narrator to play with suspense, at the same time as it describes the vast territory traversed by Efraín in his return. The death of María occurs when everything is ready for the wedding. Decades later the now old Efraín relates the entire story up to her death, when he, "torn with emotion . . . set out at a gallop over the lonely plain, whose vast horizon the night was darkening" (329/302).

Many years separate María's death and the narrator's mature evocation. About those years there is silence; they don't matter. Everything that is told about Efraín can be reduced to the circle built around his lover María. In this sense *María* is a perfect realization of the Romantic gesture: The history of the self is entirely reducible to the history of the object of love. *María,* understood as Efraín's autobiographical narrative, is nothing but his last, useless, senseless gesture of love, that is, the production of the story of his failed love. Transported to Latin America, to the war-ridden nineteenth-century Colombia, and to the tropical experience of the Jewish diaspora, the European romantic subject *radicalized* the split constitutive of all autobiography, between the speaking self and the spoken self.

The five basic moments of falling in love (Cauca), separating (Bogotá), consolidating love (Cauca), separating (England), and reencountering a corpse (Cauca), suggest a well-known pattern, except that the separations are not caused by taboos or external prohibitions, but by a consensual calculation necessary for the realization of love itself. "There is no visible social or political causality, no racial hatred, no regional conflict" (Sommer 174). The obstacle to love is immanent to love itself, so that what blocks it is its own untimeliness. As members of the same social group, Efraín and María do not face any class taboo. More than Nieto's *Ingermina,* Díaz's *Manuela,* or Carrasquilla's *Frutos de mi tierra,* Isaacs's *María* is an intraclass novel, to which peasants, servants, and even middle classes do not accede other than as part of the landscape. Neither do we see political enmity, as the reduction of social otherness to mere local color puts in parenthesis the Colombian political struggle between liberals and conservatives. That rift remains blocked away from the text. The only interdiction that could emerge between these cousins (who strangely look like siblings) would be that of *incest,* a ghost that haunts the text from afar and gets partially exorcised when the father—the key figure in the rigid patriarchal system that governs the family—promises a *future* blessing to the engagement of Efraín and María: "Your position will be a very good one four years from now, and then María will become your wife" (210/186). In England, for a year Efraín had "twice a month letters from María" (288). The last ones arrived, according to the old narrator, "filled with a melancholy so profound that the earlier ones seemed as if written in our days of undisturbed happiness" (288/258). From the last letter Efraín learned that the illness has been consuming María for a year. His father ordered his return, and apologized for "not having done so before" (290/261). The father thus implicitly assumed the blame for his son's untimely arrival, which precluded the encounter that might have saved María's life (according to novel's shaky scientific premises). The father figure closes the novel by apologizing for having delayed too much, for having fallen prey to untimeliness.

The inaugural moment in the Cauca Valley novel was quite unlike the coast's historical novel of conquest and colonization and also rather different from Bogotá's conjuctural and directly political narrative of manners. *María* is a part of another lineage, namely sentimental, Rousseau-Chateubriandian Romanticism, from which Isaacs maintains the basic rhetorical devices but not the social egalitarianism, a position that he would only embrace later. As opposed to *costumbrismo,* sentimental Romanticism allows fiction to take a certain distance from the immediate turbulence of state and political wars. Here is the difference between *Manuela* and *María,* these two tales of heroines of love and death. The accomplished sublimation of politics in *María* is part of the explanation for its overwhelming canonization. To use the Marxian phrase, *María transcends* more effectively its conditions of production.[17] In contrast with *Manuela, María* appears independent from the political clashes of nineteenth-century Colombia—it reads as "autonomous" fiction. This is not to say, of course, that it is an apolitical novel, but that unlike the exhaustive, conjunctural presence of state, political discourses in *Manuela, María* inscribes politics as *negativity,* that is, it moves politics to the terrain of the unsaid.

Such shifting of politics into unnamed zones of the text makes of *María* one of the crucial moments in the process *of relative autonomization of fiction in Latin America*—even though, of course, Isaacs is far from the moment of professionalization of the writer upon which the question of autonomization is all too often collapsed. Until *María,* Colombian fiction had narrated (either in historical or in *costumbrista* novels) events associated with the colonial or the republican state apparatus. An incipient process of autonomization, made possible by the sentimental novel, allows Isaacs to narrate an intimate domesticity not contaminated by state conflict. It therefore allows also for the elaboration of a story that carries out a more subterranean and effective politico-ideological operation.

María's critical fortune is vast, but a few lines of inquiry have been dominant:

1. A biographical reading that maps the similarity of the novel with Isaacs's days on his father's farm. This is a reading trapped in the circular tautology of all biographism, that of explaining texts by remitting them to lives to which one only accedes, quite often by definition, through those same texts. The study of Isaacs's life does tells us much, however, about the process of canonization of María: Unlike Nieto and Díaz, Isaacs is an author who travels throughout the entire country, from the coast to Bogotá, from Antioquia to the jungle, and accumulates considerable cultural capital, which helps catapult María to the status of national novel.
2. In dialogue and complicity with the biographical reading there is a historical interpretation, which, at its most verist and mimetic, takes the form of eulogies to the Cauca, the author's faithfulness to the landscape, its characters or their social history. Although the eulogies have contributed little to scholarly knowledge about the workings of the text, the historical reading has been valuable whenever it understood that texts do not "reflect" a previously stable reality but rather are constitutive of the very history that they presumably reflect.
3. A comparatist reading that brings María back to dialogue with its "sources and influences" and measures the distance from its models, especially Chateaubriand's *Atala.* This is a tradition that has shed light on the novel,

but has also partaken in the ethnocentric perception of María as an imperfect copy, and in the obliteration of its many unique traits.

4. A reading that one might call stylistic-historicist, combined or not with the comparatist reading in order to identify a list of characteristics of Romanticism (or Realism, or costumbrismo). At its most sophisticated this reading takes the form of an analysis of tropes, rhetorical devices, and the like.
5. An important sociohistorical reading that sees in the novel the response of the slave-holding, land-owning class to the severe crisis that Isaacs had experienced. An important insight in this tradition is the notion that in María the social sector whose base is "large property and slave labor generates frustrated romance, while the world of small rural properties generates successful romances." (Mejía xi)

As with all classic texts, it is a good idea to read *María* searching for what was forgotten early. In the novel's second Colombian edition, one of the country's literary patriarchs, Vergara y Vergara (also the signatory of the folkloric description of Díaz Castro) wrote a prologue in which a short recount of the story was given: "young Efraín comes back from Bogotá to the father's house and falls in love with María, an orphan raised by her uncle and aunt, Efraín's parents" (Vergara y Vergara qtd. Arciniegas 52). The reference suggests that María enters the novel as an orphan. By doing so it erases the father Solomon (still alive as action happens, although outside the plot) and the mother Sarah (whose death is reported early in the novel). Vergara y Vergara's portrayal of María as "an orphan" inaugurates a long tradition of denial of the Jewish heritage in the text. His prologue is contemporary to the portrait of María done by Alejandro Dorronsoro, to which Isaacs explicitly objected by pointing out that it was missing a more distinctively Jewish nose (later corrected to Isaacs's liking in a second version). *The erasure of Judaism is a constitutive moment in the text's history.* "Erasure" is here understood in the Derridian sense of an operation that at the same time hides and shows that it is hiding. Judaism has inhabited the novel spectrally, as a thematic that is both explicit and obvious. It is, for example, a heritage claimed in chapter 7, where Efraín makes allusions both to "our race" and "her [María's] race." Judaism is also systematically negated, with traditional recourse to the argument that Isaacs's father was a convert and that so were Isaacs's characters.

Negation as a concept, problem, and operation, both in the sense given to the word by the Jew who invented psychoanalysis as well as in the sense preferred by the Jew who invented communism, is not alien to the plot of *María,* and can in fact be a key to thinking the very inscription of Judaism in it. Radically different, the Freudian and the Marxian concepts of negation share the same insistence: What is negated is always and necessarily making possible negation itself. As you negate, a fundamental *turned-around* form of affirmation emerges. If one of Freud's most consistent axioms is that the unconscious knows no negation (what is negated is being fundamentally affirmed at another level), for Marx no true dialectics is possible unless the negative potential of any given antithesis is fully incorporated, fully preserved in the movement of the synthesis. Both in Freud and in Marx one sees an incipient theory of the ghost as a component of the concept of negation. The process of negation, both in psychoanalysis and in Marxism, lets off spectres, remainders that are not fully incorporated, and that invariably come back to haunt the act of negation itself.

Hence the strange effect that all the critics who have devoted time to negating the "Hebrew" or "Jewish" "influence" in *María* seem to become, involuntarily, characters of what the novel describes. They all seem to be transported to the scene depicted in the text. In being engulfed by the text's elastic throat, they thereby lose the possibility of reading it critically, for negation and masking are the text's very themes.[18] María had been born *Esther,* daughter of *Sarah.* The latter is, in the Bible, the legendary sterile woman who is visited by God and conceives the son of Abraham, Isaac, before dying at 127 years of age. The reference is symbolic and ironic: In addition to naming Maria's mother after the biblical mother from whom he inherits *his own name,* Isaacs makes her conceive and die young. The name *Sarah* immediately refers us to the thematic of preservation and reproduction of the race, rewritten by the moderate Isaacs as a need for subtle but firm insertion in the Christian tropical society. Neither is it accidental, of course, that Isaacs names María's widowed father Solomón, and makes him the character in charge of the "sensible" decision of handing Ester over to his Christian cousins for baptism as "María." In tropical postcolonial societies, there is good reason to believe that it is Salomonic to rebaptize Esthers as Marías.

The name abandoned by María at baptism confers on Isaacs's allegory its definitive meaning. Esther, one of the most fascinating biblical characters, is the Jewish woman with whom the Persian king Xerxes falls in love. Because of her closeness to the king, she is able to unveil a plotting by Haman to kill Jews. She successfully prevents the massacre and guarantees the survival of her people. On the day when the killing was to take place she unmasks Haman's plot. Only then does she also reveal her Jewish identity to her husband Xerxes. Esther is yet another figure of a mediator, a go-between, operating close to the enemy, violating precepts of her own tradition (such as that against marrying non-Jews), but maintaining her people's survival as a fundamental motor of her actions. Esther is for Isaacs an *emblem of conciliatory insertion as alternative to isolation.* In the subtle and hesitant Christianization of Judaism that operates in Isaacs's text, Esther is the anticipation of Mary, the Christian name par excellence. María comes to represent Esther's *Aufhebung* (sublation), in the radically contradictory Hegelian sense of being maintained and cancelled at once. In Isaacs's conciliatory strategy it was necessary that Esther be transcended so that "María" could emerge. On the other hand, naturally, María will always carry within herself a certain "Esther" who remains emblematic of the negation of identity haunting all converts.

Efraín's name is not accidental either. He is a biblical character, son to Joseph and Asenath, and he eventually leads the largest of the Israeli tribes originating in the family (Genesis 48:13–20).[19] There is no doubt that Isaacs, assiduous reader of the Bible, produces calculated effects with characters' names, symbolically referring María and Efraín's love to the question of the foundation and reproduction of a people. Judaism in the novel is systematically referred to as something that *remains,* a heritage that resists over and beyond the social and cultural transformation undergone by characters. María's eyes had "the brilliance and beauty belonging to those of the women of her race" (56/5), and her father "was a man who believed in certain prognostics and auguries, proper to his race" (translation modified, as Rollo Ogden *omits* the reference to race, 127/91). María's "light and noble walk revealed the un-subdued pride of our race, and the fascinating modesty of a pure and maiden soul [*seductivo recato de la virgin cristiana*]" (59/9). Efraín's oscillation between "su raza" y "nuestra raza" is noteworthy insofar as it establishes Jewish identity as alternately interior and exterior to the speaking subject. The dialectical tension between permanence and cancellation is inscribed in the pronouns themselves.

A reference to the Jewish origins of Antioquia is made when the narrator refers to the Antioquian José as someone whose "countenance had an appearance almost biblical—as has that of almost all old men of good habits in the land where he was born" (translation modified, as Rollo Ogden freely translates "bíblico" as "patriarchal," 71/24). The Jewish referent appears in *María* in a process defined by an erasure made to seem an inevitable, almost tragic fate. The image of a residue that no erasure is able to do away with is encrypted, in the novel, as Jewishness itself. The definitive emblem of this takes shape when we learn that the epilepsy that eventually takes María away from Efraín was "the same disease her mother had" (80/34), a kind of hereditary destiny already inscribed in the female character, implicitly and mysteriously transformed in container of the wound that prevents the couple's reunion and the consolidation of the national family.

The position of Judaism in the novel as "a vanishing mediator"—a term with which Fredric Jameson designates the mediator that only realizes its work at the cost of erasing itself as such—suggests that a revision is needed in Doris Sommer's reading of Judaism in the novel as "displacement of the much more threatening and destructive racial contrast between black and white" (195). In the racial and class politics that presided over nineteenth-century Colombia, and particularly the Cauca Valley, the Jew was not a figure that could symbolically stand for alterity as such, much less black alterity in particular. Blackness is indeed inscribed and assigned a place in Isaacs's novel, but it is not coextensive, or mutually allegorizable with Judaism. While Judaism appears as the emblem of what is covered and encrypted, blackness appears in Isaacs within a *cordialist* ideology of social relations. In the Colombian ideology of cordial relations (which shares much with the one organizing a number of Brazilian national narratives as well), the question was never "whether to satisfy the blacks' and the liberal whites' desire for change, or to control those desires and forestall and a racially mixed possibly monstrous progeny" (Sommer 198). These two options are anachronistically posed and are based on a not-quite-exact geography.

The representation of racial mixing as monstrosity never had, in Colombian literature, the prominence that it had in other latitudes. Even though positivist racism had its day too in Colombia, that day is decades posterior to the publication of *María,* and cannot be said to inform Isaacs's novel in any way. *María* handles, rather, the ideology of cordiality and assimilation, not of scandalized racial segregation. Isaacs's is another form of white supremacism and subjection of blackness, to be sure, but it is not one that resorts to the Puritan code of horror in the face of monstrosity. His strategy is the ideology of cross-class and cross-race niceness: "Lorenzo was not a slave. A faithful companion of my father, during the time of his frequent business journeys, he was loved by the whole family" (292/263). The reader can see from the beginning what is the code organizing the representation of blacks: "the slaves were well clad, and as happy as it is possible for slaves to be, and were docile and even affectionate towards their master" (60/10). This is a swamp of cordialist ideology, but one that is not to be confused with the isolationist panic of the Puritan. This led Sommer to the error of seeing Jewishness in the novel as the speakable and representable facet of a deeper antagonism involving blackness and whiteness. This does not, of course, take any merit away from Sommer's reading, for it is impossible to reshape an entire subfield, the way *Foundational Fictions* did, without getting *some things* wrong.

More than metaphor of an unspeakable other, Jewishness is, in Isaacs, the seed of alterity that all identity brings within itself. It is the seed that binds identity to a heritage that was mysteriously asked to explain the present failure. On the other hand, blackness for Isaacs is more than anything a *border* and a *limit*: It is integrated at the cost of losing its otherness, its own independent voice. Blackness, in Isaacs, has its limits as otherness, as it tends to become an internalized replica of sameness. Blackness and Jewishness are not, therefore, mutual metaphors in the text. Submitted to conversion, Jewishness persists and operates silently, as the narrator never tires of reminding us. With blackness the opposite process occurs. It is present throughout the novel, in several dialogues (chapters 5, 19, 21, 22, 49), but always speaking as it were part of the landscape. The Jewish element is silenced and remains speaking subterraneously. The black element is summoned to speak and appear in the novel, not to have a voice of its own but rather to be submerged in cordialist subjection, another form of silencing, to be sure. In this sense it is not Jewishness but blackness that is submitted to the truly violent operation in the text, even as it appears with such a "happy" and "spontaneous" face.[20]

Hierarchies of class, race, and gender do not cease to make their appearances thorough the end of the text. The oligarchy is depicted as sovereign and uncontested, never threatened by any breaks in the pact of cordiality that binds social classes. On the other hand, it pays a price for failing to overcome and reproduce itself. It pays a price for failing truly to consolidate a nation. The oligarchy in Isaacs's novel drags itself in the self-deferring pattern of sterility. It is, then, incapable of dialectics. The subjection of the feminine character, the interdict anteposed in front of her, is related to this representation of the oligarchy as a sterile body. No prohibition bars María from her desire, but the female character is led, by the text's internal logic, to renounce any claim to enjoyment, silenced as she is by the elderly masculine voice that evokes her. Insofar as violence operates in the text primarily in the form of a consensual silencing, the racial and gender violence implicit in the cordial subjection of blacks and the obliteration of the feminine become the very matrices of violence as such. Precisely because there is no violence in it, *María* inserts itself in the Colombian tradition of "narrative of violence": The brutally violent act of the text is the *erasure and denial of real processes of violence that were taking place in society.* In making "cordiality" the basic paradigm presiding over his representation of social relations, Isaacs implicitly soaks his language with paternalistic rhetoric. In a way he inaugurates in literature a particularly Colombian understanding of violence as something not deprived of a certain sweetness, cordiality, informality. He *prevents social relations from acceding, in representation, to the real violence which is their truth.* In addition to the point of view that identifies *Manuela*'s portrayal of political, partisan clashes as the foundation of "the novel of violence" in

Colombia, one would have to add *María* as the moment in which racialized exclusion *becomes language* and establishes itself imperceptibly in the very set of cordial linguistic interchanges. *María* is a novel in which violence speaks through the very silences of the text.

Hence Efraín and María's failed love story is an intraclass allegory of impossible fulfillment. Genuinely national in its plot (as Efraín is raised in the Cauca, studies in Bogotá, interacts with Antioquians, crosses the jungle during his return, etc.), Isaacs's novel is also the narrative of the sterility of one class. Witness the full absence of redemption in the death of its female protagonist: The narrator wants explicitly to link the oligarchic sterility with a female body contaminated by an "illness" *(un mal)* that is hereditary and associated with the mother's name. In taking her out of the circuit of interchange, María's death reaffirms her value as one that does not survive itself, that is, a sheer *use value* that disappears with the death of the body. Alien to all exchange (and therefore to circulation), use value is perishable, sterile by nature. María is, in a way, the name of that which will never accede to exchange value. In allegorizing it as a failed love story, the author paradoxically endowed that sterility—one that for him is particularly associated with regionalization and oligarchic decadence—with a truly national and fecund literary voice, one that created the conditions for a future Colombian canon. This is why in order to map the family/nation allegory in Colombia, reading *María* is not enough. The engagement with *María* must be supplemented with a comparative, synchronic look at the other regions of this highly segmented country. By the time the modernizing region of Antioquia produced its first novel—30 years after the publication of Isaacs's idyll in the Cauca—*economic relations,* not failed love, had taken center stage in fiction.

Frutos de mi tierra, or the Fable of Exchange Value as the Origin of Antioquia's Novel

After a lengthy interchange it was agreed:

1. that trade with the muses should, if continued at all, be done with extreme reserve, for the contraband thing that it was.

—*Tomás Carrasquilla,* Frutos de mi tierra

As the origin of more than half the gold produced in Colombia in the nineteenth century, the province of Antioquia witnessed the early constitution of a regional bourgeoisie that came to accumulate considerable capital. By the 1820s the region was already described by a series of attributes that would later be mythically associated with its inhabitants: hard-working, entrepreneurial, industrious. Around the time of independence the economic force of Antioquia was visible, as the region was the primary source of financing for the patriotic campaign. With birth and marriage rates higher than those of other regions of Colombia, the *paisas* were the protagonists of a remarkable territorial expansion. They came out of the main nuclei of Santa Fe de Antioquia, Medellín, Rionegro, and Marinilla, and travelled in all directions. *Antioqueño* migration was generally well received by the elites of other regions, such as the Cauca, who saw in the newcomers a force of whitening. By the 1840s it was possible to hear a Cauca governor relate to the president that "one Antioquia worker is worth three from here" (qtd. Palacios and Safford 177) According to one of Colombia's leading historians, Marco Palacios, Antioquia's regionalism was unique in that while in other areas regionalism was born out of "evolving situations of force between the center and the region," Antioquia's regionalism was "organic and not conjunctural," that is to say it expressed a real provincial hegemony on the part of its ruling class, and did not necessarily wish to impose itself nationally, or *become* national for that matter (Palacios, *Estado,* 120–2).

The myth of *antioqueño* exceptionalism finds one of its main pillars in the notions of whitening and prosperity, turned into ideologemes and cast as terms of a causal relationship. Like all mythical narratives, they operate out of a base that is real—in this case the indeed dynamic character of Antioquia's economy, already protocapitalist when other regions of Colombia still dragged on the legacy of slavery. The mythical narrative takes this empirical base and refers it to an imaginary soil, associating it with presumed whiteness and with some quite uncertain Jewish roots of the region. This operation is particularly efficacious as Jewishness provides the story of entrepreneurship with a figure with which to identify. Even someone as erudite as José María Samper did not escape the myth; his *Essay on the Political Revolutions and Social Conditions of the Colombian Republics* recounts the arrival of "200 families of this race," leading to a "fusion" that presumably produced the region's uniqueness. As it becomes a cultural given and is taken as natural, the mythical narrative also begins to shape the very reality that at first it simply represented in distorted form. Not only in this long reflection on the Colombian novel, but also in this book's previous essays, I have been particularly drawn to those moments when that distinction collapses, and the operation of ideology becomes indistinguishable from the shaping of the real itself.

The distortion that racially homogenizes Antioquia is interesting, as toward the late eighteenth century the region's ratio of white and black populations was not much different from that of the Cauca (from which it only differed in its substantially lower percentage of indigenous population). In some places such as Santa Fe de Antioquia and Medellín, blacks and mulattoes were actually more numerous than whites. In typical ideological fashion, this did not prevent the region from being culturally associated with whiteness, racial homogeneity, and a host of presumed economic consequences thereof. The myth has an illustrious history that includes literary criticism, where the doctrine of Antioquia's exceptionalism also set roots in versions more or less white supremacist, such as that of Antonio Gómez Restrepo's or Enrique de la Casa's who, invoking the authority of Miguel de Unamuno, proposed the sinister thesis that Antioquia's literature is more Spanish than Colombian due to the "cleanliness of blood" in the region, "with no mixes of Indian or black people" (14). It is somewhat astounding how often, over the course of the twentieth century, literary criticism has accepted to voice the most grotesquely racist premises.

In literary terms, the instructive contrast is the one that opposes Antioquia to the lettered city par excellence, Bogotá. Associated with *production,* Antioquia placed itself early on in a position antagonistic to the capital, perceived as home to an epidermic, bureaucratic, and rhetorical culture. Decades before the *antioqueño* novel was inaugurated by Tomás Carrasquilla in 1896, Juan Dios de Restrepo (1823–1894) pointed out that the bourgeoisie of Antioquia did not have time to waste on things such as poetry or novels (qtd. Palacios and Safford 173). This does not mean that the myth of Antioquia exceptionalism did not find early expression in poetry. It did, but in the poetry written by folks from elsewhere. No one less than the Cauca Valley's own Jorge Isaacs gave abundant poetic representation to Antioquia in one of his most accomplished lyric poems, "The land of Córdoba." Paradoxically, it is the relative economic progress of Antioquia that explains the belated development of its prose fiction 40 years after Bogotá's narrators of manners had established themselves around *El Mosaico* and 50 years after Juan José Nieto has inaugurated the Colombia novel in his Jamaican exile.

Lettered culture, which was a *colonial* heritage both on the Caribbean Coast and in Bogotá, emerged in Antioquia within an already modern horizon. There was no need, in other words, to bring literary language "up to date" with a postcolonial context, because lettered culture as such, for Antioquians, coincided with a fully modern, post-independence political moment. Antioquia's first press was established in Medellín and its first literary magazine, *El Oasis,* was founded in 1868. *Antioquia literaria,* the pioneering anthology edited by Juan José Medina in 1878, was primarily a collection of hybrid pieces of writing, proper to those moments when literature is still enmeshed with political discourse. As late as 1895 the novel, as a literary form, was alien enough to Antioquia's lettered culture that Tomás Carrasquilla set himself to writing one simply to win a bet against his partners in the Literary Casino, who sustained that their region did not possess novelistic material, that one simply could not write a novel set in Antioquia or about Antioquia.

Tomás Carrasquilla (1858–1940) won that bet by writing and publishing *Frutos de mi tierra* in 1896. At that moment he was already an intellectual with a considerable road behind him. Born and raised in Santodomingo, Antioquia, Carrasquilla traveled to Medellín to finish secondary school and join the university. A year after his registration in the law school in 1876, he had to return to his town due to the civil war. For years he devoted himself to tailoring before writing a story, "Simón el mago," that turned out to be his ticket into the "Literary Casino" then being formed in Medellín. The polemic within the Casino, on the existence or not of novelistic material in the state, happened in 1895. Carrasquilla composed *Frutos de mi tierra* in the "Arcadian quiet of my parish" (qtd. Levy 31) and took his first trip to Bogotá to negotiate the novel's eventual publication in 1896. Back in Santodomingo, Carrasquilla then supervised his family's definitive move to a house in Medellín, the province's undisputed cultural and economic center. In Medellín Carrasquilla wrote a good part of his oeuvre, with intervals lived in a mine in Sanandrés, Antioquia (1906–09), and again in Bogotá (1914–19). By his death in 1940, Carrasquilla was recognized as the great name of the Colombian narrative of his time, signatory of short and full-length novels such as *Salve, Regina* (1903), *Entrañas de niño* (1906), *Grandeza* (1910), *Ligia Cruz* (1920), *El zarco* (1925), *La Marquesa de Yolombó* (1926), and *Hace tiempos* (1935), in addition to an extensive array of short stories, tableaus, chronicles, essays, drama, and an autobiography.

Carrasquilla is the foremost figure responsible for the great synthesis that, departing from the epidermic narrative of manners, leads to realism's socially critical fiction of realism. In comparison with the picturesque descriptions of Díaz, Carrasquilla's narrator is a cold and intellectual pair of eyes looking at his surroundings. It is not casual that the realist critical gaze is developed in Antioquia rather in the other regions. Toward the late nineteenth century, under the centralism of the "Regeneration" period that followed Rafael Nuñez's victory over liberals and the passing of the 1886 constitution, *language* was a terrain in which a number of regional battles took place in Colombia. Bogotá, the lettered city, was associated not only with the new political power but also with the purist rhetorical norms of Rufino Cuervo's grammar. To claim the possibility of a realist, non-*costumbrista* transcription of the provinces' popular speech was, quite clearly, also a gesture of political rupture with Bogotá's lettered centralist order.

The distinction between the narrative of manners of *costumbrismo* and realism's critical social fiction is a key to understanding Carrasquilla. While *costumbrismo* establishes an external point of view from which to portray popular speech (thereby systematically producing a comical or ridiculing effect), the realist narrator intends to find a point of view *immanent* to each social group to which s/he gives voice in fiction. The fact that this realism is never "perfect"—that is to say the subject who speaks in fiction, especially if s/he is a subaltern subject, never ceases to exhibit the author's prejudices—does not invalidate this distinction. The "faithful" transcription of speech done by Díaz in *Manuela* is radically different from the "faithful" transcription carried out by Carrasquilla in *Frutos de mi tierra*. While Díaz had objectified his material (by creating tableaus and images of the province), the Antioquian realist attempted a prosopopeya. Let us explain. In Díaz's *costumbrista* fiction characters are typified, flat subjects who have a one-to-one relationship with their group: They *are* that group. In a Carrasquilla novel, on the other hand, characters are always metaphorizing a certain position in a social system of voices, even if their position changes in the course of the narrative. While in *costumbrismo* characters are relatively direct *metonymies* of the social group for which they stand, in critical realism characters tend to be metaphors of moments of their social relations. Hence the fact that the eulogy of a "faithful" transcription of popular speech never tells us much. One must ask what is the rhetoric and the politics organizing the transcription. In the case of Carrasquilla, that operation was particularly embedded in a regional struggle that was simultaneously political and linguistic.

Since his arrival in Bogotá in 1895, Carrasquilla's correspondence and autobiography did not economize on disdainful adjectives to describe a city he saw as profuse in empty intellectuals. Carrasquilla penned devastating descriptions of Jorge Roa, "who knows of Russian literature only something or other by Tolstoi," and the effete *modernista* writer Maximiliano Grillo, who "speaks with foolishness and simple-mindedness," and the patriarch Rafael Pombo, a pinnacle of Colombian Romantic poetry whom Carrasquilla describes as "an archeo-anthropological curiosity" (8). Not even the elegant symbolist José Asunción Silva, whose poetry of preciosity had achieved continental canonical status, escaped Carrasquilla's sarcastic plume, which immortalized him as "José Pretension Silva Pendolfi" (a near homophonous of *pendejo,* Spanish for "idiot"). We still miss an analysis of how the polemic between *modernismo*'s poetry of preciosity and the realism of social criticism allegorized a political and regional conflict in late nineteenth-century Colombia. In any case, by writing

Frutos de mi tierra, Carrasquilla inaugurated an important fact: For the first time in Colombia, ***money began to occupy center stage in fiction.*** Not by chance, the first novel of "entrepreneurial" Antioquia narrated the story of two love relations always already contaminated by exchange and business.

Filomena Alzata is the elder of a family of traders from Medellín. Along with her brother Agustín, she accumulates riches through the exploitation of their sisters Mina and Nieves (the latter naive and submissive, the former resentful and hurt). The novel opens with Agustín addressing Nieves in humiliating and vulgar fashion when she brings him his coffee. Described through an aesthetic of the grotesque, with his bad smells and Napoleon III moustaches (3), the figure of Agustín coalesces for the reader when the novel describes what one might call the family's primitive accumulation. When they lose their mother, Agustín requests a moment with the body and robs the grave, taking the dead woman's clothes and shoes so as to sell them later at the family store (14). Filomena is the female version of the same value system. Also described as a grotesque figure (4), Filomena exerts implacable extortion upon poor citizens who find themselves in growing difficulties after the "the Great War" of 1860. Filomena and Agustín thus conform their initial capital through theft and exploitation. Mina limits herself to obeying and complaining to her sister Nieves about the regimen of semislavery in which they live. Nieves limits herself to obeying and crying over her misery.

Carrasquilla depicts a universe in which economic value has overtaken and subsumed all moral and political values. In describing how after the war the poor "would leave their rations at the store, in exchange for food and drinks" (10), the narrator reminds us that "the Alzates were the cloth for everyone's tears" and that they "never ventured into the depths of political opinion" (10). This piece of information is crucial, as it announces the considerable autonomization of literature vis-à-vis politics represented by Carrasquilla's fiction. As is the case in all specialized discussions of the relation between literature and politics, "autonomization" here does not mean absence of political content in fiction. *Frutos de mi tierra* indeed refers to a quite clear political background, that of the creation of a confederacy of sovereign states, the United States of Colombia (1863–85) and the imposition of a centralist and authoritarian state following the conservative "Regeneration" of 1886 (Restrepo 165). But the key is that politics enters fiction in completely different fashion than what was hitherto known in Colombian fiction.

Unlike *Manuela,* where characters *are* their political affiliation, *Frutos* refers to a political background but has acquired considerable autonomy in relation to it. This is coherent with the rise of a new ruling class represented by the Alzates: They are no longer the old rich lords of "Spanish surnames inherited from the colony," but rather the nouveau riches who "have established money as their only, and powerful, weapon" (Rodríguez 22). Carrasquilla's narrator makes it clear that this is a ruling class far removed from the lettered city. In Agustín's room "there is nothing that smells of books, or any printed matter, or even a written message" (2). It was to be expected that the modernization of Colombian fiction should have come from Antioquia and not from the lettered city of Bogotá, dominated by an effete *modernismo* that would have shivered at the thought of casting money and economic relations as literary themes. This is, then, the implicit opposition between Carrasquilla and José Asunción Silva: While the latter's symbolist poetry reacts to the commodification of art and the professionalization of the writer by constructing an "ideal," "spiritual" sphere presumably alien to exchange, Carrasquilla assumes that he is living in an epoch in which literature is a commodity and handles his materials accordingly.

With the accumulation of capital, Filomena and Agustín expand their business, inaugurate a larger store, and expropriate Mina and Nieves's shares in the family inheritance. Their egos inflate as they pile up richnesses. Agustín, "a mortal enjoying the ectasis of the self" (20) is also despised by his sister and partner in crime Filomena, who thought of herself "far superior to Agustín in matters of business" (20). With their social life reduced to their economic pillage of others, the two siblings devote themselves to complaining about the neighborhood: "they declared war on everyone, and with particular feverishness on the only poor family on the street, that of Mr. Juan Palma" (22). Alternating between aggression toward their neighbors and resentful comments, the Alzates uselessly attempt to have Juan Palma's daughters arrested. After one of Agusto's scandals, Juan Palma receives the visit of his son-in-law Jorge Bengala, a Cauca Valley native of "a powder-type temperament" (46). Bengala whips Agustín publicly and leaves him bleeding on the floor under insults. The episode initiates the long decadence of Agustín, now resigned to a bitter and permanent stay home.

Although Filomena is more astute than (and just as avaricious as) Agustín, her role in the novel is not exhausted in the accumulation of capital. She is not too full of herself "not to miss something: a little husband [*maridito*], so to speak" (20). At 50 years of age she receives the visit of her Bogotá nephew César, who had married away from the family. The key here is the description of Filomena as a character who is petty and materialistic, but not enough for the reader to find her incapable of falling in love. Little by little there develops between the two a rather odd love. César's love is believable but is inevitably enmeshed with business as her aunt represents social climbing for him. For Filomena César represents the exit out of an age-old life of misery next to siblings that she despises.

The reader faces a choice that turns out to be undecidable until the very end. Are César and Filomena truly in love or do they want to take advantage of each other? Are the poor young man and the rich old woman genuinely in love and or falling into a scam? Upon César's arrival Filomena is still doing her petty calculations (will he ask me for the fare money?), but he increases his praise for her dishes and for her presumed elegance, and accompanies it with a surprising use of the informal *tú* pronoun, a gesture particularly meaningful and bold in Colombia: "*tú* here, *tú* there, what an insinuating young man!" (72). She eventually surrenders, naturally. On the part of her brother Agustín, there are no signs of jealousy, only concern over a possible financial trick by César. This ambiguity between exchange value and love value is constitutive of Carrasquilla's writing and subsists throughout the novel. His Realism consists in staging the play among the possibilities that in the affair between Filomena and César: 1. both of them are truly in love; 2. both are trying to take advantage of the other via a romantic experience; 3. César is trying to capitalize on his rich aunt to be lifted out of poverty; 4. Filomena is trying to exploit her young and refined nephew to be lifted out of her mediocre provincial world; 5. the truth is, in fact, a combination of all these hypotheses.

Of the 30 chapters of *Frutos de mi tierra,* 17 focus on the crude and cumulative saga of the Alzates, sprinkled by doubts about this affair. Interspersed with those 17 chapters, the other 13 also narrate a curious blend of exchange value and love value. The "suburban Lovelace" Martín Gala, a rich young man and a Byronian type from the Cauca Valley, seduces and is seduced by Pepa Escandón, a *paisa* (Antioquia native) from the city of Medellín, who is legendary for cruelly toying with local men's feelings. Martín arrives in Medellín because his mother, a *paisa* who moved to the Cauca Valley, "did not want to send him to Bogotá . . . as they were contaminated with the red heresy" (29). Here is your very early mention of Communism, framed through Colombia's notorious regionalism.

Martín accepts the idea of living in Antioquia in exchange for the promise of a future trip to Europe. Little by little he gets into a romance with Pepa Escandón and gains the friendship of José Bermúdez (with whom he reads Sue and Dumas). The romance starts when Pepa and her women friends humiliate him publicly with their regionalist jokes about his place of origin. Martín handles this with the honor code of an old nobleman, one that is rather different from that of nouveaus riches like the Alzates. Therefore, when he is wounded in his pride, he begins to plan a revenge in Romantic fashion: He will try to seduce her. The Antioquian young woman, who sees in the voluptuous expressions of the Caucan young man a provocation (37), ends up rising to the challenge. An obsessive war of simulation and secret gazes begins.

Up to this moment in the story we are on the terrain of sheer exchange value, as the act of enamoring the other is a mere currency with which each character attempts to play. The movement of the story is, of course, that over time that weapon begins to use the very characters who were presumably using it. The Caucan young man "no longer knew what to do in the streets, it was a constant going and coming from one point to the next, walking by the disgraceful woman's house, and almost unconsciously taking a position at the corner" (41). The utmost defeat takes place at a ball to which Martín has the unfortunate idea of wearing a costume while bringing flowers to Pepa. She laughs and scares him away one more time. Martín later has another unfortunate idea, that of returning to the ball without the costume and pretending that nothing has happened. He later sees her getting a laugh out of telling her friends that he had first come as a "clown in a costume" and then as a "clown dressed as a city slick [*cachaco*]." Completely "submerged in death," Martín felt "an attraction of greater pulling the greater was that woman's evil" (66).

When everything indicates that the Byronian young man will be defeated, he receives a card from Pepa Escandón, inviting him to a *tertulia* (a night of reading and music held at someone's house). At the *tertulia* she confesses her love, repents for her cruelty, and flagellates herself for the suffering she caused her sweetheart. The surprising turn retrospectively voids the defeat she had imposed upon him. The reader has no idea that that was a possibility, as the entire narration had been carried out from the point of view of Martín's misery. Much like Martín, Pepa makes the transit from exchange value (enamoring the other as a currency) to love value (handing oneself over to the other in a genuine act of giving).

We go from the realm of transactions and interchanges to the realm of love. The latter is by definition alien to exchange. A love that offered itself as part of a business deal, as an element in a transaction involving other things, would naturally not be love at all, but rather a mere calculation, an interested offer. The story thus takes us from exchange value to love value, but we do not remain stationary there. We are in Carrasquilla's Medellín, not in Isaacs's Cauca Valley idyll. The difference between the two is that for the Antioquian these two realms are invariably mixed, as the passage from one to the next is never definitive. When Pepa declares her love to Martín, he receives it without the slightest trace of pride, as a dead man who is lifted out of death back to life. This at first seems to resolve the argument with a mutual entrance into love and the cancelling of all business deals. This is not so because their relationship leads to marriage—

the business deal par excellence—and therein emerges the figure of the *father* as the needed endorser of the legal and real union that closes the story.

"'It is dirtier than don Pacho Escandón's mouth,' they say in Medellín to highlight the filth of something" (91): This is how Carrasquilla introduces, toward the end of the novel, Pepa's father, who comes in as a emblem of ill humor, lack of manners, and unrefined provincialism. It takes a few chapters for him to accept their marriage, as if he were submitting her daughter's fiancée to a "primitive exploitation" before accepting him in the family. The father's role here is to consummate their union as the ultimate business deal. The wedding is described by Carrasquilla *from a purely external point of view*, that is to say the focus is on the guests, the party, the costumes, the movement of money and consumer goods, and the party's impact upon the city. In other words, what was presumably the moment of culmination of love brings us back to sheer exchange value. The last mention of Martín and Pepa in the novel is their exit out of the church, narrated in mordacious manner, so as to emphasize the shallowness of the ritual. We are then told that "in the El Poblado village, at the foot of the hill . . . their nest awaits them" (138).

Paralleling that plot line, Filomena's infatuation with her Bogotá nephew César becomes obsessive: "she was the one that had inspired such violent love! in César to boot! She was the woman that had him ill" (118). When their scandalous wedding is confirmed, Filomena's doubt is that "between the fear of not being envied and the fear of being ridiculed, she did not know which one to pick: if she spread the news of her wedding, they would make jokes; if she concealed it, how would she be envied?" (119). This makes clear how in Carrasquilla's fiction exchange value and love value coexist in very unique tension. The fact that she takes the wedding as a business deal and as revenge against townsfolk does not contradict the fact that she is deeply in love. To recount that plot line Carrasquilla chooses the indirect free speech, a mode that allows him at the same time to narrate from Filomena's position to speak from the point of view of a present narrator who *knows something else*. This supplement of knowledge remains concealed from all and only is revealed when César establishes himself with Filomena in Bogotá only to flee with all the money soon afterward. César thus leaves the fierce usurer behind as the great loser in the novel.

Pepa and Martín's story leads to a wedding that announces a future "nest." In contrast, the union between Filomena and César ends with the great accumulator of capital being thrown into poverty and soon death itself, as if punished for having truly fallen in love. The end of the novel interrupts the two marriages in rather different points, but they both share the nature of being *concluded* business transactions. The wedding between Pepa and Martín allows for the regional reproduction of capital and human resources. The trick played by César on Filomena brings us to the implacable circulation of theft, the infinite chain of thieves robbing thieves.

Frutos de mi tierra thus founded Antioquia's novel by aligning itself with that sector of Latin American literature that had introduced money and exchange value as mediators in love relationships (a late nineteenth-century trend that reached its modernist heights in the mature novels of Brazilian Machado de Assis). The metaphorical dimension of the word *frutos* in Tomás Carrasquilla's title is another reminder of those relations. Whereas in a previous Romantic register that word alluded to natural elements that enriched the local landscape, in Carrasquilla the semantic web around the word "fruit" invariably suggests a particular economic order in entrepreneurial Antioquia. This displacement—the entrance of exchange value no longer as an exterior element but rather as a structuring principle of the love relationship itself, one that does *not prevent the existence of love*—is in fact continental and includes, in addition to the Colombian Carrasquilla, a host of other writers, such as Blest Gana, author of the Chilean national novel *Martín Rivas,* the Argentine Eugenio Cambaceres, author of the pioneering novel *Sin rumbo,* and the Brazilian Machado de Assis, already in his early novels from the 1870s, such as *Ressurreição* and *A Mão e a Luva,* prior to his revolutionary-vanguardist period when economic matters would acquire even more complex contours.

These are authors who clearly belong to another moment, different from the one marked by earlier figures such as Jorge Isaacs and Eugenio Díaz (Colombia), José Mármol (Argentina), and José de Alencar (Brazil), in whose novels one witnesses a clearcut separation between exchange value and love value. In those Romantic writers "feelings" and "economics" were terms that could be in conflict with one another or not, but each term was always identical to itself and uncontaminated by the other. In Jorge Isaacs's *María,* for example, Efraín and María's love does not have to face any prohibition, as characters belong to the same social class and their union seems "natural": The family's wealth is more a silent background than an explicit theme. Economic stability is a silent condition of possibility for their love to be narrated, even though the ultimate fate of that love is failure. Likewise, in José de Alencar's *Iracema* (1854) the love between the indigenous woman and the Portuguese colonizer Martim can only be conceived because the economic structure that separates them is erased or ignored. This is not to say, of course, that the realm of money and exchange did not operate in those earlier, Romantic texts. It is simply that it operated insofar as it was antagonistic to love or a condition of possibility for it. That is, in Romantic novels money was either an external condition that made love possible or an external condition that made it impossible. It was never, in any case, *internal* to love itself.

Whereas in Romanticism money was never a structuring element of love, in Carrasquilla's novel, the two realms ultimately become enmeshed into each other, as love is always already a symbolic, value-laden, economic exchange. The reader is thus led to ask: Is s/he really in love or is s/he taking advantage of him/her? Are we dealing with exchange value or love value? If the Romantic novel was characterized by the belief in the separability between these two spheres—so that love could be a redemption for the absence of wealth, for example—Machado de Assis, Tomás Carrasquilla, and Blest Gana inaugurate a period where the realms of the economic and the affective are irredeemably enmeshed and inseparable.

Carrasquilla's novel is, then, a quite appropriate regional *allegory* for protocapitalist Antioquia in the late nineteenth century. In speaking of "regional allegory," I do not mean to discuss how truthful the narrative of Antioquian entrepreneurship really was, or to confirm or deny the myth by referring it to the sociological or ontological ground that could prove the text right or wrong. When we unravel the allegorical threads of a narrative we do precisely the opposite of referring it to a facile contextual confirmation. Rather, we map how Carrasquilla's novels, in inaugurating the *fiction of exchange value* in Colombia, both *participated* in the idyllic tale of Antioquian exceptionalism and *interrupted* said mythical narrative. In founding the novel of social criticism in Antioquia, Carrasquilla had both to rely on the narrative of entrepreneurship and ultimately dismantle it in his fiction.

Carrasquilla's *Frutos de mi tierra,* Juan José Nieto's *Ingermina,* Eugenio Díaz Castro's *Manuela,* and Jorge Isaacs's *María* are novels that reproduce and deconstruct the social myths upon which each region sustained itself. This has something to do, of course, with the fact that each is a central, fundamental novel in its respective regional canon. In both articulating the dominant voice that emerged through literature and offering a powerful critique of said voice, these texts remind Latin Americanists that the recent scholarly insistence on the links between literature and power in nineteenth-century Latin American societies may have been slighted overstated. In Nieto's *Ingermina,* egalitarian liberalism is both a motor behind the novel and its first casualty. In both protesting and justifying the Spanish colonization of the Caribbean, *Ingermina* takes liberalism to the highest limits that it could reach in 1840s Colombia. Surrounded by the development of what would be the particularly war-ridden second half of the century in Colombia, *Ingermina* championed ethnic egalitarianism while singing liberalism's swan song. Likewise, Eugenio Díaz-Castro's *Manuela,* an Andean narrative that marks the provincial writer's arrival to the lettered capital of Bogotá, both *reinstates and unsettles* the *costumbrista* myths of representability, easy communication between social classes, and bump-free overcoming of antagonisms that sustained Bogotá's mid-century literary life. A decade later Jorge Isaacs's *María* would bring clear marks of the ideology of Cauca Valley's agrarian aristocracy, while at the same time giving testimony to the remarkable operations of silencing and violence upon which the ruling of that class depended. This culminates with Carrasquilla's *Frutos de mi tierra,* which champions but ultimately mourns the metaphorical system of equivalences between love and money, between getting married and building foundational social coalitions.

In different degrees, these texts reinforce and dismantle the myths that make them possible. They also announce a subsequent history of violence that shapes Colombian society and shapes the way those early literatures of violence are interpreted today. That impact, however, is different upon each author and each particular region. For Carrasquilla, the long twentieth century inaugurated in Colombia by the War of the Hundred Days (1898–1901) confirms that love and exchange, affect and politics, nesting and coalition building would remain inseparable through the incessant violence that unifies and fragments the country. Writing three decades before Carrasquilla, in 1867, Isaacs had inaugurated a truly national novelistic canon by allegorizing (in strictly historical, though eternalized fashion) the presumed Colombian impossibility of sythesizing difference, unifying regions, and social classes. The capital-city version of this split had been given a decade earlier by Eugenio Díaz Castro's *Manuela,* at once a literary point of articulation and a moderate conservative pamphlet that proposed a new (and ultimately failed) class pact. Politically, the most interesting project, however, was the humanist egalitarianism that Nieto had put forth a decade earlier, in the 1840s, in his Jamaican exile. Along with a reevaluation of the radical complexity of Nieto's anti- and postcolonial *Ingermina,* a new edition of the poetry and prose of his Afro-Caribbean contemporary Calendario Obeso would put Latin American criticism in the position of composing a new, more representative, and less elitist map of nineteenth-century Colombian literature.

AFTERWORD

Violence, Law, and Justice

On September 11, 2001, the *New York Times* reported on the lawsuit soon to be brought against Henry Kissinger by René Schneider, Jr., the son of Gal. René Schneider, constitutionalist commander of the Chilean army assassinated in October 1970, as part of a CIA-orchestrated campaign to destabilize the elected president of Chile, Salvador Allende. As is well known, the Nixon and Kissinger-led policy toward Chile in the early seventies culminated on September 11, 1973, with the bombing of the Chilean presidential palace and the establishment of a two-decade long military regime that made extensive use of murder and torture. For the most optimistic among those who continued to struggle to shorten the rift between justice and (the enforcement of) law, the news stamped on the pages of the *New York Times* that morning might have been a reason for hope. Precisely on the twenty-eighth anniversary of the inauguration of state terrorism in Chile, one of its primary and most powerful orchestrators faced the possibility of being brought to justice. On September 11, 2001, the *New York Times* brought at least one piece of promising news to those of us who would like to see the law inch a little closer toward justice.

Certainly a putative trial of someone like Henry Kissinger for his responsibilities in U.S. policy toward Chile, before and after the assassination of Gal. Schneider, would be a trial fraught with all of the obstacles and dangers that one can imagine, and perhaps others that one might only suspect. In any case, on September 11, 2001, one of the world's leading papers reported on a lawsuit that, if carried out, certainly would have a substantial import in bringing the world's attention to what happened in Chile on and after September 11, 1973. That the twenty-eighth anniversary of the Chilean coup was marked by news of that lawsuit was, or might have been, a reason for hope. Forced severely to limit his travels outside the United States, Kissinger faced the possibility of having to respond, in American territory, for charges of "summary execution, assault and civil rights violations" (Rother 5), in a $3 million civil suit filed against him by the Schneiders in Washington. The *Times,* that morning, reported on a piece of news that represented the opening of a major precedent in international justice.

In the United States, as we know, paying any heed to that piece of news printed on the *New York Times* was a possibility given only to those who could have a moment with the paper before nine o'clock or so that morning. The terrorist attacks on the World Trade Center, and the intense manipulation of them that immediately ensued, brought Henry Kissinger himself to ground zero, where he paraded with Mayor Giuliani and perorated on good versus evil for the cameras. September 11, 2001, was the morning when Mr. René Schneider, Jr.'s claim to justice, his claim to bringing to justice those responsible for ending his father's impeccable life, became a dream that was a little further way.

New Yorkers assessed their losses, searched for their loved ones, and began to mourn their dead. The city also realized that it would be intensely manipulated by Bush, precisely at the moment when he demonstrated the most obvious lack of interest for the city's life. The anger and indignation of masses of New Yorkers fueled powerful movements such as Not in Our Name and Our Grief Is Not a Cry for War. New York's protests against the war in Iraq in February 2003 were among the most massive in the country, and also the most furiously repressed. Ignoring the will of multitudes and governments around the world and ignoring the will of the very New Yorkers whose grief offered him an excuse for politicking, Bush and his oil-weaponry-insurance coalition embarked on one of the most irresponsible, scandalous, and illegal wars of all of modern history. The war effort was marked by a list of farcical-grotesque events: lies about links between a state and a terrorist organization, about the existence of weapons of mass destruction in another nation, and about that nation's commercial activities; a most embarrassing presentation at the United Nations that included plagiarizing an old undergraduate paper; and an episode in which diplomats of Security Council member states found themselves spied upon by the U.S. administration in U.S. territory. In addition, the dominant oil-media-weaponry coalition in power has an unprecedented degree of control over and censorship of the televised media, in a true version of an Orwellian Ministry of Truth.

At the cost of thousands of lives, Osama bin Laden did his former business partner George Bush one last favor: He helped him impose another round of defeat upon the Schneiders of the world. This defeat is not definitive or absolute, but it is certainly important enough to deserve careful reflection. Rethinking violence, law, and justice has become an urgent matter for the understanding of what has happened to the planet since the morning when the *New York Times* reported on René Schneider's promising, most important lawsuit—until a little after nine, when that lawsuit took a plunge into invisibility. Regardless of how this most emblematic case evolves, the struggles over law and justice evoked by it will continue for years to come. It seems that literature and cultural studies will have had quite a bit to say about those struggles after all.

Notes

Introduction

1. Facing the usual Heideggerian tale about how *Being and Time* remained unfinished (namely the claim that the 1927 volume comprises only the two first sections of the first part of a project that ultimately proved impossible to realize), Slavoj Zizek makes two most interesting points. He argues that Heidegger's later publications *Kant and the Problem of Metaphysics* and *The Basic Problems of Phenomenology* roughly cover the remaining sections of the original *Being and Time,* so that if you put the three books together you have an approximate notion of the scope of the original project. Most interestingly, Zizek postulates that "it is rather as if Heidegger's insistence that the published book is just a fragment conceals the fact that the book is closed, finished." (Zizek, *Ticklish,* 23). The "unfinished" nature of *Being and Time* has, then, more in common with that of Clausewitz's *On War* than with Musil's masterpiece *Man without Qualities,* where a *discourse on unfinishability* is very much a structuring principle of the text itself. For Musil's intricate thinking on the subject, see his *Diaries.* I share the love of long, cerebral, early twentieth-century central European narrative with my friend and colleague (and film scholar) Tatjana Pavlovic.
2. Translation modified, as Michael Howard and Peter Paret's choice, "continuation of *policy* by other means," limits meaning in a way certainly not intended by Clausewitz's text. Their edition is, however, the authoritative English text that should be used. In twentieth-century France the Prussian general commanded the attention both of progressive, radical post-1968 philosophers (see Michel Foucault's *Society Must Be Defended*) and of conservative thinkers such as Raymond Aron (see his *Clausewitz, Philosopher of War*). Contemporary philosophy's most innovative theorist of war, Paul Virilio, has never tired of acknowledging his debt to Clausewitz. A very useful introduction to the Prussian general is Michael Howard's *Clausewitz.*
3. *On the Genealogy of Morals* was undoubtedly the Nietzsche book that most intensely influenced Foucault's methodology of historical inquiry. He made frequent mention of his preference for *Genealogy of Morals* over others texts such as *Zarathustra.* The revolution carried out by Nietzsche's *Genealogy* was to displace the *entire* range of ethical and moral questions (what is good and evil, how to act, what virtue is, etc.) to the terrain *upon which that morality*

depended, namely politics. For Nietzsche politics is a package that includes both the war and the later peace of subjection and humiliation that the victorious impose upon the defeated once the actual war is over. Only as an expression and justification of that degrading process does morality arise. In other words, Nietzsche makes the realm of morality dependent upon and derivative of the political realm. The fundamental event is the result of the political battle, the interpretive war that defines the "good" that will reign next. All of Foucault's work is governed by Nietzsche's axiom that *first* there is a war, there is bloodshed. As a result of it a political order is imposed and *then* morality is invented. Never the other way around, morality first and politics later, as religious conservatives as well as secular liberals tend either naively to believe or yet claim in bad faith. Of most recent relevance for that argument, see Michel Foucault's Collège de France seminar from 1974–75, *Abnormal.*

4. The inaugural moment of postcolonial theory, Edward Said's *Orientalism* (1978), was also the canonical critique of the erasure of colonialism in Western humanistic disciplines. Said's study was a landmark account of the distorting construction of the Oriental other by Western discourses, literary, scientific, and otherwise. By the time Said returned to the literary coding of colonialism, in *Culture and Imperialism* (1994), his theses had become so influential that even though his interpretations were just as elegant and well informed, he could not help sounding a bit repetitive and predictable. Meanwhile, thanks in part to the effect of Said's work, postcolonial theory, criticism, and historiography have become immense fields. This canonization has been propelled also by the work of a number of remarkable Indian scholars who were discussing another foundational text, Ranajit Guha's *Elementary Aspects of Peasant Insurgency in Colonial India* (1983), long before its publication. The Subaltern Studies group, as they would later become known, revolutionized our understanding of a number of concepts, including the Gramscian category of subalternity and the Kantian notion of antagonism. For its unfolding in literary criticism, see the already vast oeuvre of Gayatri Spivak, especially *The Postcolonial Critic, Outside in the Teaching Machine,* and *A Critique of Postcolonial Reason.* A most lucid treatment of the national question is Partha Chatterjee's *Nation and Its Fragments.* For an analysis of how the West has obliterated its roots in colonialism and slavery, see Paul Gilroy, *The Black Atlantic.* For two particularly illuminating analyses of colonial discourse by new generations of postcolonial theorists, see David Spurr's *The Rhetoric of Empire* and Gaurav Desai's *Subject to Colonialism.*
5. In this sense, Virilio's work clearly dialogues more fruitfully with Gilles Deleuze's than with Foucault's. Deleuze was, as is well known, the twentieth century's great thinker of movement, speed, and nomadism. Throughout a four-decade philosophical career, Deleuze coined concepts such as line of flight, movement-image, time-image, war machine, deterritorialization, and many others, all of them marked by a profoundly spatial and mobile form of

thinking. For his relating of surface displacement to joy (against the seriousness and guilt of depth-hermeneutic forms of thinking) see *The Logic of Sense.* For an insight into new war machines, see Gilles Deleuze and Felix Guattari's *A Thousand Plateaus* (351–423). For Deleuze's analysis of cinema as *temporalization of the image through movement,* see his *Cinema 1: The Movement-Image* and *Cinema 2: The Time-Image.* For Deleuze and Guattari's most poignant use of the concept of deterritorialization, see their *Kafka.* Most specialists would agree that in strictly philosophical terms, Deleuze's masterpiece is *Difference and Repetition,* where the question of movement is present throughout his meticulous demonstration of how repetition is a concept of an order entirely other than Hegelian identity, much like the concept of difference is of an order not comparable with the equally Hegelian notion of contradiction. For two elegant introductions to Gilles Deleuze's philosophy, see Michael Hardt's *Gilles Deleuze: An Apprenticeship in Philosophy* and Roberto Machado's *Deleuze e a Filosofia.* For an excellent discussion of Deleuze's cinema works, see Rodowick's *Gilles Deleuze's Time Machine.*

6. It was only at 32 years of age, in 1924, that Benjamin would look Marxism straight in the face by falling in love with Bolshevik activist Asja Lacis and reading, first of all, Georg Lukács's *History and Class Consciousness.* In 1921, when he finished "Critique of Violence," Benjamin's intellectual life had revolved around a few axes: the youth movement of the 1910s, the critique and overcoming of Kantianism, his mystical theory of language, and questions of art, criticism, and the aesthetic in German Romanticism. Of special import for the argument developed in chapter 3 are Benjamin's *political* pre-Marxist writings such as "Imperial Panorama" (a section of the later published *One Way Street,* where he dissects the Germany of hyperinflation) and his critique of and clear refusal to contribute to Martin Buber's Zionist journal *Der Jude.* For well-researched yet quick and manageable biographical references on this period of Benjamin's life, see Marcus Bullock and Michael W. Jennings's "Chronology" in *Selected Writings,* vol. 1 (490–515). Illuminating for the understanding of this period are Benjamin's letters, sent primarily to Ernst Schoen and Gershom Scholem, in *The Correspondence* (66–199). For an indispensable account, all the more remarkable for the author's tremendous difficulty to understand Benjamin, see Gershom Scholem's *Walter Benjamin: The Story of a Friendship.* Unmatched in its poetic brilliance and love for Benjamin is Pierre Missac's account in *Walter Benjamin's Passages.* Brazil has a long and illustrious tradition of Benjamin scholarship. The indispensable books are José Guilherme Merquior's *Arte e Sociedade,* Sérgio Paulo Rouanet's *O Édipo e o Anjo,* Olgária Matos's *Os Arcanos do Inteiramente Outro* and *O Iluminismo Visionário,* and Jeanne Marie Gagnebin's *Walter Benjamin: Os Cacos da História.* The exploration of Benjamin's theory of translation was

started by concrete poet, essayist, and translator Haroldo de Campos in "Para além do princípio da saudade," and "A Lingua Pura," and has culminated most recently in Susana Kampff Lages's *Walter Benjamin: Tradução e Melancolia.*

7. To illustrate the Heidegger-centric lens for reading Weimar Germany, for which Derrida is, in a way, responsible, suffice it to relate an anecdote of a Heideggerian friend of mine. Upon hearing a version of what would later become chapter 3 of this book, he insisted that, however much I set Benjamin and Heidegger apart, I should admit the former's "language of man" essay was indebted to the latter's "notion" of language. It was only after being informed that Benjamin's language essay had been concluded in 1916 (and therefore could not be indebted to *anything* by the future author of *Being and Time*) that my Heideggerian friend realized he hadn't bothered to check the facts. Naturally, this does not mean that the facts would actually make him change his mind or outlook on these things. I do not suggest that Derrida would ever commit gross factual errors like this, but his work—by sounding excessively confident at times about what Heidegger "encompasses"—has indirectly justified and helped proliferate said errors.

Chapter 1

1. "Height of the military regime" is a poor synecdoque to describe 1973 Brazil. Those were also the years of, among other things, the underground resistance and first victories against the dictatorship, the emergence of a mimeographed poetry movement known as "marginal poetry" that would become a landmark, the consolidation of rock music with *maudit* icon Raul Seixas, the beginnings of *desbunde* ("tripping out"), and the heyday of structuralism in literary studies. In the intellectual context in which it happened—in Rio de Janeiro, center of the country's structuralist trends—Foucault's talk accomplished quite a bit and has in fact become *symbolic* of a certain turn in the debate on Oedipus and the Law. In this sense, it is instructive to read the Portuguese version of "Truth and Juridical Forms," as it includes Foucault's heated exchange with noted Brazilian psychoanalyst Hélio Pellegrino in the Q and A session. Pellegrino insisted on discussing the Oedipus myth as the demonstration of a universal axiom, the proof of a certain law or destiny. Clearly, then, he was *not understanding* the two most basic points made by Foucault: 1. that his was a reading of the *Sophokles play* written in a very particular moment of Greek history; 2. that the *Sophokles play* was an *agent* in the production and consolidation of a different relationship with truth, a different *way of telling* the truth. For Pellegrino "truth" could only be a transcendental concept reflected or represented by the myth, never something that literature could actually be producing. The exchange was an instance of what Lyotard calls a *differend*: that is, a difference so radical that it does not pertain to something expressable in any language. In a true

differend, the minute you name the opposition that separates the terms, *you actually take a position on the side of one of them,* as in fact I just did above when relating the Foucault-Pellegrino interchange. A differend is a difference unnameable in any one language and only expressible in the *rift* between two or more languages. For the elaboration of this notion of untranslatable difference see Lyotard, *Differend.* For a most sophisticated dialogue with Foucault's "Truth and Juridical Forms," see Julio Ramos's reading of the nineteenth-century Cuban juridical subject in *Paradojas de la letra*; ninety percent of the English-language bibliography on Foucault does not engage "Truth and Juridical Forms" at all and seems unaware of its centrality for the thinking of its author. To understand the Brazilian intellectual context in which Foucault delivers that piece, one might look at Flora Süssekind's *Literatura e Vida Literária* and Heloísa Buarque de Hollanda's *Impressões de Viagem,* and her collaboration with Zuenir Ventura and Elio Gaspari, *Cultura em Trânsito.* The new, authoritative history of that period is Elio Gaspari's *A Ditadura Escancarada.* For an extraordinary Marxist satire of the dominant literary methods of the time, see Roberto Schwarz's "19 Princípios para a Crítica Literaria." For the most sophisticated literary reflections developed at that time, very much in tune with Foucauldian critique, see Silviano Santiago's *Uma Literatura nos Trópicos* and *Vale Quanto Pesa.* The best summary of that cultural period, from a Marxist perspective, is that of Roberto Schwarz in "Cultura e política." For a study of the coalescing of a Brazilian counterculture in the 1970s, see Christopher Dunn's *Brutality Garden,* 160–87.

2. On the topic of the blood that continues to be spilled as the history of capitalism unfolds, see most recently the extraodinarily well-informed and emphatic book by Tariq Ali, *The Clash of Fundamentalisms: Crusades, Jihads, and Modernity.* Ali critically surveys "the most dangerous fundamentalism," American imperialism (281–315), the bloody history of Zionism (86–125), the India-Pakistan partition (166–202), and the entire history of Islam and the Middle East in ways that unmask the hypocrisy of U.S. foreign policy in the region. Ali's *Clash of Fundamentalisms* is a clear instance of a book *sadly confirmed* by the events on and after September 11. In the paperback edition Ali got to include an introduction and a couple more chapters that reflect on that eerie coincidence.
3. For an interesting dissection of the procedure of arriving at an identity by excluding nonidentity, see Roberto Schwarz's critique of Brazil's (and by extension Latin America's) 1960s-style nationalism, one that proceeded by searching for the nation in the place left vacant once all of the non-national was excluded. See Schwarz, "National by Elimination" in *Misplaced Ideas.* For sustained, admirable engagement with Schwarz's work, see essays in Neil Larsen's *Reading North by South* and *Determinations.*
4. For the subtle and methodical Cartesian crushing of doubt, see especially part four of *Discourse on Method,* where Descartes starts from a curious premise: "since I now wish to devote myself solely to the search for truth, I thought it

necessary to do the very opposite and reject as if absolutely false everything in which I could imagine the least doubt" (Descartes 126–7). Undoubtedly, around the same time a quite different conception of the subject was being developed by Spinoza in his *Ethics* and *Theological Political Treatise*. Spinoza scholars such as Marilena Chauí, in *A Nervura do Real*, have shown how Spinoza's "fortunate coalescing of modality and finitude, intellect and imagination" is a practice "in what we call freedom" (932). Following Chauí's monumental work, one could postulate Spinoza as the great reservoir of subversive and liberating energy of all pre-Nietzschean philosophy. For a fascinating biography of this most persecuted of all philosophers, see *Spinoza: A Life*, by Steven Nadler. Classics of Spinoza scholarship are, of course, Deleuze's *Spinoza: Expressionism in Philosophy* and *Spinoza: Practical Philosophy*. Committed to a post-Lacanian restoration of the Cartesian subject, thinkers such as Slavoj Zizek are not impressed with the wave of Spinozism. See his defense of Cartesianism in *The Ticklish Subject*. For a good sample of the work done on Descartes by Zizek's circle at the "Liubliana school," see his edited volume *Cogito and the Unconscious*. A most talented Brazilian poet and philosopher, Antonio Cícero, wrote a lean and seductive vindication of the Cartesian subject, *O Mundo desde o Fim*.

5. Here I would certainly not want my critique of Dorfman/Polanski to reinforce the simplistic, pseudo-poststructuralist notion that *all* representations of the tortured subject will necessarily betray him/her. For recent, postdictatorial feature films that ethically and aesthetically deal admirably with the topic, see the Argentine *Garage olimpo* (1999), directed by Marco Bechi, as well as the Brazilian *Que bom te ver viva* (1989), directed by Lucia Murat. For a most compelling documentary on the U.S. role in disseminating torture around the world from the Fort Bennings–based School of the Americas, see *School of Assassins* (1994), directed by Robert Richter and narrated by Susan Sarandon. A recent, impeccable documentary on the French origins of many modern techniques of torture is *Escadron de la mort: L'école francaise* (2003), directed by Marie-Monique Robin. There you learn that many of the horrors passed on to Latin Americans by their gringo teachers from Fort Benning, Georgia, were in fact first developed by the French and applied upon Algerians.
6. I enjoy much of Roman Polanski's work. And although the rhetoric in Ariel Dorfman's writings turns out to be somewhat repulsive to me, I have good memories of studying under him at Duke University and very much find myself in agreement with most of the political positions he explicitly takes. This harsh critique of the film, therefore, comes from a position that is sympathetic and politically allied, and exercises the critique that the film attempts to foreclose. For a critique that goes roughly in the same direction as mine—endowed, however, with a knowledge of the Chilean context incomparably greater than mine—see Nelly Richard's *Residuos y metáforas*. For a depiction of torture less odious but just as naive as Dorfman's, see Mario Benedetti's play *Pedro y el capitán*.

7. The expression "obscenity of understanding" arose in a particularly revealing moment in the U.S. development of trauma studies. In April of 1990, Claude Lanzmann, director of *Shoah,* appeared before the Western New England Institute for Psychoanalysis (WNEIPA). The agenda, to which he acceded beforehand, was a viewing and a discussion of a film tracing the life of Nazi doctor Eduard Wirths. After arriving in New Haven, Connecticut, and viewing the film privately, Lanzmann refused to participate in its public showing. Lanzmann critiqued the film's obscene attempt to "understand" the Nazi doctor and the discussion that ensued also included the audience's reaction to that refusal. See Cathy Caruth's edited volume *Trauma: Explorations in Memory* (200–20) for a most compelling account of that night by Lanzmann himself. Most crucial in the bibliography on trauma studies is the volume by Shoshana Felman and Dori Laub, *Testimony.* On the linking of testimony and death/disappearance, see Felipe Victoriano's recent piece "Fiction, Death, and Testimony."

Chapter 2

1. As it is never too late, I refer any interested philosophers to the relevant bibliography. To start, see the volume *Deconstruction and the Possibility of Justice*, edited by Drucilla Cornell, Michel Rosenfeld, and David Gray Carlson, as well as *The Philosophy of the Limit*, by Drucilla Cornell. See also what is in many respects the foundational text, Jacques Derrida's *Force of Law*, extensively analyzed in my next chapter. Perusal of the *Cardozo Law Review* in the 1990s will yield evidence of the quantity and extraordinary quality of that bibliography.
2. For passages of "The Ethnographer," the first set of page numbers in parenthesis refers to the original Spanish, and the second set to Andrew Hurley's translation in *Collected Fictions.*
3. U.S. American intellectual life seems to include the periodic appearance of a major work of conservative cultural criticism that rehashes the thesis on the West's superiority. In the 1980s it was Allan Bloom's *The Closing of the American Mind*, which actually got many serious and respectable scholars discussing the most ludicrous hypotheses about feminism or rock music. In the 1990s Samuel Huntington proposed the thesis of a *Clash of Civilizations*, a dangerously phrased conservative pamphlet that may have turned out to be a self-fulfilling prophesy. Huntington has presented us now, in 2004, with the even scarier "The Hispanic Challenge," an article that anounces a terrifying forthcoming book. In it Huntington argues that the "problem" of Mexican immigration "threatens to divide" the United States. As always in these cases, the mythical unit in danger of splitting turns out to be a retrospective, nostalgic, and racist mirage that never existed. Huntington's article, published in *Foreign Policy*, has already elicited a vigorous and well placed response by Carlos Fuentes, published in *El País* on March 23, 2004,

and to my knowledge not yet available in English. I refer to the Portuguese version that appeared in *Folha de São Paulo* on March 28, 2004.

4. For a foundational moment in the "interpretive turn" of cultural anthropology, see Clifford Geertz's *The Interpretation of Cultures*. For interesting reflections on the imbalance proper to the anthropological encounter, see the collection of essays edited by Clifford and Marcus, *Writing Culture*. Pieces specially relevant to the issues discussed here are Mary Louise Pratt's "Fieldwork in Common Places" and Talal Asad's "The Concept of Cultural Translation." Clifford's "On Ethnographic Allegory" is not only a key moment in the self-reflexive turn of anthropology but also one of the most refined discussions of the concept of allegory in any discipline.
5. A contemporary Chilean philosopher has reflected, in a most illuminating fashion, on the question of the absence or feebleness of a philosophical tradition in the Spanish language. In *Sobre árboles y madres*, Patricio Marchant relates the telling anecdote that to a 20-year-old Chilean it is perfectly possible and feasible to utter the sentence "I am a poet"—expressing a desire that may or may not be realized through a statement that is, however, within the domain of the sayable. Not so with the statement "I am a philosopher," which invariably invites, argues Marchant, the correction: "You mean a *professor* of philosophy" (85). In the split between philosopher and professor of philosophy, producer and reproducer of thought, Marchant reads the hierarchy I am attempting to show here. "I am philosopher" is simply not a statement that belongs in the order of the possible for that youth. The word is barred in advance. For another remarkable engagement with that question of the (marginal) language by Patricio Marchant, see his essay "En qué lengua se habla Hispanoamérica,?" posthumously compiled by Willy Thayer and Pablo Oyarzún in *Escritura y temblor*.
6. George Yúdice has offered a most emphatic critique of a multiculturalism that incorporates the other as a typical specimen that ultimately only testifies to the fact that the dominant culture "has it all to offer," and "is a mirror of the whole world." See his "We Are *Not* the World," for an analysis of how a certain U.S. multiculturalism has preferentially absorbed those Latin American images, texts, and practices which in more docile fashion replicate fantasies of an exotic identity. Yúdice has recently engaged these appropriations and flows from the standpoint of an "expediency" that makes of culture a signifier particularly malleable and appropriaple in contemporary political struggles. See specially the chapters on the globalization of culture (82–108), on the Rio de Janeiro funk scene (109–32), and on free trade (214–86) in *The Expediency of Culture*.
7. For those interested in approaching the question of the encounter between Heidegger and Nazism from the point of view of his *thinking*, over and beyond any hysterical campaigns, the key sources remain the same: Jacques Derrida, *Of Spirit*, Philippe Lacoue-Labarthe, *Heidegger, Art, and Politics*, Jean-François Lyotard, *Heidegger and "the Jews."* For definitive evidence

that the Farías book adds *nothing* to what was already known by those who take interest in Heidegger, see Derrida's interview "Heidegger, the Philosophers' Hell" in *Points.*

8. The "De Man affair" began around 1987 with the discovery of a number of war-time articles written by Paul de Man for a collaborationist newspaper in Belgium during the Nazi occupation in World War II. Of the several dozen articles, two or three made explicit anti-Semitic remarks. From there sectors of the mainstream American press, with the inestimable help of resentful academics, derived a furious campaign against deconstruction. It was fairly obvious that those conducting the campaign were not in the least interested in discussing the relations between philosophy and politics. The explicit goal was, based on two or three pathetic logical leaps, to draw the conclusion that deconstruction was a form of thought with dangerous roots in Nazism. The articles are published in Paul de Man, *Paul de Man: Wartime Journalism.* Derrida wrote a beautiful piece about the lamentable controversy, "Like the Sound of the Sea" in *Memoires: For Paul de Man.*
9. I use "post-phenomenological thought" to refer to the diverse bodies of theory loosely connected by the critique of humanism after World War II, especially in France. My preference for this term, over the shorthand "poststructuralism" popularized in the United States, stems from my perception that it was the attempt to think the unexamined premises of phenomenology, not the more localized dissatisfaction with the scientific pretensions of structuralism, that endowed all those theoretical endeavors with their coherence. This is now a hopeless terminological dispute, as the term "poststructuralism" has been established and popularized. But it is a reminder that for that entire intellectual scene the step beyond structuralism was just one among many others.
10. Another example of the sweeping disqualification of literary theory among moralistic philosophers is offered by Richard Eldridge: "To the extent that literary criticism takes place through unreflectively assuming one or another stance on the historical development of language, culture, and expression, it is itself ideological and premature . . . Perhaps we cannot establish with certainty what *the* logic of historical development and human action is; perhaps there is no such logic. But these very thoughts ought to cast some doubt on confident assertions that human agents and their expressions are nothing but effects of linguistic codes or material forces or unconscious life or gender oppositions or whatever" (10–1). It is at least curious that a philosopher about to criticize unreflective assumptions should so unreflectively establish such an organic relationship between literary criticism and unreflectiveness, especially when *not a single* literary critic is being examined to justify the assertion. It also intriguing that a philosopher criticizing "confident assertions" should assert so confidently that claiming "human agents" to be *nothing but* . . . is indeed what language-based, materialist, psychoanalytic, and gender criticisms are doing, without confronting or examining a single work. In fact, Eldridge's last sentence, rather

than reflecting what literary criticism has done, bespeaks the tremendous anxiety of a certain U.S. philosophical establishment facing theoretical references it does not handle and witnessing their growing impact upon young philosophy students.

11. No one advanced this task in our field more effectively in the 1990s than Michael Bérubé. See his detailed critique of conservative stereotypes about higher education and the role of critical theory in English departments in *Public Access*. See also his argument for the "employability" of English for our society, and conversely the renewed relevance of social and cultural questions for literary studies, in *The Employment of English*.
12. Despite all efforts to avoid moralistic dismissals, the anxiety over value leads Booth to disregard mass-cultural products "like *Jaws*" which "approach a limit of worthlessness" (206). The problem becomes clear when one compares that remark with Fredric Jameson's intricate reconstruction of the allegories of both the novel and the film, their respective representations of a certain pattern of disguised class conflict in post–civil rights America, the ideological roles of law enforcement and the science-and-technology rhetoric in the film, its veiled Utopian content, etc. ("Reification" 26–30). In this instance, clearly, aesthetic moralism has prevented the critic from confronting a rich texture of cultural and political problems present in the film.
13. See the essays collected in *Love's*, many of which deal with James. See also her elegant *The Fragility of Goodness*, an ethical analysis of the theme of luck in Greek tragedy and philosophy. Nussbaum again makes use of literature to think through philosophical questions in *Poetic Justice*.
14. For a small sample of the directly relevant bibliography by the subaltern studies group that Martha Nussbaum is missing here, see the introduction to this book, note 4.

Chapter 3

1. Benjamin's witty and acute reversal of Keller is from Konvolut N, the epistemological heart of the *Arcades Project*, and the main source for his essay on the concept of history. The totality of the *Arcades* is now finally available in English, after existing a while only in German, French, and Italian. By far the most elegant and insightful translation of that crucial Konvulut, however, is Pablo Oyarzún's version in *La dialéctica en suspenso*. Recommended even to those who read German, for it indeed *sheds light* on the original.
2. Much less read and well known than the other pieces with which it was compiled—"Plato's Pharmacy" (the exemplary reading of *Phaedrus*) and "Double Session" (the piece on Mallarmé)—"Dissemination" names the volume, however, and brings one of the most often (mis)quoted and misunderstood of Derrida's sentences: "there is nothing before the text; there is no pretext that is not already a text" (328). "Dissemination" is a web of quotes woven around Philippe Sollers's *Nombres* [*Numbers*], and consti-

tutes one of Derrida's most experimental texts, conceptually as much as syntactically and typographically. It is the announcement of the galactic proliferation that would later take place in *Glas*.

3. In addition to Derrida's works and the extensive juridical and philosophical rethinking of responsibility in Drucilla Cornell, see another important deconstructive reading of responsibility (done from a quite different angle than Cornell's) in the work of Gayatri Spivak, especially the article "Responsibility."
4. In addition to the editors, the following authors participated in the congress and contributed to the volume: Douglas Kellner, Abdul Janmohamed, Zhang Longxi, Andrei Marga, Gayatri Spivak, Carlos Vilas, Keith Griffin, Azizur Khan, Ashot Galoian, Stephen Resnick, Richard Wolff, Su Shaozhi. With the exception of a couple of essays of theoretical interest (especially the one by Gayatri Spivak), the conference papers limit themselves to putting forth a frightened defense of the relevance of Marxism while attempting to interpret a number of different national situations.
5. Fredric Jameson once pointed out to me that "tradition" is not really a word applicable to the analytic pragmatism dominant in U.S. philosophy departments. In other words, theirs is not really a body of thought that evolves the way a tradition does. Jameson had good reasons to argue that "perpetual present" would in fact be a more adequate designation.
6. What do Hamlet and Marx have in common? Not much, until Benjamin—and especially Derrida's reading of Benjamin—comes around and produces the kinship between the two. We thus have here another instance of the law unveiled by Borges in "Kafka and His Precursors": Precursors and lineages do not exist until later subjects retrospectively construe them. Every tradition is a retrospective invention.
7. Based on this status of justice in Derrida's work, Drucilla Cornell proposes to rename "deconstruction" the "philosophy of the limit" as a strategy to make "the ethical message of deconstruction" (*Philosophy* 155) more visible and to critique those who think that all deconstruction can do in the realm of politics is to provide us with a politics of suspicion. For an important rethinking of feminism in the light of the impact of deconstruction upon legal studies, see Drucila Cornell's *Beyond Accommodation.*
8. A mapping of the impact of Heidegger on Derrida is, in a way, a mapping of all of Derrida's work: the horizon of what gets called "logocentric metaphysics" in *Grammatology* (1967) and *Speech and Phenomena* (1967), to the long article dedicated to *ousia* and *grammé* in Heidegger in *Margins of Philosophy* (1972), the first critical dissection of Heidegger in *Of Spirit* (1987), the intervention on the limits between "life" and "work" in Nietzsche's thought, brought to its conclusion in *Otobiographies* (1984), the reflection on the gift of time in *Given Time* (1991), and the engagement with the problem of technology in "Heidegger's Hands," to mention just a few of the most obviously relevant in defining the centrality of Heidegger in Derrida's thought. One of the most subtle reflections on the Heidegger-Derrida

dialogue can be found in Evando Nascimento, *Derrida e a Literatura* (199–229). For an important discussion of Derrida's encounter with Heidegger through the thematic of the metaphor, see Giuseppe Stellardi, *Heidegger and Derrida on Philosophy and Metaphor.*

9. On the relationship between utopia and anonymity in Jameson, see his "On Literary and Cultural Import-Substitution in the Third World: The Case of Testimonio." On anonymity as one of the key allegories for utopia in postmodern fiction, see Avelar, *Untimely,* 186–209. For an analyisis of questions of gender particularly attentive to the issue of undecidability that I have been highlighting here, see Robert Irwin's *Mexican Masculinities.*

10. Throughout my analysis of Benjamin's "Zur Kritik der Gewalt," the reader should keep in mind the polyssemy of *Gewalt* in German. It means not only "violence" but also legitimate and legal "power" and "force" (as in *Staatsgewalt,* state force). My reading of Derrida's reading of Benjamin will also bracket a long German tradition of reflection, debate, and disagreement on the multifaceted nature of Walter Benjamin's legacy. This debate is inaugurated during Benjamin's own life, mostly in the correspondence he maintains with his contemporaries Adorno, Scholem, and Brecht. The tradition continues with Hermann Schweppenhäuser and Rolf Tiedemann's editorial work, Jürgen Habermas's attempt to rescue Benjamin for an Englightenment-friendly agenda, and Winfried Menninghaus's studies of language in Benjamin in *Walter Benjamins Theorie der Sprachmagie* and *Schwellenkunde.* On the early Benjamin, especially the theory of language, see Elisabeth Collingwood's *Walter Benjamin: La Lengua del Exilio.* Two extraodinarily lucid reflections on Benjamin are Pablo Oyarzún's "Sobre el concepto benjaminiano de traducción" and "Cuatro señas." An excellent collection of some of the fundamental, historic German pieces on Benjamin is available in English in Gary Smith's edited volume *On Walter Benjamin.* Of all that the English-language bibliography has added, in particular about the "young" Benjamin, that will occupy us here, see especially work done by Carol Jacobs, Rainer Nägele, and Timothy Bahti. These scholars, in close dialogue with Derrida's work, have been the signatories of illuminating engagements with the early Benjamin throughout the 1980s and 1990s. On Benjamin's vertiginous and abrupt interpretive procedures, see Carol Jacobs, *Dissimulating Harmony* and *In the Language of Walter Benjamin.* By Rainer Nägele, see *Theater, Theory, Speculation.* By Bahti, see *Allegories of History,* especially 204–25, 255–90. This tradition produced a most elegant book on Benjamin's theses on photography: Eduardo Cadava's *Words of Light: Theses on the Photography of History.* Of the dialogue that this cohort of scholars has sponsored, see the volumes edited by Rainer Nägele, *Benjamin's Ground* and by David S. Ferris, *Walter Benjamin: Theoretical Questions.* Especifically on violence in Benjamin see Werner Hamacher, "Afformative Strike"; on critique and violence in Benjamin see also Rodolphe Gasché, "On Critique, Hypercriticism, and Deconstruction: The Case of Benjamin." Some inter-

pretations of Benjamin carried out from this perspective seem content in repeating Derrida. See Beatrice Hanssen's *Walter Benjamin's Other History.*

11. Even though the translation of *rechtsetzungende Gewalt* as "law-positing violence," preferred by Alexander García Düttman in his "The Violence of Destruction," may indeed be a more correct and elegant rendering than Edmund Jephcott's "law-making violence," I choose to maintain the latter. Jephcott's phrase captures Benjamin's view of the abruptness, the interruptive nature of the violent act.
12. Although I have not made many references to this essay, I greatly admire Tom McCall's engagement with Benjamin in "Momentary Violence." McCall's reading of the Benjamin piece corrects some of the Derrida's hypothesis, without in fact taking issue with Derrida clearly as I do here. On "Greek" and "Hebrew," and an original, interesting argument on how philosophy has presumably privileged the latter over the former, see Lambropoulous, *The Rise of Eurocentrism.*
13. Much remains to be said about the silent dialogue between Walter Benjamin and Franz Rosenzweig. For initial important work, see Stéphane Mosès, "Walter Benjamin and Franz Rosenzweig," in Gary Smith, ed., *Walter Benjamin: Philosophy, Aesthetics, History.*

Chapter 4

1. Palacios also notes that the decade of the 1930s witnessed increasing national unification, anchored in the oligarchies' political integration. This coincided with the entrance of populism into the nation's political scene.
2. Among the most illustrious, see Octavio Paz, for whom *María* is the epitome of Spanish American Romanticism as the imperfect reflection of another reflection, namely Spanish Romanticism (122). See also Roberto González Echevarría, for whom privileging works such as Sarmiento's *Facundo* or Euclides da Cunha's *Os Sertões* over novels such as José Mármol's *Amalia* or Isaacs's *María* means choosing Latin American originals against texts that were mere copies of Europe (40, 103). That the titles of both novels discarded as imperfect copies are names of women is not at all an irrelevant point in this case.
3. Palacios's *Entre la legitimidad y la violencia* is a lucid, indispensable introduction to modern Colombian history that takes us all the way to Pablo Escobar's death in 1993 and the election of liberal Samper in 1994, already in the era of the fully national narcowar and growing American military presence.
4. The literary allegory of that pact is the publication history of *Amalia*, by José Mármol, the final text of which makes a conciliatory gesture with the populist leadership defeated in Caseros, as part of a "ni vencedores ni vencidos" (no winners no losers) pact celebrated after the liberal victory. For a reasonably short but informative account of the Rosas regime, see Túlio Halperín

Donghi's *Historia contemporánea de América Latina*. The critical bibliography on Argentina's mid-nineteenth-century literary system is of high quality and quite daunting by now. Good starting points are David Viñas, *Literatura argentina y realidad política*; Graciela Montaldo, *De pronto el campo: literatura argentina y tradición rural*; and the Halperín Donghi et al., eds., *Sarmiento, Author of a Nation*.

5. Marx inherited from Hegel the concept that designates the relationship maintained with the set by the element which is, at the same time, the name of the entire set. This is the concept of *genensätzliche Bestimmung* ("oppositional or antithetic determination"). Hegel introduces it in the Greater *Logic* to speak of the essence as a reflection of itself and to derive the thesis on the identity of identity and nonidentity (Hegel 409–43). Marx revisited the concept in the introduction to *Grundrisse*, when he defines the singularity of production in the chain that unites production, distribution, exchange, and consumption, and in *Capital*, when he speaks of finance capital as the universal actualization of capital as such. See Slavoj Zizek's use of the concept of universality as a key to contemporary left-wing politics in his debate with Judith Butler and Ernesto Laclau (Butler, Zizek, and Laclau, *Contingency*, 314–5).
6. For important initial work on Calendario Obeso, see Laurence Prescott's *Candelario Obeso y la iniciación de la poesía negra en Colombia* and the volume edited by Amir Smith Córdoba, *Vida y obra de Calendario Obeso*. See also the article by Carlos Jáuregui, "Candelario Obeso: entre la espada del Romanticismo y la pared del proyecto nacional."
7. The original reads, in Obeso's popularesque *pentasílabos* (5-syllable verses): "¿quieren la guerra / con los cachacos? / yo no me muevo / de aquí de mi rancho / si alguno intenta / subir a lo alto / !busque escalera / por otro lado."
8. Mexican tales of national identity have established, since la Malinche, a link between translation and betrayal. Already a crucial translator in the Aztec empire before the Spanish arrival (as she spoke both Maya and Nahuatl), Doña Marina became Cortés's lover and key mediator in the conquest of Monteczuma's kingdom. It is hard to overestimate to what extent this story has framed and circumscribed the representation of the feminine in Mexican culture. Echoing as a paranomasia in the unspeakable national curse *(chingar, la chingada), Malinchismo* is an ideology, a cage, and at the same time an endless source of stories. For an indispensable collection of essays on la Malinche, see the volume edited by Margo Glantz, *La Malinche: Sus padres y sus hijos*. See Glantz's feminist reading of the word, letter, and voice in "La Malinche"; see also Carlos Monsiváis's piece "La Malinche y el malinchismo," devoted to mapping the "historical expulsion" of Marina in hegemonic national narratives such as nineteenth-century liberalism and the Revolution; and Octavio Paz's essayism on "the Mexican mask." I thank Robert Irwin for this reference and for the access to the volume.

9. *Manuela* has been read from the point of view of the opposition between writing and orality but the antagonism that structures the novel is irreducible to that dichotomy. First, because there is just as much writing in the province as in the city, albeit of a different kind. Secondly, because what Díaz stages is in fact a conflict between two sets of writings: that of the conservative church, that hegemonizes provincial life, and that of empiricism and the Enlightenment, from Bacon to the Encyclopedists, who inform Demosthenes's discourse. In other words, Demosthenes would not be a representative of "oral culture" even if one could indeed speak of "oral cultures" so confidently, as if the phrase designated a real referent.
10. As is well know, the concept of lettered city is one that is developed late in Angel Rama's work. Rama coins it after a lenthy stay in Caracas, a modernized and dynamic metropolis in comparison with which, in Rama's reflection, Bogotá often appears as a still lettered bureaucratic city with a more contradictory modernization process. See Rama, *Ciudad.*
11. Rooted in the Colombian Andes, the *bambuco* is a traditional and popular music genre, canonized and nationalized by folklorists. Of regionally variable structures and instrumentations, since the early twentieth century the *bambuco* has included primarily two typical lineups: that of instrumental trios or quartets with one or two *bandolas,* a *tiple* and a guitar or else that of vocal duets accompanied by *tiple* and guitar. The *bambuco* has also become a dance generally associated with professional folk dance groups. I am most grateful to Ana María Ochoa for this information.
12. On that score, see the very interesting sociological contrast that makes itself visible when Manuela runs into Demóstenes by the river. While the "cosmopolitan" Demóstenes is horrified that a single woman can go by herself to bathe in the river, the "provincial" Manuela takes that fact most naturally, noting that only after marriage does a woman from the countryside lose her right to occupy the public space (37).
13. On Díaz's representation of class relations, see Colmenares' interesting remark: "If the *hacienda* system is represented as oppressive only in the figures of pitiless butlers, and always without the knowledge of the benevolent landowner and his family" (259).
14. For a study of Samper from the stanpoint of the history of culture, see especially Jaramillo Uribe, 31–46 and 175–191.
15. Miguel Antonio Caro's angry reaction against Isaacs's spicy protoethnography is part of a vast enterprise. Caro is the epitome of lettered power in nineteenth-century Colombia: head of the conservative "Regeneration," writer of the 1886 constitution, and grammatic president par excellence, Caro combined, with more authority than anyone else, the "correct," academic use of language, with a moral and divine order. For an excellent critical dismantling of Miguel Antonio Caro and Colombian grammaticalism, see Erna von der Walde Uribe, "Limpia."
16. The novel does narrate the peasant love affair of Tránsito and Bráulio, el Salomé and Tiburcio's love episode, Carlos' failed love pretension, and

Emigdio's adventures, in addition to Nay and Sinar's allegorical tale at the center. These are all at best counterpoints to Efraín and María's story, however, and never reach the level of being parallel plots.

17. The Marxian question regarding art never was, for sure, how certain conditions of production produce certain styles and aesthetics. From a Marxist point of view, naturally, one assumes that that will be the case. The truly important question is in fact the opposite one: How can Greek art, so visibly a product of a particular historical moment, of an "infantile" moment of humankind, still fill us with emotion? What is the eternal kernel that persists in this historical and contextual being that is art? This is how far Marx takes us in the introduction to the *Grundrisse,* before returning to the polemic with Proudhon regarding value. There is a highly significant coincidence of dates that is worth pointing out: while in London Marx prepares the endless manuscript of the *Grundrisse,* on the other side of the Channel, in Paris, Baudelaire publishes the *Flowers of Evil,* where one of the key questions is the dialectic between the two halves of art, the temporal and the eternal. The secret and allegorical relation between Baudelaire and Marx is one of the treasures hidden in Walter Benjamin's *Arcades Project.*
18. Among the most panicked denials of the Jewish question in the novel is that of Donald McGrady, who discards it with arguments that all things meaningful in the novel are characteristics of Romanticism, that the "Old Testament is an important part of the Catholic tradition," that "Isaacs was not a Jew either by heritage or by education," and finally that "unless one supposes a biological determinism it is difficult to understand how this presumed Jewish influence could operate" (McGrady, "Introducción," 35–6). It does not occur to McGrady to ask, for example, if names such as Efraín, Ester, Solomon, and Sarah might not mean something.
19. For a hypertext and multilingual edition of the Bible, see http://bible.ort.org. For an extensive compilation of biblical themes and characters in literature, see Preminger and Greenstein.
20. It is true that one of the novel's embedded stories relates the story of African royal subjects Sinay and Nay. As pointed out by critics such as Menton and Anderson Imbert, this is a tale that displays many parallels with Efraín's and María's story. Blackness is given a voice, however, at the cost of being *moved to an immemorial past.* In fact, the story's basic operation is quite Orientalist in Said's sense: A reifed otherness is imagined in order to grant the white subject a replica of his story. The sympathetic, noble, honorable portrayal of blacks in the story is made possible by what anthropologist Johannes Fabian calls *denial of coevalness.* Sinay and Nay speak, but at the cost of being converted in voices of the past.

Works Cited

Alencar, José de. *Lucíola*. São Paulo: Saraiva, 1972

———. *Senhora*. Rio de Janeiro: Aguilar, 1975.

Ali, Tariq. *The Clash of Fundamentalisms: Crusades, Jihads, and Modernity*. London and New York: Verso, 2003.

Anderson, Benedict. *Imagined Communities: Reflections on the Origins and Spread of Nationalism*. London and New York: Verso, 1983.

Arciniegas. Germán. *Genio y figura de Jorge Isaacs*. Buenos Aires: Editorial Universitaria, 1967.

Arendt, Hannah. *On Violence*. New York, San Diego, and London: Harcourt Brace and Company, 1970.

Aristotle. *Politics*. Trans. Benjamin Jowett. *The Basic Works of Aristotle*. Ed. Richard McKeon. New York: Random, 1941. 1113–1316.

Aron, Raymond. *Clausewitz, Philosopher of War*. Trans. Christine Booker and Norman Stone. New York: Simon and Schuster, 1986.

Arquilla, John and David Ronfeldt, eds. *Networks and Netwars: The Future of Terror, Crime, and Militancy*. Santa Monica: RAND, 2001.

Asad, Talal, ed. *Anthropology and the Colonial Encounter*. London: Ithaca, 1973.

———. "The Concept of Cultural Translation in British Social Anthropology." Clifford and Marcus 141–64.

Avelar, Idelber. *The Untimely Present: Postdictatorial Latin American Fiction and the Task of Mourning*. Durham and London: Duke UP, 1999.

Bahti, Timothy. *Allegories of History: Literary Historiography after Hegel*. Baltimore: Johns Hopkins, 1992.

Baudelaire, Charles. *Flowers of Evil*. 1857. Trans. James McGowan. Oxford and New York: Oxford UP, 1993.

Bauman, Zygmunt. *Postmodern Ethics*. Oxford, UK, and Cambridge, Mass.: Blackwell, 1993.

Benedetti, Mario. *Pedro y el capitán*. México: Nueva Imagen, 1979.

Benjamin, Walter. *The Arcades Project*. Trans. Howard Eiland and Kevin McLaughlin. Cambridge, Mass.: Belknap Press, 1999.

———. *The Correspondence of Walter Benjamin, 1910–1940*. Ed. Gershom Scholem and Theodor W. Adorno. Trans. Manfred R. Jacobson and Evelyn M. Jacobson. Chicago: U of Chicago P, 1994.

———. "Critique of Violence." 1921. *Reflections*. Trans. Edmund Jephcott. New York: Schocken, 1978. 277–300.

———. *La diálectica en suspenso. Fragmentos sobre la historia.* Trans., intro and notes Pablo Oyarzún. Santiago: ARCIS-LOM, 1995.

———. *One Way Street.* 1928. Trans. Edmund Jephcott. *Selected Writings.* Vol. 1. 444–87.

———. "The Right to Use Force." *Selected Writings.* Vol. 1. 231–34.

———. *Selected Writings. 1913–1926.* Vol. 1. Ed. Marcus Bullock and Michael W. Jennings. Cambridge, Mass.: Belknap, 1996.

———. *Selected Writings, 1927–34.* Vol. 2. Ed. Michael W. Jennings, Howard Wiland, and Gary Smith. Cambridge, Mass.: Belknap, 1999.

Bérubé, Michael. *The Employment of English: Theory, Jobs, and the Future of Literary Studies.* New York and London: New York UP, 1998.

———. *Public Access: Literary Theory and American Cultural Politics.* London and New York: Verso, 1994.

——— and Cary Nelson, ed. *Higher Education under Fire: Politics, Economics, and the Crisis of the Humanities.* New York: Routledge, 1995.

Bhabha, Homi. *The Location of Culture.* London: Routledge, 1994.

Blest Gana, Alberto. *Martín Rivas.* 1862. Caracas: Ayacucho, 1977.

Bloom, Allan. *The Closing of the American Mind: How Higher Education Has Failed Democracy and Impoverished the Souls of Today's Students.* New York: Simon and Schuster, 1987.

Booth, Wayne. *The Company We Keep: An Ethics of Fiction.* Berkeley, Los Angeles and London: California UP, 1988.

Borges, Jorge Luis. "El etnógrafo." *Elogio de la sombra.* 1969. *Prosa completa.* Vol. 3. Buenos Aires: Emecé, 1979. 265–67.

———. "The Ethnographer." *Collected Fictions.* Trans. Andrew Hurley. London and New York: Penguin, 1998. 334–35.

Bullock, Ed. Marcus and Michael W. Jennings. "Chronology." In *Selected Writings.* Vol. 1. By Walter Benjamin. 490–515.

Buarque de Hollanda, Heloísa. *Impressões de Viagem: CPC, Vanguarda e Desbunde, 1960–1970.* São Paulo: Brasiliense, 1980.

Buarque de Hollanda, Heloísa, Elio Gaspari, and Zuenir Ventura. *Cultura em Trânsito 70/80: Da Repressão à Abertura.* Rio de Janeiro: Aeroplano, 2000.

Butler, Judith. *Bodies that Matter: On the Discursive Limits of "Sex."* New York and London: Routledge, 1993.

———. *Gender Trouble: Feminism and the Subversion of Identity.* London: Routledge, 1990.

———. "Universality in Culture." Nussbaum et al. 45–52.

Butler, Judith, Slavoj Zizek, and Ernesto Laclau. *Contingency, Hegemony, Universality: Contemporary Dialogues on the Left.* London and New York: Verso, 2000.

Burgos Cantor, Roberto. "Prólogo." *Cantos populares de mi tierra.* By Calendario Obeso. Bogotá: Aranco y El Áncora, 1988.

Cadava, Eduardo. *Words of Light: Theses on the Photography of History.* Princeton: Princeton UP, 1997.

Cambaceres, Eugenio. *Sin rumbo.* Bilbao: Universidad del País Vasco, 1993.

Campos, Haroldo de. "A Língua Pura na Teoria da Tradução de Benjamin." *Revista USP* 33 (1997): 161–71.

———. "Para além do princípio da saudade." *Folha de São Paulo.* Folhetim. September 1, 1985. 6–8.

Carrasquilla, Tomás. *Obras Completas.* 2 Vols. Prologue by Roberto Jaramillo. Medellín: Bedout, 1958.

Caruth, Cathy. "Preface." *Trauma: Explorations in Memory.* Ed. Cathy Caruth. Baltimore and London: Johns Hopkins UP, 1995.

——— *Unclaimed Experience: Trauma, Narrative, and History.* Baltimore and London: John Hopkins UP, 1996.

Chakrabarty, Dipesh. "Reconstructing Liberalism: Notes Toward a Conversation between Area Studies and Diasporic Studies." *Public Culture* 10.3 (1998): 457–81.

Chatterjee, Partha. *Nation and Its Fragments: Colonial and Postcolonial Histories.* Princeton: Princeton UP, 1993.

———. *Nationalist Thought and the Colonial World: A Derivative Discourse.* London: Zed, 1986.

Chauí, Marilena. *A Nervura do Real. Imanência e Liberdade em Espinosa.* São Paulo: Companhia das Letras, 1999.

Cícero, Antonio. *O Mundo desde o Fim.* Rio de Janeiro: Francisco Alves, 1995.

Clausewitz, Carl von. *On War.* 1832. Ed. and Trans. Michael Howard and Peter Paret. Princeton, N.J.: Princeton UP, 1976.

Clifford, James. *The Predicament of Culture: Twentieth-Century Ethography, Literature, and Art.* Cambridge and London: Harvard UP, 1988.

———. "On Ethnographic Allegory." Clifford and Marcus 98–121.

Clifford, James, and George Marcus, ed. *Writing Culture: The Poetics and Politics of Ethnography.* Berkeley, Los Angeles, and London: U of California P, 1986.

Génesis. Biblia. Available at http://bible.ort.org. Retrieved January 30, 2004.

Collingwood, Elisabeth. *Walter Benjamin: La lengua del exilio.* Santiago: ARCIS-LOM, 1997.

Colmenares, Germán. "*Manuela,* novela de costumbres de Eugenio Díaz." *Manuela,* I-252.

Cornell, Drucilla. *Beyond Accommodation: Ethical Feminism, Deconstruction, and the Law.* Lanham, Md.: Rowman and Littlefield, 1999.

———. *The Philosophy of the Limit.* New York and London: Routledge, 1992.

Cornell, Drucilla, Michel Rosenfeld, and David Gray Carlson, eds. *Deconstruction and the Possibility of Justice.* New York: Routledge, 1992.

Critchley, Simon. *The Ethics of Deconstruction: Derrida and Levinas.* Oxford, UK and Cambridge, Mass.: Blackwell, 1992.

Cursio Altamar, Antonio. *Evolución de la novela en Colombia.* Bogotá: Instituto Caro y Cuervo, 1957.

de la Casa, Enrique. *La novela antioqueña.* México: Viscaya, 1942.

De Man, Paul. *Wartime journalism, 1939–1943.* Ed. Werner Hamacher, Neil Hertz, and Thomas Keenan. Lincoln: U of Nebraska P, 1988.

Death and the Maiden. Dir. Roman Polanski. Screenplay by Ariel Dorfman and Rafael Yglesias. 1994.

Deleuze, Gilles. *Cinema 1: The Movement Image*. 1983. Trans. Hugh Tomlinson and Barbara Habberjam. Minneapolis: U of Minnesota P,1989.

———. *Cinema 2: The Time Image*. 1985. Trans. Hugh Tomlinson and Barbara Habberjam. Minneapolis: U of Minnesota P, 1989.

———. *Difference and Repetition*. 1968. Trans. Paul Patton. New York: Columbia UP, 1994.

———. *The Logic of Sense*. 1969. Trans. Mark Lester with Charles Stivale. Ed. Constantin V. Boundas. New York: Columbia UP, 1990

———. *Spinoza: Expressionism in Philosophy*. 1968. Trans. Martin Joughin. New York and Cambridge, Mass.: Zone Books and MIT Press, 1990.

———. *Spinoza: Practical Philosophy*. 1981. Trans. Robert Hurley. San Francisco: City Lights, 1988.

Deleuze, Gilles and Felix Guattari. *Kafka: Toward a Minor Literature*. 1975. Trans. Dana Polan. Minneapolis: U of Minnesota P, 1986.

———. *A Thousand Plateaus: Capitalism and schizophrenia*. 1980. Trans. Brian Massumi. London: Athlone Press, 1988.

Der Derian, James. *Virtuous War: Mapping the Military-Industrial-Media-Entertainment Network*. Boulder: Westview Press, 2001.

Derrida, Jacques. " Le derniers mot du racisme." *Psyche: Inventions de l'autre*. París: Galilée, 1987.

———. *Dissemination*. 1972. Trans. Barbara Johnson. Chicago: U of Chicago P, 1981.

———. "The Ends of Man." 1969. *Margins of Philosophy*. Trans. Alan Bass. Chicago: U of Chicago P, 1982.

———. *Force of Law: The "Mystical Foundation of Authority."* 1990. *Acts of Religion*. Ed. Gil Andijar. London: Routledge, 2002. 230–98.

———. *The Gift of Death*. 1992. Trans. David Wills. Chicago and London: U of Chicago P, 1995.

———. *Given Time: I. Counterfeit Money*. 1991. Trans. Peggy Kamuf. Chicago and London: U of Chicago P, 1992.

———. *Glas*. 1974. Trans. John P. Leavey and Richard Rand. Lincoln: U of Nebraska P, 1986.

———. *Of Grammatology*. 1967. Trans. Gayatri Spivak. Baltimore: Johns Hopkins UP, 1976.

———. "Interpretations at War: Kant, the Jew, the German." 1991. *Acts of Religion*. Ed. Gil Anidjar. London: Routledge, 2002.

———. *Memoires: For Paul de Man*. Trans. Cecile Lindsay. New York: Columbia UP, 1989.

———. *Of Spirit: Heidegger and the Question*. Trans. Geoffrey Bennington and Rachel Bowlby. Chicago: U of Chicago P, 1989.

———. "Ousia and Gramme." 1971. *Margins of Philosophy*. Trans. Alan Bass. Chicago: U of Chicago P, 1982.

———. "Passions: An Oblique Offering." 1993. *On the Name.* Ed. Thomas Dutoit. Trans. David Wood, John P. Leavey, Jr., and Ian McLeod. Stanford: Stanford UP, 1995. 3–31.

———. *Points . . . Interviews, 1974–1994.* Ed. Elisabeth Weber. Trans. Peggy Kamuf et al. Stanford: Stanford UP, 1995.

———. *Positions.* 1972. Trans. Alan Bass. Chicago: U of Chicago P, 1981.

———. *Specters of Marx: The State of the Debt, the Work of Mourning, and the New International.* 1993. Trans. Peggy Kamuf. New York and London: Routledge, 1994.

———. *Speech and phenomena.* 1967. Trans. David B. Allison. Evanston, Northwestern UP, 1973.

———. "Des Tours de Babel." 1977. *Difference in Translation.* Ed. Joseph F. Graham. Ithaca: Cornell UP, 1985. 165–207.

———. "Violence and Metaphysics: An Essay on the Thought of Emmanuel Levinas." 1964. *Writing and Difference.* Trans. Alan Bass. Chicago: U of Chicago P, 1978. 79–153.

Desai, Gaurav. "Rethinking English: Postcolonial English Studies." *A Companion to Postcolonial Studies.* Ed. Henry Schwarz and Sangeeta Ray. Malden, Mass. and Oxford: Blackwell, 2000. 523–39.

———. *Subject to Colonialism: African self-fashioning and the colonial library.* Durham: Duke UP, 2001.

Descartes, René. *Discourse on Method.* 1637. *The Philosophical Writings of Descartes.* Vol. 1. Trans. John Cottingham, Robert Stoothoff, and Dugald Murdoch. Cambridge: Cambridge UP, 1985. 109–51.

Díaz Castro, Eugenio. 1856. *Manuela.* Bogotá: Círculo de Lectores, 1985.

DuBois, Page. *Torture and Truth.* New York and London: Routledge, 1991.

Dunn, Christopher. *Brutality Garden: Tropicália and the Emergence of a Brazilian Counterculture.* Chapel Hill: U of North Carolina P, 2001.

Düttmann, Alexander García. "The Violence of Destruction." Ferris 165–84.

Eldridge, Richard. *On Moral Personhood: Philosophy, Literature, Criticism and Self-Understanding.* Chicago and London: U of Chicago P, 1989.

Engels, Fredrick. *Anti-Dühring.* Trans. Emile Burns. New York: International Publishers, 1966.

Escadron de la mort: L'école francaise. Dir. Marie-Monique Robin. 2003.

Esther. The Anchor Bible. Trans. Carey A. Moore. New York: Doubleday, 1971.

Fabian, Johannes. *Time and the Other: How Anthropology Makes Its Object.* New York: Columbia UP, 1983.

Fanon, Frantz. *The Wretched of the Earth: The Handbook for the Black Revolution That Is Changing the Shape of the World.* 1961. Preface by Jean-Paul Sartre. Trans. Constance Farrington. New York: Grove Weidenfeld, 1968.

Felman, Shoshana and Dori Laub. *Testimony: Crisis of Witnessing in Literature, Psychoanalysis, and History.* New York and London: Routledge, 1992.

Ferris, David S. *Walter Benjamin: Theoretical Questions.* Stanford: Stanford UP, 1996.

Foucault, Michel. *Abnormal: Lectures at the College de France, 1974–1975.* Ed. Arnold I. Davidson. Trans. Graham Burchell. New York: Picador, 2003.

———. *Discipline and Punish: The Birth of the Prison.* 1975. Trans. Alan Sheridan. New York: Random House, 1977.

———. *History of Sexuality.* Vol. 1. Trans. Robert Hurley. New York: Pantheon, 1978.

———. *The Order of Things: An Archaeology of the Human Sciences.* 1966. Unidentified collective translation. London: Tavistock Publications, 1970.

———. *Society Must Be Defended: Lectures at the Collège de France, 1975–76.* Ed. Mauro Bertani and Alessandro Fontana. Trans. David Macey. New York: Picador, 2003.

———. "Truth and Juridical Forms." *Power: The Essential Works of Michel Foucault III.* Trans. Robert Hurley et al. New York: The New Press, 2000.

———. *La verdad y las formas jurídicas.* Trans. E. Lynch. Barcelona: Gedisa, 1980.

———. "A Verdade e as Formas Jurídicas." Trans. J.W. Prado Jr. *Cadernos da PUC* 16 (1974): 5–133.

———. "La vérité et les formes juridiques." *Dits et Écrits 1954–1988.* Vol. II: 1970–75. París: Gallimard, 1994.

Franco, Jean. *Plotting Women: Gender and Representation in Mexico.* New York: Columbia UP, 1989.

Freud, Sigmund. *Inhibitions, Symptoms, and Anxiety.* 1926. Trans. Alix Strachey. Ed. James Strachey. New York and London: Norton, 1959.

———. "Mourning and Melancholia." 1916. *The Standard Edition of the Complete Psychological Works of Sigmund Freud.* Vol. 14. Trans. James Strachey et al. London: Hogarth, 1953–66.

Fuentes, Carlos. "O Racista Mascarado." *Folha de São Paulo.* March 28, 2004.

Gagnebin, Jeanne Marie. *Walter Benjamin: Os Cacos da História.* São Paulo: Brasiliense, 1982.

Galván, Manuel. *Enriquillo.* Havana: Casa de las Américas, 1977.

Garage olimpo. Dir. Marco Bechi. 1999.

Gasché, Rodolphe. "On Critique, Hypercriticism, and Deconstruction: The Case of Benjamin." *Cardozo Law Review* 13.4 (1991).

Gaspari, Elio. *A Ditadura Escancarada.* São Paulo: Brasiliense, 2002.

Geertz, Clifford. *The Interpretation of Cultures: Selected Essays.* London: Hutchinson, 1975.

Gilroy, Paul. *The Black Atlantic: Modernity and Double Consciousness.* Cambridge: Harvard UP, 1993.

Glantz, Margo, ed. *La Malinche: sus padres y sus hijos.* México: Taurus, 2001.

González Echevarría, Roberto. *Myth and Archive: A Theory of Latin American Narrative* Cambridge: Cambridge UP, 1990.

Guha, Ranajit. *Elementary Aspects of Peasant Insurgency in Colonial India.* Delhi: Oxford UP, 1983.

Guillory, John. *Cultural Capital: The Problem of Literary Canon Formation.* Chicago: U of Chicago P, 1993.

Habermas, Jürgen. *The Structural Transformation of the Public Sphere: An Inquiry into a Category of Bourgeois Thought.* 1962. Trans. Thomas Burger with Frederick Lawrence. Cambridge, Mass.: MIT Press, 1989.

Hamacher, Werner. "Afformative Strike," *Cardozo Law Review* 13.4 (1991).

Halperín Donghi, Tulio. *Historia contemporánea de América Latina.* Madrid: Alianza, 1969.

——— et al. *Sarmiento, Author of a Nation.* Berkeley: U of California, 1994.

Hanssen, Beatrice. *Critique of Violence: Between Poststructuralism and Critical Theory.* London and New York: Routledge, 2000.

———. *Walter Benjamin's Other History: of Stones, Animals, Human Beings, and Angels.* Berkeley: U of California P, 1998.

Hardt, Michael. *Gilles Deleuze: An Apprenticeship in Philosophy.* Minneapolis: U of Minnesota P, 1993.

Hegel. *Science of Logic.* 1812. Trans. A. V. Miller. Atlantic Highlands: Humanities P, 1969.

Heidegger, Martin. "The Anaximander Fragment." 1950. *Early Greek Thinking.* Trans. David Farrell Krell and Frank Capuzzi. New York: HarperCollins, 1975.

———. *The Basic Problems of Phenomenology.* 1927. Trans. and Intro. Albert Hofstadter. Bloomington: Indiana UP, 1982.

———. *Being and Time.* 1927. Trans. John Macquarrie and Edward Robinson. New York: Harper and Row, 1962.

———. *Kant and the Problem of Metaphysics.* 1929. 5th ed. Trans. Richard Taft. Bloomington: Indiana UP, 1997.

Howard, Michael. *Clausewitz: A Very Short Introduction.* Oxford and New York: Oxford UP, 2002.

Huntington, Samuel. *The Clash of Civilizations and the Remaking of World Order.* New York: Simon and Schuster, 1996.

Irigaray, Luce. *Speculum of the Other Woman.* 1974. Trans. Gillian Gill. Ithaca: Cornell UP, 1985

———. *This Sex Which Is Not One.* 1977. Trans. Catherine Porter with Carolyn Burke. Ithaca: Cornell UP, 1985.

Irwin, Robert. *Mexican Masculinities.* Minneapolis: U of Minnesota P, 2003.

Isaacs, Jorge. *Camilo: capítulos de una novela inconclusa.* Bogotá: Incunables, 1984.

———. *Estudio sobre las tribus indígenas del Magdalena.* Bogotá: Ministerio de Educación Nacional, 1951.

———. 1867. *María.* Ed. Donald McGrady. Madrid: Cátedra, 1986.

———. *María, a South American Romance.* Trans. Rollo Ogden. New York: Harper and Brothers, 1890.

———. *La revolución radical en Antioquia.* Bogotá: Gaitán, 1880.

Jacobs, Carol. *The Dissimulating Harmony: The Image of Interpretation in Nietzsche, Rilke, Artaud, and Benjamin.* Baltimore: Johns Hopkins UP, 1978.

———. *In the Language of Walter Benjamin*. Baltimore, Md.: Johns Hopkins UP, 1999.

Jameson, Fredric. "On Literary and Cultural Import-Substitution in the Third World: The Case of the Testimonio." *Margins* 1 (1991): 11–34.

———. *Marxism and Form: Twentieth-Century Dialectical Theories of Literature*. Princeton: Princeton UP, 1971.

———. "Marx's Purloined Letter." *New Left Review* 209 (1995): 75–109.

———. *The Political Unconscious: Narrative as a Socially Symbolic Act*. Ithaca: Cornell UP, 1981.

———. "Reification and Utopia in Mass Culture." *Signatures of the Visible*. New York and London: Routledge, 1992. 9–34.

———. *The Seeds of Time*. New York: Columbia UP, 1994.

Jaramillo Uribe, Jaime. *El pensamiento colombiano en el siglo XIX*. 4th. ed. México: Alfaomega, 2001.

Jáuregui, Carlos. "Candelario Obeso: entre la espada del Romanticismo y la pared del proyecto nacional." *Revista Iberoamericana* 189 (1999): 567–590.

Kafka, Franz. "In the Penal Colony." *The Metamorphosis, the Penal Colony, and Other Stories*. New York: Schocken, 1975.

KrauthHammer, Charles. "In Defense of Secret Tribunals." *Time Magazine* 158.23 (November 26, 2001).

Kristeva, Julia. *Revolution in Poetic Language*. 1974. Trans. Margaret Waller. New York: Columbia UP, 1984.

Lacoue-Labarthe, Philippe. *Heidegger, Art, and Politics*. Trans. Chris Turner. Oxford and Cambridge: Blackwell, 1990.

Lages, Susana Kampff. *Walter Benjamin: Tradução e Melancolia*. São Paulo: Edusp, 2002.

Lambropoulous, Vassilis. *The Rise of Eurocentrism: Anatomy of Interpretation*. Princeton, N.J.: Princeton UP, 1993.

Larsen, Neil. *Determinations: Essays on Theory, Narrative, and Nation in the Americas*. London and New York: Verso, 2001.

———. *Reading North by South: On Latin American Literature, Culture, and Politics*. Minneapolis and London: U of Minnesota P, 1995.

Laub, Dori. "Truth and Testimony: The Process and the Struggle." Caruth, ed. 117–48.

Leiris, Michel. "L'ethographe devant le colonialisme." *Brisées*. Paris: Mercure de France, 1966. 125–45.

Levinas, Emmanuel. *En découvrant l'existence avec Husserl et Heidegger*. Paris: Vrin, 1974.

———. *Otherwise than Being or Beyond Essence*. 1974. Trans. Alphonso Lingis. The Hague, Boston and London: Murtinus Nijhoff, 1981.

———. *Totality and Infinity: An Essay on Exteriority*. 1961. Trans. Alphonso Lingis. Pittsburgh: Duquesne UP, 1969.

Levy, Kurt L. *Vida y obras de Tomás Carrasquilla.* Medellín: Bedout, 1958.

Licona, Carlos A. Caicedo. *Jorge Isaacs, su María, sus luchas.* Medellín: Quibdo, 1989.

Losada, Alejandro. *La literatura en la sociedad de América Latina: Perú y el Río de la Plata, 1837–1880.* Frankfurt: Verlag Klaus Dieter Vervuert, 1983.

Ludmer, Josefina. *El género gauchesco. Un tratado sobre la patria.* Buenos Aires: Sudamericana, 1988.

Lukäcs, Gyorg. *History and Class Consciousness.* Trans. Rodney Livingstone. Cambridge, Mass.: The MIT Press, 1968.

Lyotard, Jean-François. *Differend: Phrases in Dispute.* Trans. Georges Van Den Abbele. Minneapolis: U of Minnesota P, 1988.

———. *Heidegger and "the Jews."* Trans. Andreas Michel and Mark S. Roberts. Minneapolis: U of Minnesota P, 1990.

McCall, Tom. "Momentary Violence." Ferris 185–206.

McGrady, Donald. *La novela histórica en Colombia 1844–1959.* Bogotá: Kelly, 1962.

Machado, Roberto. *Deleuze e a Filosofia.* Rio de Janeiro: Graal, 1990.

Machado de Assis, José Maria. *A Mão e a Luva.* São Paulo: Mérito, 1962.

———. *Ressurreição.* Rio de Janeiro: Civilização Brasileira, 1975.

MacIntyre, Alasdair. *After Virtue: A Study in Moral Theory.* Notre Dame: U of Notre Dame P, 1981.

Manual de literatura colombiana. 2 vols. Bogotá: Planeta, 1988.

Magnus, Bernd and Stephen Cullenberg. *Whither Marxism? Global Crisis in International Perspective.* New York and London: Routledge, 1995.

Marchant, Patricio. "¿En qué lengua se habla Hispanoamérica?" *Escritura y temblor.* Ed. Pablo Oyarzún and Willy Thayer. Santiago: Cuarto Propio, 2000. 307–18.

———. *Sobre árboles y madres.* Santiago: Gato Murr, 1984.

Mármol, José. *Amalia.* 1851–55. La Habana: Casa da las Américas, 1976.

Marx, Karl. *Capital.* Vol. 1. 1867. Trans. Ben Fowkes. Intro. Ernest Mandel. New York and Toronto: Vintage, 1977.

———. *Communist Manifesto.* 1848. Ed. Frederic Bender. Trans. Samuel Moore. London and New York: Norton, 1988.

———. *The Eighteenth Brumaire of Louis Bonaparte.* 1852. Trans. Ben Fowkes. *Surveys from Exile: Political Writings, vol. 2. London:* Penguin and New Left Review, 1973.

———. *Grundrisse: Foundations of the Critique of Political Economy.* Trans. Martin Nicolaus. New York: Vintage, 1973.

Matos, Olgária. *Os Arcanos do Inteiramente Outro: A Escola de Frankfurt, a Melancolia e a Revolução.* São Paulo: Brasiliense, 1989.

———. *O Iluminismo Visionário: Benjamin, Leitor de Descartes e Kant.* São Paulo: Brasiliense, 1993.

McGrady, Donald. *Bibliografía sobre Jorge Isaacs*. Bogotá, 1971.

———. "Introducción." *María*. By Jorge Isaacs. Madrid: Cátedra., 1986.

———. *La novela histórica en Colombia, 1844–1959*. Austin and Bogotá: Institute of Latin American Studies and Kelly. s.d.

Mejía, Gustavo. "Prólogo." *María*. By Jorge Isaacs. Caracas: Ayacucho, 1978.

Menninghaus, Winfried. *Walter Benjamins Theorie der Sprachmagie*. Frankfurt am Main: Suhrkamp, 1980.

———. *Schwellenkunde: Walter Benjamins Passage des Mythos*. Frankfurt am Main: Surhkamp, 1986.

Mercado, Tununa. "La casa está en orden." Unpublished typescript.

Merquior, José Guilherme. *Arte e sociedade, em Marcase, Adorno e Benjamín*. Rio de Janeiro: Tempo Brasileiro, 1969.

Missac, Pierre. *Walter Benjamin's Passages*. Trans. Shierry Weber Nicholsen. Cambridge, Mass: MIT Press, 1995.

Molloy, Sylvia. *At Face Value: Autobiographical Writing in Spanish America*. New York and Cambridge: Cambridge UP, 1991.

Monsiváis, Carlos. "La Malinche y el malinchismo." Glantz 183–193.

Montaldo, Graciela. "Transculturación y discurso emancipador." *Latin American Literatures: A Comparative History of Cultural Formations*. Ed. Mario Valdés and Linda Hutcheon. México: Fondo de Cultura Económica. Forthcoming.

———. *De pronto el campo. Literatura argentina y tradición rural*. Rosario: Beatriz Viterbo, 1993.

Mosès, Stéphane. "Walter Benjamin and Franz Rosenzweig." *Walter Benjamin: Philosophy, Aesthetics, History*. Ed. Gary Smith. Chicago: U of Chicago P, 1989.

Nascimento, Evando. *Derrida e a Literatura*. Niterói, RJ: EdUFF, 1999.

Musil, Robert. *Diaries*. Trans. Philip Payne. Ed. Mark Mirsky. New York: Basic Books, 1998.

———. *Man without Qualities*. Trans. Sophie Wilkins. Ed. Consultant Burton Pike. New York: Random House, 1995.

Nadler, Steven. *Spinoza: A Life*. Cambridge, U.K. and New York: Cambridge UP, 1999.

Nägele, Rainer. *Theater, Theory, Speculation. Walter Benjamin and the Scenes of Modernity*. Baltimore, Johns Hopkins UP, 1991.

———, ed. *Benjamin's Ground: New Readings of Walter Benjamin*. Detroi: Wayne State UP, 1988.

Newton, Adam Zachary. *Narrative Ethics*. Cambridge, Mass. and London: Harvard UP, 1995.

Nieto, Juan José. *Ingermina o la hija de Calamar*. 1844. Medellín: EAFIT, 2001.

Nietzsche, Friedrich Wilhelm. *The Birth of Tragedy in the Spirit of Music*. 1872. Trans. Walter Kaufman. New York: Random House, 1967.

———. *On the Genealogy of Morals*. 1887. Trans. Walter Kaufmann and RJ Hollingdale. New York: Random House, 1967.

———. *Thus Spoke Zarathustra: A Book for All and None.* 1883–85. Trans. Walter Kaufmann. *The Portable Nietzsche.* New York: Penguin, 1968. 103–439.

Nussbaum, Martha. *The Fragility of Goodness: Luck and Ethics in Greek Tragedy and Philosophy.* Cambridge, UK: Cambridge UP, 1986.

———. *Love's Knowledge: Essays on Philosophy and Literature.* New York and Oxford: Oxford UP, 1990.

———. "Patriotism and Cosmopolitanism." Nussbaum et al. 2–17.

———. *Poetic Justice: The Literary Imagination and Public Life.* Boston: Beacon Press, 1995.

———. "Reply." Nussbaum et al. 131–44.

Nussbaum, Martha et al. *For Love of Country: Debating the Limits of Patriotism.* Boston: Beacon Press, 1996.

Obeso, Candelario. *Cantos populares de mi tierra.* 1877. Bogotá: Arango y el Áncora, 1988.

———. *Lecturas para ti.* Bogotá: Librería Nueva, 1897.

———. *Lucha de la vida. Cantos populares de mi tierra.* Bogotá: Biblioteca Popular de Cultura Colombina, 1950.

———. *Secundino el zapatero. Teatro colombiano del siglo XIX de costumbres y comedias.* Bogotá: Tres Culturas, 1989.

Ortega, José J. *Historia de la literatura Colombiana.* Bogotá: Escuela Tipográfica Salesiana, 1934.

Ortega, Julio. *Crítica de la identidad: La pregunta por el Perú en su literatura.* Mexico: Fondo de Cultura Económica, 1988.

Oyarzún, Pablo. *De lenguaje, historia y poder.* Santiago: Universidad de Chile, 1999.

———. "Cuatro señas sobre experiencia, historia y facticidad en el pensamiento de Walter Benjamin." *De lenguaje* 167–98.

———. "Heidegger: Tono y traducción." *Seminarios de Filosofía* 2 (1989): 81–101.

———. "Sobre el concepto benjaminiano de traducción." *De lenguaje* 131–66.

Pachón Padilla, Eduardo. "El cuento: Historia y análisis." *Manual de literatura colombiana.* 2 vols. Bogotá: Planeta, 1988. I-143–73 and II-511–88.

Palacios, Marco. *La delgada corteza de nuestra civilización.* Bogotá: New Biblioteca Colombiana de Cultura, 1986.

———. *Entre la legitimidad y la violencia: Colombia 1875–1994.* Bogotá: Norma, 1995.

———. *Estado y clase social en Colombia.* Bogotá: Procultura, 1986.

———. *Parábola del liberalismo.* Bogotá: Norma, 1999.

Palacios, Marco and Frank Safford. *Colombia: Fragmented Land, Divided Society.* New York and Oxford: Oxford UP, 2002.

Parker, David. *Ethics, Theory, and the Novel.* Cambridge and New York: Cambridge UP, 1994.

Payno, Manuel. *El fistol del diablo.* Mexico: CONACULTA, 2000.
Paz, Octavio. *Hijos del limo. Del romanticismo a la vanguardia.* Barcelona: Seix Barral, 1974.
Perrone-Moisés, Leyla. "Que Fim Levou a Crítica Literaria?" *Folha de São Paulo.* Suplemento Cultural "Mais!" August 25, 1996.
Piglia, Ricardo. "Notas sobre *Facundo.*" *Punto de Vista* 8 (1980): 15–8.
Pineda Botero, Álvaro. *La fábula y el desastre: Estudios críticos sobre la novela colombiana, 1650–1931.* Medellín: EAFIT, 1999.
Pinsky, Robert. "Eros Against Esperanto." Nussbaum et al. 85–90.
Pratt, Mary Louise. "Fieldwork in Common Places." Clifford and Marcus 27–50.
———. *Imperial Eyes: Travel Writing and Transculturation.* New York and London: Routledge, 1992.
Preminger, Alex and Edward Greenstein, ed. *The Hebrew Bible in Literary Criticism.* New York: Ungar, 1986.
Prescott, Laurence E. *Candelario Obeso y la iniciación de la poesía negra en Colombia.* Bogotá: Instituto Caro y Cuervo, 1985.
Que bom te ver viva. Dir. Lucia Murat. 1989.
Rama, Angel. *La ciudad letrada.* Hannover: Ediciones del Norte, 1984.
———. *Transculturación narrativa en América Latina.* Mexico: Siglo XXI, 1981.
Ramos, Julio. *Divergent Modernities. Culture and Politics in 19th Century Latin America.* Trans. John D. Blanco. Durham and London: Duke UP, 2001.
———. "El don de la lengua." *Paradojas de la letra* 3–21.
———. "La ley es otra: Literatura y constitución del sujeto jurídico." *Paradojas de la letra* 37–70.
———. *Paradojas de la letra.* Caracas: eXcultura, 1996.
Rejali, Darius. *Torture and Modernity: Self, Society, and State in Modern Iran.* Boulder: Westview P, 1994.
Restrepo, António Gómez. *Historia de la literatura colombiana.* Bogotá: Cosmos y Ministerio de Educación, 1953.
Reyes, Carlos José. "El costumbrismo en Colombia." *Manual de literatura colombiana.* I-175–245.
Richard, Nelly. *Residuos y metáforas: Ensayos de crítica cultural sobre el Chile de la Transición.* Santiago: Cuarto Propio, 1998.
Rodowick, David Norman. *Gilles Deleuze's Time Machine.* Durham, NC: Duke UP, 1997.
Rodríguez, Angela Rocío. *Las novelas de don Tomás Carrasquilla.* Medellín: Autores Antioqueños, 1988.
Rojas, Cristina. *Civilización y violencia: La búsqueda de la identidad en la Colombia del siglo XIX.* Trans. Elvira Maldonado. Bogotá: Norma, 2001.
Ross, Andrew. "Defenders of the Faith and the New Class." *Intellectuals: Aesthetics, Politics, Academics.* Ed. Bruce Robbins. Minneapolis: U of Minnesota P, 1990. 101–132.
Rother, Larry. "For Chilean Coup, Kissinger is Numbered among the Hunted." *The New York Times,* 28 May 2002.

Rouanet, Sérgio Paulo. *O Édipo e o Anjo: Itinerários freudianos em Walter Benjamin*. Rio de Janeiro: Edições Tempo Brasileiro, 1981.
Said, Edward. *Culture and Imperialism*. New York: Vintage, 1994.
———. *Orientalism*. New York: Vintage, 1978.
Samper, José María. *Ensayo sobre las revoluciones políticas y condición social de las repúblicas colombianas*. Paris: Thurnot, 1861.
Sánchez, Efraín. *Gobierno y geografía: Agustín Codazzi y la comisión corográfica de la Nueva Granada*. Bogotá: Banco de la República and El Áncora, 1999.
Sánchez López, Luis María. *Diccionario de escritores colombianos*. Barcelona: Plaza y Janés, 1978.
Santiago, Silviano. *Uma Literatura nos Trópicos*. São Paulo: Perspectiva, 1978.
———. *Vale Quanto Pesa: Ensaios sobre Questões Político-Culturais*. Rio de Janeiro: Paz e Terra, 1982.
Sarlo, Beatriz. "Los estudios culturales y la crítica literaria en la encrucijada valorativa." *Revista de Crítica Cultural* 15 (1997): 32–38.
Sarmiento, Domingo. 1845. *Facundo, o civilización y barbarie*. Caracas: Biblioteca Ayacucho, 1977.
Sartre, Jean-Paul. "Preface." *The Wretched of the Earth*. By Frantz Fanon 7–31.
Scarry, Elaine. *The Body in Pain: The Making and Unmaking of the World*. Oxford: Oxford UP, 1985.
Scholem, Gershom. *Walter Benjamin: The Story of a Friendship*. Trans. Harry Zohn. New York: Schocken Books, 1988.
School of Assassins. Dir. Robert Richter. Narrated by Susan Sarandon. 1994.
Schmitt, Carl. *Concept of the Political*. 1927. Trans. George Schwab. New Brunkswick: Rutgers UP, 1976.
———. *The Crisis of Parliamentary Democracy*. 1923. Trans. Ellen Kennedy. Cambridge, Mass.: MIT, 1985.
———. *Political Theology: Four Chapters on the Concept of Sovereignty*. 1922. Trans. George Schwab. Cambridge, Mass.: MIT, 1985.
Schwarz, Roberto. "Cultura e Política, 1964–68." *O Pai de Família* 61–92.
———. "National by Elimination." *Misplaced Ideas: Essays on Brazilian Culture*. Ed. John Gledson. London: Verso, 1992.
———. *O Pai de Família e Outros Estudos*. São Paulo: Paz e Terra, 1978.
———. "19 Princípios para a Crítica Literaria." *O Pai de Família* 93–94.
Scott, George Ryley. *History of Torture Throughout the Ages*. 1940. London: Sphere, 1971.
Shakespeare, William. *Hamlet*. Ed. Cyrus Hoy. New York: Norton: 1996.
Siebers, Tobin. *The Ethics of Criticism*. Ithaca and London: Cornell UP, 1988.
Smith, Barbara Herrnstein. *Contingencies of Value: Alternative Perspectives for Critical Theory*. Cambridge, Mass.: Harvard UP, 1988.
Smith, Gary, ed. *On Walter Benjamin: Critical Essays and Recollections*. Cambridge, Mass. and London: MIT, 1988.
Smith Córdoba, Amir, ed. *Vida y obra de Calendario Obeso*. Bogotá: Centro para la Investigación de la Cultura Negra, 1984.

Sommer, Doris. *Foundational Fictions: The National Romances of Latin America.* Berkeley, London, and Los Angeles: U of California P, 1991.

Sorel, George. *Reflections on Violence.* 1919. Trans. T. E. Hulme. New York: AMS, 1975.

Spinoza, Baruch. *The Ethics.* 1677. *The Spinoza Reader. The Ethics and Other Works.* Trans. Edwin Curley. Princeton, N.J.: Princeton UP, 1994. 85–265.

———. *Theological Political Treatise.* 1677. Trans. Samuel Shirley. Indianapolis: Hackett Pub, 2001.

Spivak, Gayatri Chakravorty. *A Critique of Postcolonial Reason: Toward a History of the Vanishing Present.* Cambridge, Mass. and London: Harvard UP, 1999.

———. *Outside in the Teaching Machine.* New York and London: Routledge, 1993.

———. "The Politics of Translation." *Outside* 179–200.

———. *The Postcolonial Critic: Interviews, Strategies, Dialogues.* Ed. Sarah Harasym. New York and London: Routledge, 1990.

———. "Responsibility." *boundary* 2:21 (1994): 19–64.

———. "Scattered Speculations on the Question of Cultural Studies." *Outside* 255–84.

———. "Subaltern Studies: Deconstructing Historiography." *In Other Worlds: Essays in Cultural Politics.* New York and London: Routledge, 1988.

Spurr, David. *The Rhetoric of Empire: Colonial Discourse in Journalism, Travel Writing, and Imperial Administration.* Durham: Duke UP, 1993.

Stellardi, Giuseppe. *Heidegger and Derrida on Philosophy and Metaphor: Imperfect Thought.* Amherst, NY: Prometheus, 2000.

Sun-Tzu. *The Art of War.* New York: Spark, 2003.

Süssekind, Flora. *Literatura e Vida Literária.* São Paulo: Zahar, 1985.

Thayer, Willy. La crisis no moderna de la universidad moderna (Epílogo del conflicto de las facultades). Santiago: Cuarto Propio, 1996.

Toker, Leona. "Introduction." *Commitment in Reflection: Essays in Literature and Moral Philosophy.* Ed. Leona Toker. New York and London: Garland, 1994. xi-xxxii.

Trotsky, Leon. *The Balkan wars, 1912–13: The War Correspondence of Leon Trotsky.* New York and Sydney: Monad and Pathfinder, 1980.

Vergara y Vergara, José María. "Biografía." *Novelas y Cuadros de Costumbres.* By Eugenio Díaz Castro. 2 vols. Bogotá: Procultura, 1985.

Viñas, David. *Literatura argentina y realidad política.* Buenos Aires: Jorge Alvarez, 1964.

Victoriano, Felipe. "Fiction, Death, and Testimony." *Discourse* 25.1–2 (2003): 211–230.

Virilio, Paul. *Desert Screen: War at the Speed of Light.* Trans. Michael Degener. London and New York: Continuum, 2002.

———. *Ground Zero.* Trans. Chris Turner. London and New York: Verso, 2002.

———. *Pure War.* Interviews with Sylvère Lotringer. 1982. 2nd ed. Trans. Mark Polizotti. New York: Semiotext(e), 1997.

———. *Strategy of Deception.* Trans. Chris Turner. London and New York: Verso, 2000.

von der Walde Uribe, Erna. "Limpia, fija y da esplendor: El letrado y la letra en Colombia a fines del siglo XIX." *Revista Iberoamericana* 178–9 (1997): 71–83.

Vries, Hent de. *Religion and Violence: Philosophical Perspectives from Kant to Derrida.* Baltimore and London: Johns Hopkins, 2002.

Weinberg, Félix. "La época de Rosas. El romanticismo." Vol. 1: desde la Colonia al Romanticismo. *Historia de la literatura argentina.* Buenos Aires: Centro Editor de América Latina, 1980.

Wettstein, Germán. "Lenguaje alegórico e ironía pedagógica en el quehacer poético de Bolívar." *Casa de las Américas* 21 (1984): 143.

Williams, Bernard. *Ethics and the Limits of Philosophy.* Cambridge, Mass.: Harvard UP, 1983.

Williams, Raymond. *The Colombian Novel, 1844–1987.* Austin: U of Texas P, 1991.

———. "*Manuela:* La primera novela de la violencia." *Violencia y literatura en Colombia.* Ed. Jonathan Tittler. Madrid: Orígenes, 1989. 19–29.

Yúdice, George. *The Expediency of Culture: Uses of Culture in the Global Era.* Durham and London: Duke UP, 2003.

———. "We Are *Not* the World." *Social Text* 31–2 (1992): 202–16.

Zizek, Slavoj. *The Plague of Fantasies.* London: Verso, 1997.

———. *The Ticklish Subject: The Absent Centre of Political Ontology.* London and New York: Verso, 1999.

———, ed. *Cogito and the Unconscious.* Durham and London: Duke UP, 1998.

Index

CPSIA information can be obtained at www.ICGtesting.com
Printed in the USA
BVOW072240241111

276749BV00002B/21/P